Stig Børsen Hansen
Philosophers of Technology

Stig Børsen Hansen

Philosophers of Technology

—

DE GRUYTER

ISBN 978-3-11-061987-4
e-ISBN (PDF) 978-3-11-062207-2
e-ISBN (EPUB) 978-3-11-061951-5

Library of Congress Control Number: 2020937333

Bibliographic information published by the Deutsche Nationalbibliothek
The Deutsche Nationalbibliothek lists this publication in the Deutsche Nationalbibliografie;
detailed bibliographic data are available on the Internet at http://dnb.dnb.de.

© 2022 Walter de Gruyter GmbH, Berlin/Boston
This volume is text- and page-identical with the hardback published in 2020.
Cover image: Stefan Schweihofer
Printing and binding: CPI books GmbH, Leck

www.degruyter.com

In Memoriam: Robert Joensen

Acknowledgements

This book has been a long time in the writing, and it gives me great pleasure to record my gratitude to some of those who have helped it take shape. Feedback from and conversations with students at the University of Copenhagen encouraged me to pursue the task of putting the material into book form in the first place. Thanks are due to the late Stig Andur Pedersen for discussing with me the overall theme and structure of the book. A book on the same theme written by him would likely look very different, but I hope this is a work he would have wanted to consult.

Almost two decades ago, assisting Graeme Gooday in his teaching at the Centre for the History and Philosophy of Science at the University of Leeds got me interested in the philosophy of technology. This was a stimulating intellectual environment. Fortunately, the interest that was sparked there withstood the precariousness and dynamics of an academic career as well as other tasks and duties. Teaching at the HumTek degree program at Roskilde University offered an opportunity to meet and listen to one of the philosophers treated in the book, Langdon Winner. Just as importantly, working closely with the students, as they designed and reflected on technical artefacts, I could frequently see the relevance of combining technical insight with the philosophical issues discussed in the book. It was a great place to work, and several colleagues there engaged critically with parts of the manuscript.

Thanks are due to participants at research colloquia at my own institution, the University of Southern Denmark, as well as ones held at the Universities of Aalborg and Aarhus. On these occasions, I have benefitted from the opportunity to discuss the overall plan of the book as well as aspects of its chapters. Dylan Cawthorne, Michael May, Hans Fink, Asger Sørensen, Anne Gerdes, Nafsika Athannasoulis, Mikkel Bille and Søren Harnow Klausen have given generously of their time by offering detailed comments on the material and helped me avoid more than a few embarrassing mistakes. Maja Louise Nielsen was an invaluable help in preparing the manuscript, and Tim Vogel at Walter de Gruyter has been a source of encouragement in steering the manuscript through the publication process.

Without Sonia, Kasper and Jonathan, I imagine this book would have been finished a lot sooner. I am grateful that they in so many ways put the frequently all-consuming process of writing and preparing a book manuscript into perspective. This book is dedicated to them.

Contents

Abbreviations —— XI

1   Introduction —— 1
1.1   Philosophy of technology: vagueness squared —— 1
1.2   A flawed but promising history of the philosophy of technology —— 9
1.3   Plan of the book —— 13

2   Karl Marx: What machines do —— 16
2.1   Rousseau's challenge —— 16
2.2   Work and objectification —— 18
2.3   From craftsman to machine appendage —— 22
2.4   Frustrated objectification: alienation —— 27
2.5   Marx and the Machine —— 34
2.6   Marx as an Enlightenment Thinker —— 39

3   Herbert Marcuse: One-Dimensional Man and the technological veil —— 42
3.1   Introduction: Marcuse the Marxist —— 42
3.2   Marcuse's pessimism: one-dimensional machine man and the happy consciousness —— 48
3.3   The missing technics in Marcuse's reception —— 54
3.4   Marcuse the optimist: the art of living and a new logos of technics —— 59
3.5   Marcuse's challenge to value sensitive design in education —— 65

4   Langdon Winner: Tools without handles —— 70
4.1   A strange idea and ritual forswearings —— 70
4.2   Forms of determinism —— 77
4.3   Technology: Whose control, what mastery? —— 82
4.4   The mechanics of autonomous technology – imperatives and reverse adaptation —— 86
4.5   Caring for monsters —— 92

5   Martin Heidegger: thinking beyond technology —— 98
5.1   Heidegger's Mysticism —— 98
5.2   Being —— 102

5.3	Metaphysics and technology —— 109
5.4	On being a thing and building for dwelling —— 113
5.5	What to do? How to think? —— 118

6	**Albert Borgmann local technologies** —— 122
6.1	Technology: force and character —— 122
6.2	A pattern of disengagement —— 128
6.3	Things: orientation and the good life —— 136
6.4	Reform and design as antidotes for akrasia —— 146

7	**John Dewey: The making of tools** —— 149
7.1	Introduction —— 149
7.2	The inquiring organism and its tool of tools —— 155
7.3	The world well built: a history of philosophers' view of technology and creation —— 164

8	**Bruno Latour: Networks and fabrications** —— 171
8.1	Introduction: from situations to networks —— 171
8.2	The network behind reference to things —— 179
8.3	Dummett and Latour on primitives and their images of reality —— 187

Bibliography —— 196

Index —— 209

Abbreviations

QCT	Heidegger, Martin (1977). The Question Concerning Technology. In *The Question Concerning Technology. And other Essays.* London and New York: Garland Publishing.
AT	Winner, Langdon (1977). *Autonomous Technology: Technics-out-of-Control as a theme in Political thought.* Cambridge, MA.: MIT Press.
MECW	Marx, Karl & Engels, Friedrich (1975–2004). *Collected Works of Karl Marx and Friedrich Engels.* 50 Vols. London: Lawrence and Wishart.
ODM	Marcuse, Herbert (1964). *One-Dimensional Man: Studies in the Ideology of Advanced Industrial Society.* Boston: Beacon Press.
EW / MW / LW	Dewey, John (1996). *The Collected Works of John Dewey 1882–1953.* Jo Ann Boydston; Larry Hickman (Eds.) Charlottesville, Va. : InteLex Corporation.

1 Introduction

1.1 Philosophy of technology: vagueness squared

Historian of technology David E. Nye once suggested to me: "Sometimes you have to give a collection a name. Then it becomes somebody's job to take care of it". He was talking about collections of objects of technical and historical interest and the demands they place on the institutions that house the collections. His observation seems an apt description of the field of philosophy of technology and outlines the task of this book. The remark points to the occasional creative nature of acts of naming – acts that achieve something new, rather than describe what already is somehow a natural collection. Philosophy of technology is now frequently spoken about as a field or collection of thoughts, philosophies and philosophers that can be taught and enlisted for different intellectual purposes. This book is written out of a perceived need for providing an overview of philosophy of technology – to take care of a collection that can prove unwieldy for a newcomer, and whose items I suggest can require dusting off, for those familiar with the objects. Highlighting and rearranging objects, as well as giving a more prominent positioning to some items in the collection, is occasionally the job of custodians of museums and academic fields alike.

This is a book on a theme that academics, policymakers and laymen alike are drawn to. Currently, technology is perhaps the most pivotal concept when we seek to make sense of ourselves, our times and societies. It informs a range of policies. As I am writing this, a new subject is being introduced into the Danish public school, a subject which is perhaps best translated as "Technological literacy" or more directly "understanding of technology". The contents of the subjects are largely concerned with the use of computers and information technologies as they are encountered in everyday life; how to code software; how to be aware of various pitfalls when using communication technologies and how to use computers to construct things. This reform of the schooling of the nation's youth – and the changes it entails to teacher's colleges – is one among many witnesses to the work of political forces, to what we find important in our society and to what is perceived to be required for its continued flourishing.

When one starts reading about the motivations and reasons for having such a subject, it soon emerges that views of the future are deeply shaped by one of many prevalent technologies: the personal computer. The proposed school subject does not differ much from academic and popular discussion of technology. It immediately raises a question of definition. Technologies surely concern more than the use of computers and their information processing. The naming of the school subject – technological literacy – might suggest a tendency to work with a simplified, prototypical definition, according to which "technology" simply means a range of devices – computers – as their workings increasingly get our attention and to some appear to impact our daily lives in the most profound way. While such an understanding of "technology" might be close to the mark when it comes to popular use, no-one who offers the concept of technology a modicum of sustained reflection will be persuaded by the prototypical definition.

The fundamental challenge to definition is that of vagueness. After offering some thoughts on the history of the idea of punishment, Nietzsche mused: "all ideas, in which an entire process is semiotically summarized elude definition. Only something which has no history is capable of being defined" (2009, p. 62). The concept of technology is a case in point. It is regularly drawn on by philosophers, historians, educators, policymakers, sociologists, cultural critics and others, to understand contemporary societies and their development and to make sense of ourselves as human beings. Yet, the word itself has a confusing and multifarious history, which indeed seems to render the concept an expression of an entire process "semiotically summarized."

Nietzsche's disparaging remarks did not make attempts at definitions of words with a history slow down. Academics regularly offer the kind of definitions that are commonplace in philosophy. For example, a book-length study, *Narratives of Technology,* duly offers not one, but several definitions as an introduction to, and framing of, its fascinating topic. For reasons that will become clear, I shall not try to outdo the definitional work that the book relies on. One of the more recent attempts cited by the author defines technology as "the methods, practices, and devices a culture uses to make things function" with the following three features: "'(1) a means to fulfil a human purpose'; (2) an 'assemblage of practices and components'; and (3) 'the entire collection of devices and engineering practices available to a culture'" (Arthur, 2009, 27 f., cited in van der Laan 2016, p. 6).

Such conceptual work is best seen as an attempt at offering a descriptive definition. Such definitions seek to be faithful to ordinary usage and as a consequence, in this case they become extremely inclusive. Van der Laan emphasises means and ends when understanding technology. Should one sing a lullaby to make one's child sleepy with a view to making the following workday an acceptable experience, the song would count as a technology, based on aspects of the definition above (given, of course, that we agree what a thing is). The point of discussing songs and things is not to offer a counterexample with a view to somehow refine the definition of technology. Understanding tunes as tools might well be an interesting and worthwhile intellectual exercise that helps us understand our culture and its practices. The point is that the definition seems to have lost one of the useful features of good definitions: they leave a sufficient number of things and phenomena out. Further attempts will typically make use of additional concepts such as "rationality", "science", "system", "power" and "efficiency". This opens the definitional exercise to another charge. It is using words that themselves stand in need of clarification and in some cases are only marginally clearer than the word they serve to define.

Though enjoying no legislative powers over the use of language, philosophers will often try to somehow set the history of a word straight by offering a normative, rather than a descriptive, definition. While registering a multitude of actual uses of a word, they will insist that there are uses of the word that are somehow truer to an origin of the word, and importantly, more fruitful for conducting the intellectual and practical pursuits that lead us to doing the definitional work in the first place. For example, according to one normative definition, neither the lullaby, drying racks, Kaplan turbines nor the latest smartphone (a prototypical specimen) is a technology. Taking notice of the "logos" that can be traced in the word "technology", philosophers such as Bruno Latour and Larry Hickman have suggested that the word already implies a general and reasoned discourse about things technical, rather than talk about the technical things themselves. We don't talk about "biologies," but about giraffes and amoebas, while reserving "biology" and its branches for a systematic study of living things. This usage of "ology" is in many cases well-established but has mostly been abandoned in the case of "technology". Schatzberg (2018) suggests that European languages, not counting English, for most parts of the 20th century made a distinction between variants of "technique" and "technology", where the latter had to do with the science of, and education in, the former. Eventually, this was muddled by the influence of the concept as it had developed in the English language, primarily through adoption in a North American context. Pointing to the "technics" and "logos" that make up the word "technology" is worthwhile, and Marcuse made a point of distinguishing the two. Yet, it remains foreign to ordinary usage of the word in the academic lingua franca, English.

In discussing technology, philosophers have historically used words that were in some ways different from those currently in use. Heidegger's very influential lecture was not addressed to a question concerning technology, but to one of *Technik*. Ellul's stake of the century concerned "La Technique". Only at a late stage in the development of his thinking does Dewey consider that speaking of technology, rather than of instruments or simply, arts, might have served him better in getting his thoughts across to his readers. Then, use of "arts", though increasingly prefaced by "industrial" or "useful" was a widespread way of talking about what we today mean by "technology". Today, however, "art" has retained a different meaning and at times is contrasted with technology. Marx rarely used the word technology, and when he did, he relied on what is called a Kameralist understanding of "technology", that was on the vane, and in some respects, foreign to our use (Schatzberg, 2018). In different ways, these philosophers relied, more or less consciously, on words already in use in the wider culture, among engineers, educators and, in Marx's case, scholars of state administration.

So far, I have pointed to some challenges of defining the word in a way that is faithful to both contemporary usage and the use made of it by different philosophers. While the meaning of the word "technology" is remarkably complex and multifarious, one can trace its complex history.[1] The Oxford English Dictionary suggests the first usage to have occurred in 1612, and a landmark in the use of the word is considered to be Johann Beckmann's 1777 *Anleitung zur Technologie*, where technology was understood to be a science of the processing of natural materials and knowledge of handicrafts. This use was itself not without a history as it drew on Greek terminology. The subsequent use of the word in its travels in European and North American contexts has left us with a concept that can only offer to us a confused "semiotic summary". Moments of notice in its varied use was the need for a word to describe the process that concerned Karl Marx – the industrialization and widespread use of machinery that had occurred primarily in the 19th century in parts of Europe. Leo Marx (2010) describes this need as a semantic void that was filled by "technology". The concept that did the filling was not entirely plastic. It had already been shaped by the adoption of the German "Technik" by American social scientists and changed in the process. The history of the concept is fascinating, and in virtue of the deep concerns and hopes that cultural and historical analyses have placed on technology, the concept has found application in many regions of the intellectual life of Western cultures. Schatzberg finds that three distinct meanings, each with their own history, but with porous boundaries, are contained in contemporary use of the concept of technology: "*Technology* as industrial arts, as applied science and as technique" (2018, p. 13). These different meanings continue to rear their heads in contemporary use of the words, and they bring with them both the practical contexts of engineering and deepfelt pessimism about the ways our culture uses tools.

---

[1] For this paragraph, see for example Nye (2006), Marx (2010) and in particular, the magisterial account of the concept of technology given by Schatzberg (2018).

In this way, the phenomenon of vagueness seems particularly acute in the case of "technology". Vagueness is frequently presented as a technical problem in philosophical logic: the meaning of some words (such as "bald", "heap", "poor") is such that they have no clear boundaries. This allows for deriving a paradox – a symptom of a disease in our thought – and technical, philosophical work in formal logic can begin. Wittgenstein's contribution to the question is often restricted to that which can be gathered from his concept of family resemblance. However, in the passage below, Wittgenstein suggested we think about the vagueness of concepts as a more general phenomenon, that in many cases upsets the expectations we have of our concept: to be clear, precise and fit for expressing thoughts:

> "If a concept refers to a certain pattern of life then it has to contain a degree of indefiniteness". I am thinking of something like this: On a strip of paper we have a continuous and regular pattern of drawing or painting, which we describe in relation to the pattern, since the relation is what matters to us. If the patterns were to run: a b c a b c a b c etc. I would have a special concept, for example, for something red that is on a *c*, and something green that appears on the following b.
>
> Now once anomalies occur in the pattern I will be in doubt as to which judgement ought to be made. But couldn't my instruction have provided for this? Or *do I simply assume* that in being instructed in the use of the concept, that particular pattern was just taken for granted, but was never itself described? (Wittgenstein, 1982, §206)

Wittgenstein is reminding us that our concepts are embedded in the hurly burly of everyday life, our form of life. We may instruct ourselves and others in the use of a concept. Such an exercise is, however, done on the background of existing usage and practical matters of concern to us. Wittgenstein's picture is meant to bring into focus the reliance on potentially changing background for words to have their meaning. The "background is the bustle of life. And our concepts refer to something within *this* bustle. And it is this very concept 'bustle' that brings about this indefiniteness. For a bustle only comes about through constant repetition. And there is no definite starting point for 'constant repetition'" (Wittgenstein (1980), § 625–626). Rather than being a secluded topic in logic, vagueness as a linguistic phenomenon has meta-philosophical repercussions. We can, on occasions of writing a book or introducing a new policy, define concepts like "technology", and interesting conceptual work can certainly be done. When we today use the concept of technology, it brings with it a rich, and at times contradictory, history. However, there are rich studies of the history of the word that achieve much in terms of bringing out the different backgrounds on which engineers, historians, sociologists and "ordinary people" have made use of this concept, and their point of doing so in different contexts.

These studies are interesting in their own right, but our interest here is ultimately philosophical, not historical. Rather than hope for a Pentecost miracle, or try to legislate a certain use of a word without appropriate legislative powers, this book will let each philosopher's use of the concept speak for itself, as it is placed on the background of academic and practical "hurly burly of everyday life". Rather than offering definitions, Wittgenstein's characterisation of our quandary suggests that our task is as much a matter of making clear the background pattern that allows one to go on using a concept in the way it was used on a certain occasion. For example, when an exposition of Marx's thoughts makes him speak of technologies, it is in many ways on a very different background from the one on which Albert Borgmann speaks of them. Their concepts of technology can be made clear by bringing out the pattern they are repeating and sometimes slightly altering. Importantly, they used rough equivalents of our concept of technology to talk about what mattered to them and still matters to us.

The multiplication of vagueness suggested by the title of this section comes from prefacing "technology" with "philosophy of". This should be seen as part of a larger change in the organization and specialisation of academic philosophy. As an attempt at making philosophy applicable and useful, we begin getting "philosophies of" from the 1970's. Philosophers have different ways of compartmentalising their discipline and combined with these different compartments in the form of traditions, schools and fields, there is a constant tendency toward division and separation. This is partly a result of the organisation of academia, but it tends to make the collection of items in the philosophy of technology harder to survey. For example, Don Ihde features prominently in what is called post-phenomenological philosophy of technology, a more recent field within philosophy of technology. It is described by central proponents as follows:

> Post-phenomenologists study the relationships that develop between users and technologies. This perspective addresses questions such as: How do technologies shape our choices, our actions, and our experience of the world? How are technologies at once objects we use for our own purposes, and at the same time objects that have an influence on us? How do technologies inform our politics, ethics, and our understandings of the basic features of our everyday experience?... [P]ostphenomenology brings together the phenomenological approach and the ontological commitments of the American pragmatist tradition of philosophy. (Rosenberger & Verbeek, 2015, p. 1)

This characterisation points to a range of important questions. It is likely specific versions of these that draw people to the field of philosophy of technology in the first place, and perhaps, to post-phenomenology specifically. Rosenberg & Verbeek's description of this "distinctive philosophical approach" (2015, p.1) within philosophy of technology surely needs more detail (the authors offer this on other occasions) as well as examples of the many interesting studies carried out under its banner. Yet, off its own bat, the description would leave the uninformed and informed reader alike none the wiser. The phenomenology presented by Husserl, the Heidegger that wrote *Being and Time* and the one that penned "The Question Concerning Technology" display considerable variety, to mention but a few historical phenomenologists. While American pragmatism was underway in the early 20th century, Arthur Lovejoy could identify thirteen different kinds of pragmatism. Contemporary American pragmatists have sought inspiration in the tradition of James, Dewey and Peirce, but no clear agreement between Hilary Putnam, Richard Rorty and Robert Brandom has emerged on the question of how to understand the ontological commitments that pragmatism can be seen to involve.

We soon find ourselves in the same quandary with "philosophy" as we did with "technology". While it ought to be possible to reach an agreement in the case of "technology", likely with the help of disambiguation, philosophy seems a fit candidate for what Gallie (1956) called an essentially contested concept. Originally suggested in the context of treatments of art and justice, essentially contested concepts involve fervent and continued disagreements, but mutually recognized reason-giving about open ended phenomena. While collectively, we are not ready to abandon philosophy, it is in the nature of philosophy that there is no universal agreement on what its goals and methods are. Each mode of philosophy comes with its own metaphilosophy, and it is an integral part of philosophy to try to say what philosophy is.[2]

The reader might be exasperated by the vagueness surrounding the two concepts that define the collection, and the prospects of gaining a representative overview will seem dim. This feeling might only be compounded by a key statement that is found in what is probably the most influential paper in the philosophy of technology to come out of the 20th century – one of many papers that saw "*Technik*" become "technology" in its translation: "[T]he essence of technology is nothing technological" (QCT, p. 35). However, rather than add to our despair, it suggests something important about the use of the concept technology. The concept has continued to fill a void in the writings of different philosophers, and the meaning has been made clearer by seeing how their concepts of technology relates to other key concepts found in their thinking. If one wants to under-

---

[2] Offering, and arguing for, new definitions is a part of the ongoing contestation. Philosopher of information, Floridi, is deeply involved in discussions of technologies and has done definitional work of a philosophical problem in the light of his philosophy of information (Floridi, 2013).

stand Marx's discussion of technologies, one should at the very least explore some of the cases he discusses and the concepts of value and work, objectification and alienation. Conceptions of metaphysics, causality and ideas surrounding the concept of dwelling are important to those approaching Heidegger's philosophy of technology. It is in relation to such concepts and examples that we see their point of discussing tools, acts of building and use of machines. Their philosophical outlook is an important part of the "background bustle" on which their concepts of technology are shaped and their concerns expressed. Of course, philosophers cannot do whatever they want with concepts. Each concept comes with a history, but it is one that is sometimes altered and shaped by those philosophers. Concepts are, after all, the material that philosophers in different ways give shape to. This activity is an essential part of their craft.

With "philosophy" considered an essentially contested concept and "technology" a radically vague concept, this book does not set out by offering definitions. The structure and contents of the book is informed by the conditions for thinking and thinking philosophically, so well described by Dewey:

> There is no thinking which does not present itself on a background of tradition, and tradition has an intellectual quality that differentiates it from blind custom. Traditions are ways of interpretation and of observation, of valuation, of everything explicitly thought of. They are the circumambient atmosphere which thought must breathe; no one ever had an idea except as he inhaled some of this atmosphere. (LW6, p. 13)

This in turn makes traditions of thought the background on which the questions concerning philosophy are treated. Rather than describe these traditions in the abstract, this book is structured around the development of traditions as they are made concrete in the writings of historical philosophers, and the way the traditions they worked in have been carried forward by more contemporary philosophers. By focusing on people, and not questions, one runs the risk of engaging in a degenerate form of philosophy that becomes mere scholasticism, being one unnecessary step away from what truly matters: the kind of questions and problems suggested by Rosenberger & Verbeek's description of a field within philosophy of technology. That is a genuine risk. The material in this book is arranged historically also from acknowledging the converse risk. If not presented historically, one might miss important patterns in answering and raising the type of questions that Rosenberger & Verbeek point to. When it comes to identifying the kind of patterns that makes it possible to go on and continue doing philosophy of technology, historical modes of thought deserve our attention.

1.2 A flawed but promising history of the philosophy of technology

Fortunately, "philosophy of technology" does not work in a way comparable to a definite description, where we identify what is talked about by combining the meanings of two terms. Rather, it functions as a proper name of a collection that has already been delimited and arranged in a certain way by other academics having taken on the role of a custodian. One way of arranging the collection has acquired sufficient stability, to be widely referred to in discussions of the technologies that currently capture our imagination. Here, it is found in an excerpt from an engaging and influential discussion of machine ethics:

> While old-style philosophy of technology was mostly reactive, and often motivated by the specter of powerful processes beyond people's control, a new generation of philosophers of technology are more proactive. (Wallach & Allen, 2009, p. 38)

This excerpt expresses what I suggest is a flawed, but widely held view of the history of philosophy of technology, even when there is large agreement on what philosophers and concepts should be in the collection. Yet, it also expresses a genuine hope for one of the roles that philosophy of technology can serve.

As to its flaws, received history of the philosophy of technology suggests a movement from a state of play where academics are hurling stones from ivory towers, to one where they constructively engage with the design of technical artefacts. They bring to the practice of design of systems and artefacts an awareness of values and the importance of human practices in all their diversity that are at stake when technologies mesh with humans, their families and institutions. Thinkers like Heidegger, Ellul and Marcuse and possibly Marx, are cast in the role as old-style or classical philosophers. Supposedly, they saw the phenomenon of technology as a monolithic force that has a corrosive effect on societies and its mores. Then, in the late 1970's, philosophy of technology begins what is called the empirical turn. An influential academic custodian was Hans Achterhuis, whose *American Philosophy of Technology: The Empirical Turn* suggested that a substantial change took place as philosophers like Andrew Feenberg, Langdon Winner, Albert Borgmann and Donna Haraway began "to look at the manifold ways in which technology manifests itself" (2001, p. 3).

Karl Marx, who at a distance might seem to fit the bill of a classical philosopher of technology, seemed deeply committed to the collection, analysis and presentation of empirical material. One manifestation of this is the way that extensive data material was updated by Marx for the second edition of the first volume of *Capital*. While concerned with industrialization, Marx's remarks in *Cap-*

ital about seeing education in that light – for example as a sausage factory – has entered Danish vernacular and informed countless analyses of education, academics, teachers and students in academia. In what I suggest is the same tradition and also lumped with the classics, Herbert Marcuse certainly saw and described the influence of technologies in more arenas of life. While not predominantly conducting empirical studies in an academic setting, he was also a man who was deeply engaged in the ongoings of societies. He worked for years as an analyst for the precursor for the American Central Intelligence Agency and followed and influenced social movements in the 60's. A constant theme in Marcuse's mode of engagement was a discussion of different kinds of technologies and their effect on the human subject. More examples, some found in this book, abound. They make it hard to see a clear partition in the history of the field between those philosophers who did or did not "refrain from addressing concrete technological practices" (Achterhuis, 2001, p. 5).

I suggest that further markers of the change from classical to empirical philosophy of technology are overstated. Albert Borgmann, one empirical philosopher of technology also treated in this book, does seem to see in technology a certain force, or character, that transforms our society, and in a relevant sense, he can be seen to be reactive. Philip Brey (2010) has maintained the distinction between empirical and classical philosophy of technology, and suggests that the philosophers belonging in the latter category are characterised by a distinct pessimism about technologies in the aftermath of the First and Second World Wars. As we explore in the chapters to come, this picture lacks accuracy. Influential philosophers of technology, empirical as well as classical, have expressed optimism and pessimism quite independently of the horrific events of the 20th century. In short, when Marcuse is presented predominantly as a pessimist, as Brey joins many others in doing, I suggest that at least one of the objects in the collection of philosophers deserves a dusting off. As this book progresses, it should become clear that more of the classical, and even empirical philosophers, similarly deserve a second and more detailed look in the context of discussing philosophy and technology.

This is not to say that changes in moods associated with philosophical analyses of technology cannot be discerned when one surveys philosophers' engagement with technology in the latter half of the 20th century. Furthermore, philosophers such as Jacques Ellul, counted among the classical philosophers, fit the bill quite well. The point of questioning the discontinuity between classical and later philosophers of technology is rather to stress the relevance of classical philosophy to more recent developments. This is the promising aspect of the history of philosophy of technology. While the intellectual history is complex, one turn from the classical mode was carried out by Science and Technology Studies.

1.2 A flawed but promising history of the philosophy of technology — 11

Here there was a reaction against overarching narratives about technology and a perceived lack of attention to detail, and many interesting cases of design and uptake (or lack of uptake) of technologies have been subject to empirical exploration.

What I take to be a more promising history is that which traces and seeks to further engagement between those with technical knowledge – tinkerers, designers and engineers – and those who think hard about the kinds of questions concerning technology that we saw absorb post-phenomenological as well as most other philosophers of technology. These are questions of agency, value, fairness, subjectivity, the good life and the nature of reality, among others. An anecdote involving what I take to be an overlooked, "classical" philosopher of technology exemplifies the promise.[3] Tinkerer and engineer Lee Felsenstein was one of the many pioneers of the now global communication network. During the early 1970's, when he played a central role in setting up the first publicly available computer network, called "community memory", at a music store in Berkeley, his father sent him a copy of *Tools for Conviviality* by Austrian born, theology trained Ivan Illich. Upon reading it – Felsenstein and Illich later met – Felsenstein found that many of his instincts about the importance of tools for the formation of communities (and vice versa) and about the way tools should be designed, were crystallised in Illich's concept of conviviality. This concept was otherwise at home mainly in Roman Catholic theology. It gave Felsenstein the idea of giving specifications for "A Convivial Cybernetic Device" which helped shape the thinking among other developers who eventually thought that a tool for computing should be personal. The rest is, as they say, history, though it is in many ways out of tune with Illich's and Felsenstein's instincts and convictions about our tools.

There are more such examples. Some of Illich's ideas feature in Christopher Alexander's thought and practice in architecture. Alexander's ideas about design patterns were in turn studied by software programmers and influenced the development of object-oriented programming. The more general idea, which many throughout history have seized on, is combining the concepts and ideas typically at home in philosophy and other areas of the humanities, and having those concepts play into the design of the technologies we surround ourselves with: to not come late to the technological developments, but play a role in shaping them. Marcuse expressed the idea and the hope very clearly. Cur-

---

3 See Isaacson (2014) for an account of the early beginnings of the development of some of the technologies – such as the internet and the personal computer – that in many ways shape lives and societies today.

rently, value sensitive design – also with origins in software design – is one attempt at putting into practice, in a systematic fashion, the lessons of the interaction between Felsenstein and Illich.[4] Many schools in design have shown a clear awareness of the interplay between human values and the design of technologies; what characterises value sensitive design is the breadth of fields, values, and technologies the methodology allows for.

Achterhuis took great care to emphasise the importance of the lessons learned from the classical philosophers of technology as the empirically inclined philosophers took over. An exposition of value sensitive design by Albrechtslund (2007) opens with drawing attention to the background in Langdon Winner's work. Langdon Winner, in turn, was addressing themes that had clearly emerged from the writings of Karl Marx. As mentioned, the very idea of value sensitive design found clear expression in another Marxist thinker, Marcuse. These connections are but one example of how the historical patterns and traces can assist contemporary attempts at engaging in a very practical mode of philosophy.

Exploring the development of the history of philosophy of technology can serve different purposes in addition to being a resource for those involved with or interested in such design processes. Firstly, themes in philosophy of technology can inspire, assist, and invigorate other areas of philosophy. Much academic discussion of virtue theory is carried out without considering the ways technologies shape our actions and frame conditions for the fostering of virtue. While questioning the distinction between means and ends that features so centrally in one of the formulations of the categorical imperative, Latour suggests that the moral law is also in our apparatuses (2002). Such examples suggest that drawing the disciplines of ethics and philosophy of technology even closer holds promise. Discussions of the nature of the mind are often carried out by modelling the mind on informational technologies, and the concept of a mechanism has been influential in our attempts at understanding the mind. The new policy in the Danish public schools is based on a movement in education called computational thinking; in addition, there are computational theories of mind. I shall not here begin to disentangle the complex history of the word "compute", but concepts of tools and machines would be integral to such an attempt. Secondly, philosophy of technology can assist other areas of academic and practical study. For example, when historian Francis Fukuyama (2012) reflects on the continued movement of history, this soon involves a discussion of the possibility of

---

[4] Working under a mottos of "frontloading ethics" or "engineering activism" (Nissenbaum, 2001), value sensitive design has a history of more than 20 years. A recent overview is provided by Friedman & Hendry (2019).

human control over technological systems and their development, as well as discussions of human nature. These emerge as key themes, in very different ways, in the work of several of the philosophers surveyed in the chapters to come. As the discipline of design spreads and finds the need to systematize the kind of thinking and approaches characteristic of design, more have looked to the thought of Dewey, while claiming inspiration in specific designs from Borgmann (e.g. Dalsgaard, 2014). Finally, anyone may simply desire to understand oneself and one's environment and find that this soon involves sustained reflection on the nature of technology.

1.3 Plan of the book

The material in this book cuts across a range of well established fields in philosophy, such as virtue ethics, metaphysics, philosophy of science and philosophy of language. Being about technologies and the way they shape us and our environment, it necessarily draws on developments that are typically studied by other academic branches, such as history, sociology, communication and economics. While I shall have recourse to critically discuss the reception and understanding of some of the philosophers of technology at the hands of contemporary scholars, the nature of the material means that many questions cannot be explored in depth. As a custodian seeking to draw out historical patterns of thought, in order to make them fit for use in other intellectual pursuits, I try and steer clear of the sometimes internecine fights and long standing, often highly intricate discussions that characterise and surround discussion of much philosophy.

In addition to treating questions that have a long and sophisticated history of discussion in different branches of philosophy, the presentation has to find a compromise between squabbling over the latest communication platforms and gadgets and trying to discuss something inherently practical and worldly in terms too abstracted from the technological world we inhabit. I have on occasion drawn attention to critical discussions of technologies in higher education. This is an environment that most readers will be familiar with, and it is certainly one that academics have found worthy of attention.

A minority of the philosophers of technology presented in the following chapters have identified themselves in that way. Some are beyond any straightforward categorisation, while others are key figures in critical theory, phenomenology and pragmatism. Reading and discussing these thinkers as philosophers of technology is unquestionably a distortion of their overall philosophy. It amounts to putting a magnifying glass to their texts – some elements are clearer while others are out of focus and distorted. However, concepts of technology have played a sufficiently central role in their writings to warrant such a reading. The selection of philosophers is made with a view to first bring into focus questions concerning technology, and then explore how these questions and traditions of working with them have shaped continued development in later philosophers. There are excellent and weighty philosophers of technology that are not treated in the chapters. One of my own favourites, Ivan Illich, does not fit into the historical and philosophical narratives that the book tries to bring into focus. On that count, he and others have been left to one side. Others, such as Andrew Feenberg, have their own books dedicated to them, and Feenberg in particular serves as an aid to understanding on multiple occasions. Other philosophers of technology serve as conversation partners in the arranging of objects.

Chapters 2, 3 and 4 on Marx, Marcuse and Winner set out with an account of how technologies used in production had a detrimental effect on the worker. In Marx's thought, work is a crucial avenue of the development of the human subject and flourishing, and his is a tale of technology leaving the worker severely impoverished. The theme of the subjectivity of the worker and the spread of technologies originally at home in production is a theme that Marcuse explores in depth. Though being a close witness to two wars and the demise of the revolution in the 60's, Marcuse continued to display not just pessimistic, but also hopeful strands of thought in relation to technology. Other themes from Marx are those of the role of technologies in the development of history and our perceived lack of a role in shaping history, as technological systems seem to take on a life of their own. This is a theme that Winner has explored in detail.

Heidegger's works, explored in chapter 5, have started a tradition in the philosophy of technology that aligns themes in metaphysics, technology, culture and human dwelling. Heidegger's last written words, in the form of a greeting, questioned the possibility of a homeland in a world made uniform by technology. Chapter 6 explores how Albert Borgmann has taken this question as his point of departure in his entire authorship. Relying on the concept of a thing inspired by Heidegger, he analyses in more detail the way technologies structure the possibilities of flourishing in one's environment, which is orientated around the home. Borgmann integrates a distinct virtue theoretic line of thought to those themes more clearly present in Heidegger, and chapter 6 contrasts Borgmann's approach with more recent discussions of technology that draw on virtue theory and emphasize the need for a global ethics.

Finally, chapters 7 and 8 explore key thinkers in the tradition of pragmatism that Rosenberger & Verbeek relied on when describing their field. Placing Dewey next to Latour is perhaps the biggest rearrangement of items in the collection as I found it. In these two cases, separating the philosophy – and philosophy of technology – from other strands in their thinking is difficult and doing it might distort their thought the most. Yet, their approaches display a very similar structure. They both place technologies at the centre of a treatment of a question that has vexed much philosophical thought: the relation between words and things. They bring empirical approaches to questions of reference and realism, and in their own ways contribute to some of the most intricate questions in philosophy. Challenging and replacing Plato's myth of the demiurge as the chief artisan of reality, they explore and challenge ideas of making and tool use as they contribute to a discussion of the understanding that philosophers (Dewey's focus) and scientists (Latour's focus) have of reality.

2 Karl Marx: What machines do

2.1 Rousseau's challenge

Karl Marx wrote in the context of a culture having long sought to understand its character and plot its trajectory. While a widespread sense of superiority had pervaded European self-understanding for some time, 18th-century thinkers had begun to moderate the tale of progress achieved through increased measures of freedom and reliance on reason. At the outset of the 18th century, Giambattista Vico had addressed what he took to be a general lack of proper judgement of individuals consumed by instrumental reasoning. About half a century later, Jean Jacques Rousseau would express the point of view that the Enlightenment, with its increase in knowledge and exercise of reason, was being achieved at the price of moral downfall and widespread unhappiness. The literary device of a noble savage was widely employed to criticise those convinced that the Europeans were an example of civilisation *par excellence.*

Today, when we see optimism and belief in progress expressed in connection with new technologies, from discussions of artificial intelligence to hopes for new energy forms, it should be seen as a faint echo of a more deep-seated optimism that pervaded European thinkers in the 18th and 19th centuries. A widespread response to Rousseau's challenge was to make good the claimed superiority by describing societal ailments as an integral element of a civilisational ascent. Kant, Fichte and Hegel all subscribed to varieties of this response which made history remain a tale of progress. According to Fichte, history consisted of five epochs and humankind had just begun to enter the third, characterised by freedom. With liberation from priesthoods and dogmas came indifference, greed and selfishness, and later stages were to do away with these harmful elements of the third stage of history.[1] Removed from the continent, Adam Smith subscribed to a different historical narrative. He suggested that there are four, increasingly advanced, stages of history. He considered England, a then leading country in commerce and industry, to be in the final, commercial stage. In so far as this epoch provided for man's basic desires (security and vanity, among others) and fit his nature well, Smith did not foresee any further stages of the development of civilisation. While the means of providing food served to demarcate the first three stages (hunting, shepherding and agriculture), the commercial stage was characterised by an increased division of labour and corresponding developments in trade. A characteristic of Marx was that he made productive

---

[1] See Fichte's 1806 *The Characteristics of the Present Age* (2009).

technologies an integral part of his own version of a similar narrative of civilisational progress.

Smith had studied the preconditions for the creation of wealth and had predominantly focused on the legal systems that had allowed for progressively complex kinds of commerce. In his writings, Smith alternates between an optimistic, teleological account of history with frequent reference to progress and a more pessimistic view. Though Smith did not suggest that there were markedly different stages on the horizon, he had a keen eye for the darker side of the emerging commercial and industrial societies. Slavery had not been universally abolished, and slaves were, in fact, worse off due to the greater protection from interference that their owners enjoyed by virtue of property laws. What Smith called "intellectual, social, and martial virtues" (1776, p. 603) suffered as a consequence of increased wealth, and labourers had become "mutilated and deformed" (1776, p. 607) in their mind and character as a result of the division of labour.

Smith primarily discussed production under the aegis of consumption[2] and he had correlated legal frameworks, allowing for increasingly sophisticated kinds of property, with the different stages. In *Capital,* Marx emphasised production and the use of tools as a guide to the stage of history, as well as to an understanding of the worker:

> Relics of bygone instruments of labour possess the same importance for the investigation of extinct economic forms of society, as do fossil bones for the determination of extinct species of animals. It is not the articles made, but how they are made, and by what instruments, that enables us to distinguish different economic epochs. Instruments of labour not only supply a standard of the degree of development to which human labour has attained, but they are also indicators of the social conditions under which that labour is carried on. (MECW 35, p. 189 f).

This does not amount to the claim, once held by some commentators, that Marx thought that technologies in themselves were *the*, or even *a*, driving force in the unfolding of history.[3] The general tenor of the first volume of Marx's *Capital* suggests that the desire to increase what he called relative surplus value could fill that role, at least in recent history, as it was shaped by capitalism. Nevertheless, to characterise and understand a particular stage of history *qua* economic devel-

---

2 For example: "Consumption is the sole end and purpose of all production; and the interest of the producer ought to be attended to only as far as it may be necessary for promoting that of the consumer. The maxim is so perfectly self-evident that it would be absurd to attempt to prove it" (Smith, 1776, p. 512).
3 See Shaw (1979) for a version of this position. It is one of the themes from Marx that we return to in chapter 4.

opment and "social conditions", Marx relies on the nature of the tools used in production. In some of his early works, such as *The German Ideology*, Marx located different historical stages that were marked by different social circumstances surrounding production – mainly to do with division of labour and ownership. Starting from tribal ownership, Marx suggested that human societies had progressed through city-states and feudalism. With production being arranged in a capitalist fashion, workers, in particular, could look forward to a future communist stage.

A set of tools is of course more than a mere marker for a historical stage. As suggested by the quote above, and as we explore in this chapter, there is an intimate connection between what Marx calls instruments of labour and the societal conditions that prevail at any given stage. Central to Marx's approach to technology is the understanding of history embodied in what has become known as historical materialism. According to this, there is a Hegelian-inspired progression in history. With Marx, the basis of historical development is man's material production. What drives history is the continued development of productive forces (people's aggregate productive capacities) coupled with recurring tensions in the dominant social relations (such as capitalism) under which the productive capacities are exercised. More specifically, Marx's account of technology is chiefly an account of how an emerging element of the productive forces – the machine – was a materialisation of increased tensions in the social arrangements in which it was placed – capitalism – and how these tensions would eventually lead to the appearance of a more harmonious stage in history.

2.2 Work and objectification

Throughout his works, Marx stresses the centrality of productive activity in understanding human beings.[4] To Marx, one would be wrong to consider work as something one should get over and done with in order to somehow realise oneself in leisurely or contemplative activities. Rather, work itself is a fundamen-

---

[4] When comparing Marx's emphasis with different philosophical accounts of human beings, it stands out more clearly. Quite generally, a lot of philosophy, from Descartes to branches of Artificial Intelligence, have in different ways conceived of man primarily as a thinking, rational being. Allen Wood suggests that Marx in fact provides little argument for ascribing such fundamental importance to production as the essential human function. He ascribes to Marx the position that "...human history ... is best made intelligible in terms of the fundamental human aspiration to develop and exercise the productive powers of society" (2004, p. 30). In a Marxist setting, the emphasis on work has been thoroughly criticised by Weeks (2011).

tal need, and fulfilling it is by no means necessarily unpleasant or denigrating. The focal point of Marx's treatment of technology is what he calls instruments of labour. Marx was primarily concerned with developments that had led to the widespread existence of complex, machine-based factories, and the conditions such factories offered its workers.

Marx would look to Engels when thinking about "prehistoric" man, and in his conception of work, Marx leaned on various philosophers and scientists in order to characterise both the nature of work and, in his view, its utterly deformed state in middle 19th century England. Humans have needs for nourishment and security that are shared with large parts of the animal kingdom. Humans are characterised as beings that seek to shape nature to their wants and needs. With Aristotelian inspiration, Marx claims that the labourer "effects a change of form in the material on which he works" (MECW 35, p. 188). When appealing to form, Marx distinguishes human labour from that of animal labour. Many animals, such as the spider and the beaver, will similarly adjust the environment and build complex structures while other animals appear to use tools. Humans, however, do it in accordance with a preconceived mental representation and are conscious of the object of this representation in different ways. For instance, the less attractive the work is, the more the human labourer will have to align her will with his purpose actively; further, she may identify more or less with her labour and its product.

Interspersed between the human being and the subject of his work, we find the instruments of labour. In primitive states of development, tools may be supplied by the environment (such as stones for cutting). As humans evolve, tools become increasingly complex and the idea of humans working wilfully to sculpt and arrange nature with tools of increasing sophistication in order to provide for wants and needs, hardly even begins to capture the fullness of the concept of work that Marx draws on in his treatment of technology. Perhaps most significant is the fact that labour is performed under various social conditions. Marx expresses this in his 1849 *Wage Labour and Capital:* "In production, men enter into relation not only with nature. They produce only by co-operating in a certain way and mutually exchanging their activities. In order to produce, they enter into definite connections and relations with one another and only within these social connections and relations does their relation with nature, does production, take place" (MECW 9, p. 211). The worker could be a member of a guild, a manager, a slave, a university lecturer or some other defining social category.

To designate the particularly human worker, Marx uses the term "*Gattungswesen*", taken from Hegel and translated as "species being" or "species essence". In the course of his writings, Marx would frequently replace this expression with

"*Gemeinwesen*", which indicates that it is essential for humans to stand in *some* social relations, be it a family, a guild or a commune. Further, in addition to stressing that humans belong to and depend on a community, in his early *Economic and Philosophical manuscripts of 1844*, Marx emphasises that they are aware of this belonging and dependence. A human being is a species being in more than one way: "[N]ot only because in practice and in theory he adopts the species (his own as well as those of other things) as his object, but – and this is only another way of expressing it – also because he treats himself as the actual, living species; because he treats himself as a universal and therefore a free being" (MECW 3, p. 275). Whatever else belongs to the self-understanding of human beings, being an instantiation of a species is always a part of it. This understanding might be highly articulate in contexts of social and philosophical thought, but whether articulated or not, it remains present in the practical and material activity that concerns Marx.

A central social phenomenon is that of ownership. Locke had described labour as a way of extending property from one's body to previously untouched nature. This notion had revolutionary content in a largely feudal context, where the owners of land were far removed from manual and practical work on it. Adam Smith and other economists had pointed out that Locke's model of property by the annexation of untouched nature made for a poor model of Western European conditions and worked on a different model of the relationship between labour and property. While being well aware of these explanatory problems in law and economics, Marx retained the emphasis on the close association with labour and, if not property, a set of moral rights. To Marx, the moral rights have their source in the fact that when at work, human beings engage in objectification ("*Vergegenständlichung*") – best described as self-actualisation. It is an idea that can be traced to both Aristotle as well as the expressivist trains of thought that were flourishing in German Romanticism.[5] Marx combines several of the ideas just outlined in an early manuscript on James Mill: "In the individual expression of my life I would have directly created your expression of your life, and therefore in my individual activity I would have directly *confirmed* and *realised* my true nature, my *human* nature, my *communal nature*" (MECW 3, p. 228). To succeed and flourish as a human is to exercise and develop a distinct set of human skills, and in doing so, bring to expression one's humanity. Like a sculptor may wish to bring something to expression in a statue, so too does the worker make an imprint of himself as an individual, as well as his general humanity, in

---

[5] It has been suggested that Fichte, in particular, expressed many of the ideas Marx was relying on with his notion of objectification. See *e.g.* Rockmore (1980) and Seigel (2005), chapter 11.

2.2 Work and objectification — 21

the object that he produces. In addition to having mixed labour with nature and possibly created property, the worker has created an object distinct from himself, in which he can recognise himself and his humanity.

We can sum up the different aspects of the objectification with a description of the labour of the traditional shoemaker. First, the production of a pair of shoes serves a given purpose, and the production accordingly has a certain use: protection from the environment, comfort or display of financial means. This bestows the product with use-value. Secondly, having worked on various natural materials, the shoemaker will have formed nature in accordance with his will and design. He might be proud of the design of the shoe, and he might have had to convince himself to spend his efforts on the shoe at the expense of a range of other possibilities, under the heading of leisure. Thirdly, the shoes will have been produced under certain social circumstances: he might be at the top of a hierarchy in the shoemaker shop, which in turn might be located in premises rented from a landowner. He might praise the work of the leather carver whose efforts and skills are on display in the shoe. Such social circumstances can change, but only slightly through the efforts of the individual, to whom they will appear largely as a given. Fourthly, the actual use of the shoe will remind the worker of features of his inherent humanity – his species being – according to what the shoe will be used for (it may carry associations of vanity or belligerence, depending on the type of footwear), and he will consider himself in the light of his product. He *is* a shoemaker, and in the shoe his powers and capabilities reach an expression.[6] In Marx's vocabulary, here from *The German Ideology*:

> The way in which men produce their means of subsistence depends first of all on the nature of the means of subsistence they actually find in existence and have to reproduce. This mode of production must not be considered simply as being the reproduction of the physical existence *of* the individuals. Rather it is a definite form of activity of these individuals, a definite form of expressing their life, a definite *mode of life* on their part. As individuals express their life, so they are. What they are, therefore, coincides with their production, both with *what* they produce and with *how* they produce. (MECW 5, p. 31f.)

When Marx in other contexts speaks of an appropriation between the worker and the object he produces, a Lockean account of property might suggest itself to the reader. As noted, Marx the economist knew well that Locke's model was inappropriate for Western Europe, and he was loath to take the explanatory route that

---

[6] We have exemplified objectification in a case where labour results in a physical product. Much work, such as that of transportation, cannot immediately mirror itself this way. Accordingly, we should take Marx to understand "object" in a quite general way such as "bringing about a change in external states of affairs".

Smith and other economists had taken, which relied on the notion of the worker receiving a fair pay for putting his labour into a product that he did not end up owning. Instead, when Marx speaks of appropriation of objects on behalf of the worker, we should emphasise its close relation to the process self-making, and indeed, a platform from which one can criticise a one-sided focus on relating to an object as somebody's legal property.

2.3 From craftsman to machine appendage

It is on this background that productive technologies attain a key role in Marx's diagnosis of the nature of production and the conditions of self-making under capitalism. Marx sought to confront the philosophy of his immediate predecessors to the extent that he considered them too far removed from considerations of material life. He devoted himself to a detailed study of the conditions of the emerging factory worker. In this, he was aided by the studies of Friedrich Engels and Charles Babbage in particular. Marx understood capitalism as a process of valorisation – the creation of value. The capitalist is not interested in the usevalue of the product, but in the product as something that can be exchanged at a price. This interest is purified as the relevance of local restraints of production and consumption diminishes with increased access to international markets. Capitalism as a particular, social ordering of production is set in motion by the concentration of means (money and land) in the hands of a rising class of merchants.[7] Alongside the amassing of capital, a group of previously independent artisans become wage-earners. As such, they are reliant on the means of production that are now owned and made available by the capitalist, who also owns what was produced utilising tools and later, machines.

Marx's account of technological development in production was not intended as a historically accurate description. His account of the rise of complex machine technology was informed by stages he calls co-operation, manufacture and modern industry. An overarching theme in Marx's account of technology

---

[7] Views of capitalism might influence accounts of its rise. Adam Smith ascribed the emergence of division of labour to a humanly innate "propensity to truck, barter and exchange" (Smith, 1776, p. 15), and capitalism was considered as a matter of fully realising human potential, through increasingly complex exchange between individuals, groups and nations. Marx held capitalism to have been initiated by contingent historical circumstances (primarily, gains from colonies) that led to the concentration of capital which was invested rather than consumed. Both views have fundamentally shaped subsequent accounts of European economic history. See *e.g.* Duplessis (1997).

is the fact that in the capitalist mode of production, work is predominantly viewed from a different angle than that of use-value and self-making. The theme is here expressed in *Capital:*

> We have now to consider this labour under a very different aspect from that which it had during the labour process; there, we viewed it solely as that particular kind of human activity which changes cotton into yarn; there, the more the labour was suited to the work, the better the yarn, other circumstances remaining the same… Here, on the contrary … we consider the labour of the spinner only so far as it is value-creating… (MECW 35, p. 199).

The value Marx mentions is exchange-value for commodities on a market, and not the particular use-value of a given product. Under this new view of things "…the addition of new value takes place not by virtue of his labour being spinning in particular, or joinering in particular, but because it is labour in the abstract, a portion of the total labour of society; and we see next that the value added is of a given definite amount, not because his labour has a special utility, but because it is exerted for a definite time" (MECW 35, p. 211). As we explore in this section, such a shift was, to a great extent, made possible by developments in production technologies. As a consequence of this new, dominant way of viewing labour – *i.e.* primarily as something abstract and a matter of creating exchange-value – the notion of skilled labour became increasingly relativised to the requirements of capital, rather than the inherent complexity of the work process.[8] The account of technology goes through stages and culminates with the machine, which Marx presents as an expression of the utter deskilling and personal impoverishment of the worker.

The capitalist is eager to create surplus value, which is a matter of commodities that can be exchanged at a higher value than the aggregate of values that goes into producing them (such as labour, raw materials and depreciation of instruments of labour). There are two ways of increasing surplus value. Initially, it

---

[8] In *Capital*, Marx points out: "Accidental circumstances here play so great a part, that these two forms of labour [skilled and unskilled] sometimes change places. Where, for instance, the physique of the working-class has deteriorated, and is, relatively speaking, exhausted, which is the case in all countries with a well developed capitalist production, the lower forms of labour, which demand great expenditure of muscle, are in general considered as skilled, compared with much more delicate forms of labour; the latter sink down to the level of unskilled labour. Take as an example the labour of a bricklayer, which in England occupies a much higher level than that of a damask-weaver" (MECW 35, p. 208). One can compare this with the challenge that Moravec's paradox presents to the contemporary drives for automation, nicely summarised by Marvin Minsky: "Easy things are hard" (1988, p. 29), such as physically moving, assembling and installing the furniture in our homes. In contrast, practicing law and medicine might prove comparatively easy, allowing for automation entering these fields.

is achieved by way of increasing what Marx calls absolute surplus value. This would be accomplished by seeking to reduce workers' idleness or waste of raw materials in the production process, by lengthening the working day or through "small thefts of time", such as shortening breaks. In this state of play, where "moments are the elements of profits" (MECW 35, p. 251), the capitalist could do little but introduce night shifts and allow women and children into his workforce, as employment of these people was subject to fewer legal constraints. Such ways of proceeding will quickly result in increased tension between the employers and employees, and another route to surplus value must be taken by the capitalist:

> At first, capital subordinates labour on the basis of the technical conditions in which it historically finds it. It does not, therefore, change immediately the mode of production. The production of surplus value – in the form hitherto considered by us – by means of simple extension of the working day, proved, therefore, to be independent of any change in the mode of production itself. It was not less active in the oldfashioned bakeries than in the modern cotton factories. (MECW 35, p. 314)

Changing the "technical conditions" is the second route to surplus value. We here move from what Marx calls a mere formal subordination of labour to a material subordination. This is the route of relative surplus value, described in the central part IV of *Capital*. Now, the strategy of the capitalist is not to prolong the number of working hours or number of workers, but to increase the efficiency with which the work is done. The mode of production becomes the variable: "The technical and social conditions of the process, and consequently the very mode of production must be revolutionised, before the productiveness of labour can be increased" (MECW 35, p. 320).

On the surface, the first stage of production, referred to as "cooperation", was anything but technically sophisticated. It consisted of making a large number of workers work simultaneously. Employing large numbers of workers has the effect of smoothing out deviations in labour quality, allowing the capitalist to calculate with "average labour-power". Further, it allows the capitalist to purchase fewer tools for his labourers, as the tools can be shared, and he has fewer costs from housing a labourer when there are more of them under one roof. Moreover, social contact in the workshop "begets in most industries an emulation and a stimulation of the animal spirits that heighten the efficiency of each individual workman" (MECW 35, p. 331). Finally, having workers cooperate creates new powers (e. g. when it comes to lifting) and "a body of men working in concert has hands and eyes both before and behind, and is, to a certain degree, omnipresent" (MECW 35, p. 332). This style of cooperation is by no means particular to the capitalist mode of production, but cooperation is now orchestrated by the capitalist, who is the one able to organise a sufficient number of wage-earners. Meanwhile, the antagonism between wage-labourer and capitalist remains. To both orchestrate the cooperation and negotiate the resistance of workers, a particular kind of wage-earner is born: the manager, also called the supervisor, with whom a new set of specialised skills emerge.

The next stage from cooperation is the period and arrangement of production that Marx calls manufacture. What characterises this period is the widespread introduction of division of labour. Different types of craftsmen are put under one roof in order to produce, say, a carriage. The craftsmen naturally become specialised, as for instance when the locksmith ceases to perform the full breadth of his craft. A revolutionary kind of division of labour is that made famous by Smith in his description of needle-making. A labour process is broken down into a set of smaller operations and in time replaces a handicraft. In spite of the specialisation found in manufacture, it fundamentally remains manual labour of a kind Marx calls detail labour.[9] It is more efficient by virtue of its repeated employment of a narrower range of skills, and the capitalist has achieved the desired increase in productive powers gained from the labourer. The detail labourer is more efficient because he does not have to change tools in the course of his work. All day long he will work with the same tool, and as a consequence, the tools of the labourer also become highly specialised. As an example, Marx recounts how 300 varieties of hammers at one point were in production in Birmingham (cf. MECW 35, p. 346).

Manufacture lays the grounds for the use of machines which characterises the next stage, modern industry. In the sense of "machine" that we will now explore, the machine was already present under manufacture: "The collective labourer, formed by the combination of a number of detail labourers, is the machinery specially characteristic of the manufacturing period" (MECW 35, p. 354). While manufacture embodies a human, tool-using labour force, in modern industry, the tool is to a great extent taken away from the hand of the worker and replaced with non-human, "cyclopean"[10] versions of the human tool users. The transfer was made possible by the specialisation of both labour

---

[9] Marx's usage of "manufacture" thus deviates from what has become the general accepted meaning of the word, which includes and often emphasises mechanised production in factories. Its Latin etymology, *manu factus*, made by hand, is, in exposition of Marx, more helpful, as "hand" is most often taken to include tools in this usage.

[10] Wendling (2009, p. 145 ff.) provides an overview of how Marx employs figures such as the monster, the werewolf and the cyclop to describe machinery in modern industry. We return to this theme in chapter 4 when we discuss analyses of Mary Shelley's Frankenstein.

and tools that had taken place in manufacture, and now, giant hammers, lathes, drills and more were driven by a powerful motor mechanism.

Marx analyses the machine as a combination of three elements: the motor mechanism, the transmitting mechanism and the tool, also called working machine. While huge developments had taken place in the available motor mechanisms such as the steam engine, Marx ascribes the biggest industrial significance by far to the working machine: "The machine proper is therefore a mechanism that, after being set in motion, performs with its tools the same operations that were formerly done by the workman with similar tools" (MECW 35, p. 377). While the machine, such as Hargreaves' spinning Jenny, is freed from the physiological restrictions that come with reliance on a craftsman, this only becomes significant with the increase of the number of tools wielded by the machine, which increases the need for power. Enter the steam engine, which Marx describes in a philosophically pregnant way as a prime mover, whose power is nevertheless entirely under man's control. In sum, we have gone through a historical process where first, ownership of tools was transferred to the capitalist, to a situation where "workmen are merely conscious organs, co-ordinate with the unconscious organs of the automaton, and together with them, subordinated to the central moving-power" (MECW 35, p. 422).

A well-known theme in Marx's thinking is the tension between the classes that are defined according to ownership of production technologies. During manufacture, the capitalist would employ managers and foremen with the job of keeping pressure on the workforce. Now, the "... automaton, as capital ... is endowed, in the person of the capitalist, with intelligence and will" (MECW 35, p. 406). Quite generally, "machinery... revolutionises out and out the contract between the labourer and the capitalist, which formally fixes their mutual relations" (MECW 35, p. 399). The use of machinery in the production of goods allows for even more widespread enrolment of women and children in the workforce. The result of this is that "...machinery at last breaks down the resistance which the male operatives in the manufacturing period continued to oppose to the despotism of capital" (MECW 35, p. 405). Marx suggests that women and children are more docile in the face of the demands of the capitalist, but most importantly, "the implements of labour become automatic, things moving and working independent of the Workman" (MECW 35, p. 406).

It is now the machine, rather than a manager, that confronts the worker as an alien and sometimes hostile will that imposes a gruelling work schedule. While the length of the workday was reduced with the *Factory Acts* of the mid-19th century, machine owners compensated for the reduction by intensifying the labour done at the machines. With capitalism, the antagonism between tool owner and tool user did not initially leave any trace in the tools themselves or their operation. With the advent of the machine, "workmen are merely conscious organs, co-ordinate with the unconscious organs of the automaton, and together with them, subordinated to the central moving-power with use of machinery" (MECW 35, p. 422). With the machine, the "inversion [of tool user and tool] for the first time acquires technical and palpable reality" (MECW 35, p. 426).

We conclude Marx's account of the significance of production technologies with his response to "factory apologist", Andrew Ure. Ure maintained that large-scale mechanisation was for the benefit of all parties involved: "The constant aim and effect of scientific improvement in manufactures are philanthropic as they tend to relieve the workman either from niceties of adjustment which exhaust his mind and fatigue his eyes, or from painful repetition of effort which distort or wear out his frame" (Ure, 1835, p. 69 cited in MECW 35, p. 425). Marx's collaboration with Engels, as well as his study of H.M. Inspectors of Factories reports, allowed him to go to great lengths in painting a picture of factories that showed no sign of philanthropy at work: widespread use of child labour, crippling working conditions and increasingly fast-paced work. In short, the introduction of the machine resulted in anything but a reduction in human toil and fatigue. Apart from the dire consequences of the introduction of the machine, Marx maintained that the intentions of the capitalist rest squarely with profits. Thus, when labour becomes cheaper, it will become competitive with machinery: "In England women are still occasionally used instead of horses for hauling canal boats, because the labour required to produce horses and machines is an accurately known quantity, while that required to maintain the women of the surplus-population is below all calculation" (MECW 35, p. 397). Such practices would seem to support the claim that the prime purpose of the introduction of the machine was that of maximising surplus value.

2.4 Frustrated objectification: alienation

The chapters of *Capital* dedicated to the developments in tool use, culminating with a machine that wields both humans and tools, very much read as a moral defence of the worker against the onslaught of unbridled, technology-enhanced capitalism. The tenor of the moral indictment over the condition of workers is summed up in Marx's quotation of David Urquhart: "To subdivide a man is to execute him, if he deserves the sentence, to assassinate him if he does not... The subdivision of labour is the assassination of a people" (Urquhart, 1855,

p. 118 cited in MECW 35, p. 368).[11] Large parts of Marx's account of the worker's plight are carried out in terms immediately understood by most: hazardous and monotonous work, lowering of earnings and precarious employment. Such states of affairs can be found in many kinds of social circumstances surrounding production other than capitalism. However, when describing the ailments of the capitalist mode of production, Marx would throughout his authorship utilise the notions of alienation (*"Entaüsserung"*) and estrangement (*"Entfremdung"*). Marx's most immediate influence were the writings of Hegel and Feuerbach, but the concept is also found, among other places, in Fichte, Rousseau, Adam Smith and Aristotle.[12]

Marx's account of the machine emphasises that it is derived from human labour. In addition to this, the machine also displaces and impoverishes human labour and makes for an alienation of human labour. At a societal, macro-level, the connection between alienation and tool use is perhaps most concisely accounted for by showing how the structure of Marx's criticism mirrored the criticism of religion found in Feuerbach. The criticism is crystallised in two adaptations – those of Marx and Feuerbach – of a piece of Christian scripture. The scripture has it: "For you know the grace of our Lord Jesus Christ, that though he was rich, yet for your sakes he became poor, so that you through his poverty

---

[11] Marx was by no means the first to display a critical awareness of the detrimental effects of the division of labour. Utopian thinkers like Charles Fourier and Robert Owen had emphasised the crippling effects of fragmented labour, and Adam Smith is also very clear in his description: "… the understandings of the greater part of men are necessarily formed by their ordinary employments. The man whose whole life is spent in performing a few simple operations … has no occasion to exert his understanding… [He] generally becomes as stupid and ignorant as it is possible for a human creature to become" (1776, p. 603). After describing the stupidity of the detail labourer, Smith continues: "The uniformity of his stationary life naturally corrupts the courage of his mind… It corrupts even the activity of his body and renders him incapable of exerting his strength with vigour and perseverance in any other employments than that to which he has been bred. His dexterity at his own particular trade seems in this manner to be acquired at the expense of his intellectual, social, and martial virtues. But in every improved and civilised society, this is the state into which the labouring poor, that is, the great body of the people, must necessarily fall, unless government takes some pains to prevent it" (1776, p. 603).

[12] It is beyond the task pursued here to trace these different influences in detail. In brief, Aristotle's contribution is the distinction between an item's proper use, such as the shoe's use-value, and its improper use as an object of exchange that serves to amass limitless wealth in disregard of the proper functioning and purpose of a household. From Fichte and Hegel, Marx acquires the dynamics of self-making and activity, which in the Hegelian case gets its dynamic from states of alienation. In *The Phenomenology of Spirit*, Hegel expounds a four-stage theory of production, which includes appropriation, objectification, alienation and reappropriation (cf. Levine, 2012).

might become rich" (NIV, 2. cor 8:9). In Feuerbach's influential *The Essence of Christianity*, we see a by now familiar emphasis on the need for objectification in order for man to grasp himself: "Man is nothing without an object... But the object to which a subject essentially, necessarily, relates is nothing else than this subject's own, but objective nature. In the object which he contemplates, therefore, man becomes acquainted with himself" (2008, p. 4f.). In the case of Christianity, Feuerbach insisted that this objectification had become a case of alienation, in so far as the human projection of God assumes its own life and becomes a vehicle of a negative valuation of human beings. Thus, Feuerbach seems to mock the Pauline expression when he exclaims: "To enrich God, man must become poor: that God must be all, man must be nothing" (2008, p. 22). In the hands of Marx, the Pauline quote became: "In manufacture, in order to make the collective labourer, and through him capital, rich in social productive power, each labourer must be made poor in individual productive powers" (MECW 35, p. 367). As we have seen, the assembly of labourers in manufacture – the collective labourer – was an important step on the way to mechanised production. In religion, man is dominated by a twisted creation of his own mind. In practical, material life, he is dominated by a twisted creation of his own hands.

In speaking of alienation, Marx's overall contention is that the individual has become a stranger to his own being, and *inter alia*, a stranger to other individuals and the surrounding world. In the 1844 fragment entitled "Estranged Labor", which was written at a time when Marx was yet to carry out his detailed study of work processes and conditions, the starting point is very much the account of objectification described above: "The object of labour is, therefore, the objectification of man's species-life: for he duplicates himself not only, as in consciousness, intellectually, but also actively, in reality, and therefore he sees himself in a world that he has created" (MECW 3, p. 277). Given Marx's emphasis on the activity of work and his view of work under capitalism, we can appreciate his early diagnosis of the working conditions and self-making, a diagnosis that was offered in far more empirical detail in *Capital*. "Life itself appears only as a *means of life*,… [the human being's] life-activity, his *essential being*, [becomes] a mere means to his *existence*" (MECW 3, p. 276). While Hegel and Feuerbach seemed in agreement in emphasising the right way of thinking as a way out of alienation, Marx emphasised a careful description of activitiy as well as a call for a change in social structures. Alienation is naturally felt in the consciousness of the worker, but it has its source in his technical and material life. Below, I shall survey the different aspects of alienation.

With Marx, we have seen an emphasis on two elements in the development of the capitalist mode of production. The ownership of the tools is transferred from the tool user to the capitalist (the formal subsumption), and the character of the tools is then changed with a view to an increase in relative surplus value - the material subsumption of work under capital. Given the centrality of work and tool use in Marx's philosophical anthropology, the changes surrounding tools attain profound significance. Regarding the will of the worker, work is now forced, rather than free. While the shoemaker described above had to align his bodily movements with his own will, work is now a matter of being confronted with an alien will: the will of the capitalist who gathers and orchestrates the work process, by means of managers or by means of the machine.

> ...the co-operation of wage-labourers is entirely brought about by the capital that employs them. Their union into one single productive body and the establishment of a connexion between their individual functions, are matters foreign and external to them, are not their own act, but the act of the capital that brings and keeps them together. Hence the connexion existing between their various labours appears to them, ideally, in the shape of a preconceived plan of the capitalist, and practically in the shape of the authority of the same capitalist, in the shape of the powerful will of another, who subjects their activity to his aims. (MECW 35, p. 336 f.)

As a consequence, the labourer only considers himself free when not working and the object he produces primarily reflects his servitude to the capitalist: "Since, before entering on the process, his own labour has already been alienated from himself by the sale of his labour-power, has been appropriated by the capitalist and incorporated with capital, it must, during the process, be realised in a product that does not belong to him" (MECW 35, p. 570). Labour objectifies itself in an alien product. In the alienated will at work in labour, we also see one of the manifestations of alienation between human beings, here expressed in the 1844 fragments, "Alienated labour":

> We must bear in mind the previous proposition that man's relation to himself only becomes for him objective and actual through his relation to the other man. Thus, if the product of his labour, his labour objectified, is for him an alien, hostile, powerful object independent of him, then his position towards it is such that someone else is master of this object, someone who is alien, hostile, powerful, and independent of him. If he treats his own activity as an unfree activity, then he treats it as an activity performed in the service, under the dominion, the coercion, and the yoke of another man. (MECW 3, p. 278 f.)

We have witnessed a progression in this aspect of the alienation. While the capitalist may initially have pitted himself, in person, against the worker, this role will later be performed by the manager, and ultimately – and most efficiently – by the machine.

Further, let us recall one of the main reasons that the shoemaker and other artisans perform their labour in the first place: the use-value of the final product – that which satisfies wants and needs of the one using the product. In so far as products have to be exchanged with others, to become a commodity, the worker must "not only produce use-values, but use-values for others, social use-values" (MECW 35, p. 51). We noticed how the shoemaker would be aware of his species-being, in so far as his product would be of some kind of use to his fellow man. To the extent that a commodity has use-value, Marx ascribes it qualitative worth, while Marx takes exchange-value to be primarily a quantitative relation. A large part of *Capital* concerns the economical question of the complex interplay between the two – the use and the price of a given item – and the increasing dominance of exchange-value is the starting point for much of the criticism that is levelled in *Capital*.

With the double character of the value of products of labour, Marx also operates with two kinds of labour: concrete and abstract. Marx perceived that the widespread deskilling of labour meant two things: firstly, the worker no longer, by his own efforts, produces an item that can be used. That is, the shaping and expression of the self that was involved in production became severely fragmented and alien to the labourer. Giving form to products increasingly became the work of a restricted group of workers: designers. For example, this had taken place at Wedgwood's pottery factories, where artists were hired to give form and patterns to pots. It was mainly these designers that had the task of considering the whole product (Forty, 2005; Parsons, 2016). Secondly, Marx emphasises how the alterations in productive technologies in both manufacture and modern industry meant that the worker himself was increasingly viewed as an object of exchange and his labour as abstract labour. His labour is a commodity that decreasingly appears different from other commodities. The technological developments had allowed labour to become increasingly deskilled and standardised and it thereby became viewed and conceived of, by worker and capitalist alike, primarily under the general heading of objects of exchange. So, in Marx's *Outlines of the Critique of Political Economy*, abstract labour "... is therefore developed the more purely and adequately, the more labour loses all craft-like character, the more its particular skill becomes something abstract, irrelevant, and the more it becomes purely abstract, purely mechanical activity, hence irrelevant, indifferent to its particular form" (MECW 28, p. 223). In short, through technological developments combined with developments in labour markets, capitalism has changed labour into abstract labour, and *inter alia*, into an alienating activity.

The skills once possessed by the worker have been standardised and transferred to the machine. The palpable reality of the machine means that there is a physical object that expresses the profound change in the condition of the worker and so offers an – arguably misguided – scene of opposition and battle for the worker. With the same analogy of belligerence, Marx maintains that "... it would be possible to write quite a history of the inventions, made since 1830, for the sole purpose of supplying capital with weapons against the revolts of the working-class" (MECW 35, p. 439). This revolt would, with increased frequency, target the machines themselves. In the following passages from *Capital* we see both the revolt and the different elements of alienation being portrayed:

> ... the character of independence and estrangement which the capitalist mode of production as a whole gives to the instruments of labour and to the product, as against the workman, is developed by means of machinery into a thorough antagonism. Therefore, it is with the advent of machinery, that the workman for the first time brutally revolts against the instruments of labour. (MECW 35, p. 435)

And in his summary description of modern industry:

> [The means for the development of production] mutilate the labourer into a fragment of a man, degrade him to the level of an appendage of a machine, destroy every remnant of charm in his work and turn it into a hated toil; they estrange from him the intellectual potentialities of the labour-process. (MECW 35, p. 639)

Marx presents the machine as the pinnacle of a development that thwarts human work, which in turn is an integral element of human development and flourishing. Rather than freely shaping the material on which the worker works to produce an object, the worker is now met with a system of machinery and, as repeatedly emphasised by Marx, is reduced to being an appendage to this system. At times, Marxist-inspired criticism will focus on questions of unjust distribution, but a more fundamental and scathing criticism remains one that emphasises the alienating character of work, quite regardless of its financial compensation.

Marx's line of criticism is by no means restricted to its historic expression in terms of abolition of artisan production. In *Contributions to the Critique of Political Economy*, Marx suggested that "... [n]o social formation is ever destroyed before all the productive forces for which it is sufficient have been developed" (MECW 29, p. 262). To take a more contemporary example, the development of productive forces in higher education increased with the spread of technology-driven capitalism, which has for decades concerned philosophers and historians of technology as well as educational scientists. In 2000, one could read in *Business Week* that "...corporate training firms that focus on classroom-type training will shrink unless they adapt to e-learning" and moreover that "... in the online world, corporate training programs are in the vanguard. But higher education isn't far behind" (*Business week*, 2000, Jan 10). Andrew Feenberg, also an early developer of online educational technologies, has in several writings discussed the potential change of ownership of both the means of production and the resulting teaching materials that are produced by university lecturers.[13] David Noble's (1998) work in many ways duplicates the concerns that Marx had for the skilled worker, but applies it to a university setting, while Slaughter & Leslie (1997) have given the concept of academic capitalism widespread currency.

Academics are potentially subject to many of the processes that we have surveyed in the previous sections. These processes are partially driven by the wish for increased productivity and aided by the development of information technologies. Central is the notion of unbundling, which is "the process of disaggregating educational provision into its component parts" combined with different technologies for lecture capture and storage.[14] This allows for drastically increased access for students, lower prices for those funding the universities, and freedom from the traditional degree programme. Freed from the restraints of local production, course content can be unbundled from its traditional institutional settings and its inherent relation with an academic worker and her traditional tools of lecture production: the lectern, the lecture hall, the PowerPoint presentation, the whiteboard and such. New roles and professions emerge at the university, called third-space professionals, whose function is more management-like than academic (Whitchurch, 2008), and some academics might become rebranded as "content experts" (Hamilton & Feenberg, 2005).

How might alienation resurface here, in universities increasingly reliant on replacing information technologies – the traditional productive technology of academics – in the service of productivity? To answer this, we can emulate some of the aspects of alienation that we have surveyed above. Firstly, the academic can be alienated from the product of his labour. One can consider the lecture as the product of the skilled, expressive activity of the lecturer (cf. Friesen 2011), which makes the idea of lecture capture and reproduction subject to a criticism analogous to the one Marx levelled. When teaching, the lecturer works with humans and it is not unnatural to describe a student as the student of a particular lecturer, in so far as the student works and thinks in certain ways. Rather than seeing a speck of yourself and your understanding of an academic

---

13 See *e.g.* Feenberg (2001, 2017).
14 My description of recent developments is itself based on participation in a 2019 MOOC, offered jointly by The University of Leeds and University of Cape Town: *The Unbundled University, the Market and Digital Technology*. Quotes are from the course, available on the platform, Future Learn (https://www.futurelearn.com).

subject in a graduate student, academics will be more likely to see drudgery in the activity of teaching, now spread out in nano-courses taken in a geographically and spatially dispersed arena, rather than clearly identifiable in human beings. If one instead considers a module or a degree programme to be the product, ownership of this could be taken away by widespread lecture capture and offer less influence in the educational design processes for the lecturer. There is, in other words, a loss of realisation for the worker, and potentially, the product (a lecture or a course) is no longer his or hers. Secondly, the process of production will become alien, and this is perhaps where educational technologies have the greatest sway. Characteristically, in *Education is not an app* Poritz & Rees, discussing a wealth of digital technologies in their educational setting, complain: "...like it or not, your class room is no longer entirely your own" (2017, p. X). Further, many have seen in educational technologies the danger of widespread deskilling. With specialisation in the production process, there is less of a need to have an overview of your subject as the academic workers produce more and more specialised learning objects. The wide set of skills required to put together a degree programme in co-operation with other academic workers becomes much less widespread, and work becomes drudgery requiring fewer and simpler skills. Finally, academics can be alienated from one another, in so far as their work is orchestrated to a greater extent by university managers, and less by the peculiarities of their own subject, its history and particular modes of engaging students in the lecture halls, laboratories and other avenues of learning. In so far as competition of various kinds informs this orchestration, the relations between academics can become antagonistic. In their case, it is not alienation from nature, but from each other, their lectures and the students that they seek to leave an imprint on through their teaching.

2.5 Marx and the Machine

Let us take stock. We have described the work of a shoemaker and a university lecturer in the philosophically laden terminology of objectification employed by Marx and his immediate philosophical predecessors. Moving from this presumed state of flourishing activity and life expression, we have offered an account of technologies of industrialisation as utterly devastating to the human subject. In doing this, we might seem to have assumed that Marx's writings, from the 1844 Fragment on Alienated Labour to the publication of the first volume of *Capital*, make for a continued exploration of this idea. Such an assumption seems natural, in so far as the pages of *Capital* teem with expressions of indignation over the character of work in manufacture and modern industry, and it lies in direct extension of his earlier pronouncements concerning alienated labour.

The relationship between Marx's early and later thinking, and indeed, those very categories, remains contested. While surveying or contributing to this discussion is beyond the task undertaken here, we can on the background of topics treated so far point to what might appear as a tension in Marx's writings, which in turn suggests a development in Marx's concept of labour. The modern, machine-based production was portrayed as inimical in its nature to the flourishing life as suggested by the idea of objectification through work. However, for such an account to be theoretically viable, it would seem that one needs something like a substantive conception of human nature, a universal potential that will be actualised in different degrees under different conditions. In so far as we have presented industrial technology as opposed to something essentially human, we would also seem to have suggested a reversal of the dependency espoused in a passage from *The German ideology:* "Hence what individuals are depends on the material conditions of their production" (MECW 5, p. 32). That is, we seem to have proposed something like a substantial account of human nature, loosely based on an idea of craftmanship, and presented this substantial account independently of actual material conditions. The tension between rejecting a universal account of the human subject while levelling the kind of criticism that Marx does, can be gleaned from a remark on philosophical anthropology in *Capital:* "By thus acting on the external world and changing it, he at the same time changes his own nature. He develops his slumbering powers and compels them to act in obedience to his sway" (MECW 35, p. 187). Here, we see both the notion of "slumbering powers" at work, which could suggest a substantive concept of a human nature, which in turn allows us to say that a human being has realised her potential to a greater or lesser extent. But we also see the opposite contention of the very notion of human potential being determined by his productive activity. In short, the possible tension is this: we have presented the very notion of the self that is realised as dependent on labour, while also maintaining that a certain kind of technologically-shaped labour is alien to this very self. It would seem that Marx, if true to the passage from *German Ideology* quoted above, ought to say that under modern industry, the self changes in so far as the nature of labour changes drastically. The discipline of modern industry required new habits and attitudes, and such traits were gradually adopted and internalised. And so, it would seem that something very basic in the makeup of human subjectivity was transformed, or re-engineered.[15]

---

15 Such a foundational transition in human mentality was suggested by Rousseau. In his *Dis-*

A solution lies in pointing to Marx's Hegelian heritage. The notion of a subject undergoing a dynamic development and being spurred on by states of alienation and disharmony makes for a distinct Hegelian theme in Marx's writings.[16] Hegel confronted the assumption of a universal conception of the self and offered instead a historically situated account. Accordingly, in *The German Ideology* Marx will speak of a sublation ["*Aufhebung*"] of labour, which is the Hegelian expression for a combined cancellation *and* preservation of opposites, the existence of which ultimately drives history. Alienation, in a manner of speaking, contains the seed for its overcoming. In Marx, human productive potential was the lead character in the historic narrative of objectification, alienation and sublation. The positive aspect of alienation with its historically and dynamically developing subject, was an integral part of Marx's inheritance from Hegel. This ultimately allowed Marx to offer more than a "humanistic" critique of the state of the society of his time and to see the potential for a development away from an alienated state of human society and its subjects. This is a theme that we shall explore in detail as Marx's thinking was developed by Marcuse. What unites the two is seeing the development of subjectivity as intimately connected with development of technologies.

A change can be seen to occur in Marx's concept of labour that points away from a sole focus on alienation. There are different conceptions of labour, and *inter alia*, of a human being, that find expression in *Capital*. On the one hand, there is the one we have been exploring, of humans pitting their limbs and tools against nature, thereby objectifying their species being. The other conception was inspired by German scientific materialists and their concomitant ener-

---

course on Inequality, he suggests that "in the state of nature – primitive man – is a creature of few needs and no concerns beyond them. He desires only to live and be free from labour.... Civilized man, on the other hand, is always moving, sweating, toiling, and racking his brains to find still more labourious occupations" (cited in Sayers, 1998, p. 52). A multitude of avenues of re-engineering humanity by means of technologies is explored by Frishmann & Selinger (2018), with entirely different approaches to the question of a human essence. We shall return to this theme in chapter 3 as it is taken up by Herbert Marcuse.

16 In the Preface to *Phenomenology of Spirit*, we see a similar movement expressed: "Spirit becomes object because it is just this movement of becoming an *other to itself*, i.e. becoming an *object to itself*, and of suspending this otherness. And experience is the name we give to just this movement, in which the immediate, the *unexperienced* i.e. the abstract ... becomes alienated from itself and then returns to itself from this alienation" (Hegel, 1977, §36). With Marx, the monstrous character of alienation is emphasised and it is a matter of productive forces (humans and their skills, organisation, consciousness and tools) rather than spirit.

geticist account of work.[17] According to such conceptions, man is not set against nature but on par with it and part of its self-transformation through expenditure and transformation of energy. Accordingly, Marx increasingly describes labour in terms otherwise at home in thermodynamics. Labour simply is a flow of energy, nothing more and nothing less, and from this increasingly dominant point of view, there is no difference between a machine operation, human thought, animal toil and human operation. Thus, Marx, albeit with a critical edge, can describe man on analogy with a machine: "A certain mass of necessaries must be consumed by a man to grow up and maintain his life. But the man, like the machine, will wear out and must be replaced by another man" (MECW 20, p. 129). And in *Outlines of the Critique of Political Economy*, he can describe machinery as human essence objectified and *not* alienated:

> Nature does not construct machines, locomotives, railways, electric telegraphs, self-acting mules, etc. They are products of human industry; natural material transformed into organs of man's will over Nature, or of man's activity in Nature. *They are organs of the human mind which are created by the human hand*, objectified power of knowledge. (MECW 29, p. 92)

The core concepts of the first law of thermodynamics, heat, energy and work, would soon spread to the discussion of morality and politics as an increasing range of also mental phenomena were modelled on the steam engine.[18] On this understanding, the human creative mind, so central in the notion of work inherited from German romanticism, is in essence no different from other transformations of energy that take place in nature. Accordingly, the lack of will to work is now seen as a matter of an inappropriate allocation of energy to the human worker, leaving him fatigued. As a consequence of this re-conceptualisation of the worker, the care for him is thought of as one thinks of maintaining a machine: for instrumental, rather than moral, reasons does one ensure the

---

[17] See in particular Rabinbach (1990, chapters two and three) and Rabinbach (2018, chapter two) for an account of the development in the conception of labour in the latter half of the 19th century.
[18] This was of course far from the first time in intellectual history that the machine would serve as a model for rather different phenomena. Just like the clock served to model a range of phenomena in medieval times and would later play a central role in cybernetics, so too the suggestion of an analogy between a steam engine and cosmology, politics, morality, the human mind and labour was particularly pronounced from the mid-19th century onwards.

proper maintenance and correct energy supply to one's means of production, be they human or not.[19]

These two ways of conceiving of work – as being fundamentally on par with everything else as described by physics or as something that carries a specifically human stamp – is expressed in Marx's changing use of "labour power" ("*Arbeitskraft*"[20]) and "labour" ("*Arbeit*"). Despite being influenced by scientific accounts of energy in his later works, Marx never abandons the romanticist, "self-making" conception of labour. In so far as labour and its conditions play a central role in Marx's overall thinking about history, politics and morality, the tension between the two conceptions has given rise to a range of interpretations.[21]

We can see the ambiguity when we consider Marx's imagined plea of the worker as he enters into a contract with the capitalist: "What you gain in labour I lose in substance. The use of my labour-power and the spoliation of it are quite different things" (MECW 35, p. 242). This plea to the capitalist is made in terms of power, associated with instrumental reasoning, rather than the moral reasoning associated with the notion of labour. It is the capitalist's focus on the mere continued existence of labour power that will serve as moral grounds for Marx's attack on the capitalist way of production. According to Marx, it allows for no more than replenishment of labour-power, while utterly stunting the possibility of self-creation that lies in labour.[22] Yet, alienation remains a term of diagnosis and moral criticism throughout Marx's works.

---

[19] Physiologists would soon take part in labour struggles on the side of workers, but armed with scientific instruments and reasoning, rather than moral reasoning. See Wendling (2009, p. 79f.) for an overview.

[20] The term "*Kraft*" was used by Helmholz to describe the energy created by machines as they convert chemical energy into mechanical energy. With the term "*Arbeitskraft*", the application to machinery was extended. Ideas and notions at home in natural science flowed more freely and rapidly to other subject areas than they tend to do today. See Rabinbach (1990, p. 46f.).

[21] The tension can be negotiated in a variety of ways. One may simply hold that ultimately inconsistent strands of thought are present in *Capital* and accordingly charge Marx of inconsistency, as Arendt does (cf. 1958, p. 101ff.). Also, the suggestion has been made that a predominantly scientific way of describing labour was undertaken by Marx in order to speak a more politically acceptable language and thereby dodge the considerable post-revolutionary censorship. Finally, one may engage in a quite sophisticated hermeneutical manoeuvre: In *Capital*, Marx exposes both a scientific and a humanistic illusion inherent to capitalism. The scientific illusion is the naturalistic levelling of humans. The romantic illusion is a longing for handicrafts and their concomitant privileges and political life (See Wendling 2009, p. 131ff.).

[22] An important issue in the development of Marx's thinking becomes the relationship between leisure and work as well as a fundamental change of the emphasis on labour as a route to entitlement that Locke introduced. A challenge consists of making room for leisure as an avenue of

2.6 Marx as an Enlightenment Thinker

At the outset of this chapter, we saw how Marx underscores the significance of technology for an interpretation of societal stages in history. In *Capital*, Marx used the word "indicate" to speak of the relation between technology and societal stages. The attention afforded to technologies of production in Marx's works suggests a stronger relation. Perhaps the strongest is Marx's oft-quoted remark from *The Poverty of Philosophy:* "The hand-mill gives you society with the feudal lord; the steam mill, society with the industrial capitalist" (MECW 6, p. 166). This seems to ascribe incredible transformative powers to relatively simple technological means. More balanced is Marx's view that ascribes fundamental determining and transformative powers to productive forces, rather than tools. Much like the term "armed forces", productive forces – a term otherwise at home in the thinking of Ricardo and Smith – include both men, their skills and their tools.[23] While the tools do not firmly settle relations involving production, *Capital* remains an account of how they nevertheless have an overarching influence on *e.g.* division of labour, development of skills and the degree of realisation of human potential they offer. Marx frequently uses "*bestimmen*" in connection with the relation of productive forces to other phenomena, and when one narrows "productive forces" to "technology", one gets a version of the oft-discussed position called "technological determinism". The German "*bestimmen*" is used in the context of a "compelling external agency" such as when a court determines or settles something. Another sense is drawn from the context of setting boundaries or limits (such as in the determination of a lease), within which there is freedom.[24] We shall return to technological determinism in subsequent chapters on Langdon Winner and Herbert Marcuse, as they in different ways work on the questions and challenges left from Marx's thought on technology.

Fatigued appendages to machines might seem unlikely in the role of revolutionaries or societal transformers of any kind. Accordingly, there is a marked change from Marx's early and famed encouragement of the proletariat to rise up and overthrow the unjust material and technological structures under which they suffered, to the description of the machine worker, whose conscious-

---

human development and self-creation that was previously (and remains) closely associated with labour, rather than being something that purely serves to regenerate the otherwise labouring subject. See *e.g.* Sayers (1998, chapter 8) for a discussion of work carried out along these lines.
23 See in particular Harvey (2006, p. 98 ff.) for an account of the concept "productive force" in Marx.
24 See Williams (1977), which Mackenzie (1984) relies on in his discussion of "bestimmen" in Marx.

ness is numbed, his potential stunted and attacks on the machine futile, misguided and tragi-comic, when considered as acts of revolution. Meanwhile, Marx shares with the enlightenment thinkers, initially surveyed in this chapter, a teleological account of history and more particularly, the notion of a stage in history, whose moral deficit is made good by a future stage, that requires the current stage in order to arrive on the world scene.

Especially in his later years, Marx tends to see the future communist stage not achieved primarily by the efforts of human subjects. Rather, it is tied to a crisis in a system that by all means appears to run independently of human subjects, workers and capitalists alike, and as Marx describes it, appears to run worse and worse. The faulty running of the system is primarily a matter of decreasing surplus value for the capitalist held together with the increased pressure on the work*force*. The second law of thermodynamics influences conceptions of societal development. When energy is converted, as in production, some is irreversibly lost to the environment. When this principle from physics was transposed into a characterisation of capitalist society, we got an understanding of history, here summed up by Wendling: "Capitalism is like a poorly designed steam engine that must be run at top speed, despite the fact that this speed contributes to a greater overall loss of heat" (2009, p. 91).[25] The appalling working conditions, together with the enormous increase in productive powers, would lay the ground for an abolition of the capitalist mode of production. Marx was critical of measures that seek to fix and adjust the machine temporarily. He reasoned that policies that increase the immediate welfare of workers only serve to extend the misery of alienation.[26] Thus, Marx can be seen to espouse a particularly cynical version of the enlightenment visions of Kant, Fichte and others: unbridled capitalism will break down sooner than capitalism kept in check, and should be allowed to run its course, notwithstanding the technologically mediated misery.

The most influential vestiges of Marx's philosophy of technology are the following three topics. Firstly, that technologies deeply influence, or even, in some sense, determine other phenomena. In Marx's case, the determined phenomena concern primarily issues of distribution of wealth and power relations between

---

[25] Wendling relies on Rabinbach's treatment of the spread of the second law of thermodynamics (cf. Rabinbach 1990, p. 78 ff). For an account of Marx's account of falling rates of profit and the ensuing crisis, see *e.g.* Harvey (2006, p. 176 ff.).

[26] In Babbage's *Economy of Machinery and Manufactures* (1835), profit sharing and communal ownership of means of production were suggested as a way to ensure continued technological development, which would otherwise frequently suffer at the expense of short-sighted extortion of profits.

different classes in society as well as possibilities of human flourishing through work. Secondly, there is the notion that technology runs its course quite independently of conscious human intervention. Thus, the steam engine, and the industrial machinery it forms part of, not only settles the working conditions but also the power relations. When Marx draws on the idea of a prime mover, he in effect suggests the appearance of machinery and technology being independent agents in the theatre of history. Finally, there is the notion of a projected revolution – the final implosion of capitalism at the burden of its inherent tensions – that is yet to appear. It was far from the last time that people would peg such hopes on new technology. Crucially, the state of the worker in capitalism was a critical question in this optimism.

In their simplest versions, the first two ideas – technological determinism and autonomy – are relatively easy to refute. A tool, of its own accord, cannot settle as much as Marx at times can be seen to suggest, and the idea that technology is in fact a force that runs a course that ultimately is set independently of human wishes and planning is indeed incredible. When questions in philosophy of technology are presented in such a relatively simple way, as might be suggested by the title of a 1994 anthology *Does Technology Drive History?*, answers are easy to come by. However, when the positions are situated in the context of Marx's thinking, they become far more complex. It is with the themes of technological determinism, autonomy and possibilities of radical political action in light of the nature of technology, that we in the following two chapters move about a century forward, to Langdon Winner and Herbert Marcuse.

3 Herbert Marcuse: One-Dimensional Man and the technological veil

> If Marcuse already seems to come from another era, this may be due less to the implausibility of his speculative projections than to the increasing resignation of intellectuals in the West, less and less able to imagine a truly radical break with the present.
>
> (Feenberg, "The Bias of Technology", 1988, p. 254)

3.1 Introduction: Marcuse the Marxist

Providing an overview of Marx's influence on reflections on technology in the years following the publication of *Capital* would be, both conceptually and historically, a bewildering task. Fortunately, it is one we can largely bypass when exploring Marcuse's continuation of Marx's thought on technology. In the early 1930s, Marcuse wrote a thorough review of Marx's, then newly published, early manuscripts, which helped set the reception of Marx's thought back on the path largely identical to that presented in chapter two. A primary concern for much political thought at the time when Marcuse started writing was the question of revolution. In 1918, Marcuse had played his small part in the ultimately failed revolutionary activities in Berlin, being asked to take up arms against right-wing snipers. In the latter half of the 1960s he was a prominent, star-like figure among The New Left, the counterculture of the San Francisco hippies, and the students with their joint and failed revolution in Paris. *One-Dimensional Man* and *Eros and Civilization*, the latter with a new "Political Preface", were published in paperback versions in 1966, and in particular the former had a wide readership.

In the year of the crash at the New York Stock Exchange, Henryk Grossman published *The Law of Accumulation and Collapse of the Capitalist System* (1929). While not being specific in any way about the timing of an actual demise of capitalism, he confronted reasons for thinking that capitalism could go on indefinitely. He emphasised the role of workers in seizing the right moment and becoming conscious agents in history when the circumstances were appropriate. Grossman was then the chief economist at the Marxist *Institute for Social Research*, which was still located in Frankfurt when Marcuse joined it in 1932, after studying in Freiburg under Heidegger. At the institute, Marcuse worked with Horkheimer on a concept of critical theory that would remain central to his own work. Consciousness and agency of the workers was exactly the problem in at least two fundamental ways. Firstly, their consciousness, and secondly, their status as a class.

Concerning the first problem, Lukács had argued that "the rational mechanization extends right into the worker's soul" (1923, p. 98), and this is a theme that reverberated with Marcuse, especially as he went on to study forms of propaganda during WW2. Lukács' analysis of Marx, carried out in the light of Hegel's *Phenomenology of Spirit*, was vindicated when Marx's early *Economic and Philosophical Manuscripts* were published in the late 20s. The manuscripts take us to one of Marcuse's early writings, which was also one of the first essays on the newly discovered manuscripts. Marcuse's exposition of Marx was one that placed the concept of alienation at the centre of a Marxist understanding of society and the worker. His was the "humanist" Marx, rather than the scientific Marx and Engels, that had dominated much of Marx's reception and development. The background for Marcuse's work on *Reason and Revolution* (1941) had been to emphasise the Hegelian, dialectic aspects of Marx at the cost of a presumed scientific one. "The soul of the worker" was the foundation of Marcuse's concern in the decades to come, and concepts of alienation, production, and technology continued to play a substantial role throughout, as Marcuse responded to what had long been known as "the crisis of Marxism": the absence of a revolutionary change in society, in some way along the lines envisaged by Marx. Like Grossman, Marcuse did not project any specific time for a revolution. Andrew Feenberg, a student of Marcuse's, recalls how Marcuse "elaborated the conditions of its possibility" (2010, p. 241). Late in his work, Marcuse increasingly drew on aesthetic thinking and saw a change in sensibility as a prerequisite for such a change.

We approach Marcuse as someone responding to the lack of a new stage of society and someone who, in his most influential work, *One-Dimensional Man*, clearly perceives Marx's focus on labour in his understanding of man: "we live and die rationally and productively" (ODM, p. 149). The concern is seen in the subtitle to One-Dimensional Man, "studies in the ideology of Advanced Industrial Society", and is expressed in his 1960 piece, *From Ontology to Technology:* "Up to the present, technical progress remains the progress of an alienated labor, of a repressive productivity" (2011a, p. 138). Having read Husserl's *Crisis of European Sciences and Transcendental Phenomenology* and studied under Heidegger in the late 1920s, phenomenology remained a resource for Marcuse in thinking about science, technology and the human subject, and it continued to be visible in his response to the crisis.[1] Further, Freud was relied upon when thinking

---

[1] In particular, Marcuse's concept of the technological a priori in chapter 6 of ODM, has strong

about the human subject, instincts, needs, and mechanisms of repression. Yet, Marcuse's 1932 review reiterates the themes that were explored in chapter two and that also make up the main axis of Marcuse's response to the crisis: The human essence (*Wesen*) is closely tied up with the idea of objectification through labour, but in a capitalist society, "…the existence of man does not become, in estranged labor, the "means" for his self-realisation. The reverse happens: man's self becomes a means for his mere existence" (2005b, p. 104).

Marcuse reminded the reader that Marx's writings were no mere exercise in philosophy, but the "foundation of a theory of revolution" (2005b, p. 104) with practical intent. He further addressed the conundrum that we encountered in Marx, of combining two ideas: first, that of an essence in the labourer that is being thwarted by technological means – instruments of labour eventually wielded by the machine. Second, the overall dialectical outlook, according to which reality – essences – develops through opposition and sublation: "If historical facticity thus reveals the total inversion of all the conditions given in the determination of the human essence, does it not prove that this determination lacks content and sense, and that it is only an idealistic abstraction, which does violence to historical reality?" (2005b, p. 105). Marcuse suggested that this should initially be seen as a matter of Marx's fighting on different fronts. For example, appeal to a human *Wesen* served as a tool of critique in interaction with the "bourgeois political economy" and as a more practically oriented platform for opposing Hegelian-inspired forms of idealism. More fundamentally, Marcuse insists that "[w]e are no longer dealing with an abstract human essence, which remains equally valid at every stage of concrete history, but with an essence that can be defined in *history* and *only* in history" (2005b, p. 105, Marcuse's emphasis). Focus on the human essence and its material, real-life realisation (existence) is the driver for revolution: "It is precisely the persistent focus on the essence of man that becomes the inexorable impulse for the initiation of radical revolution. The factual situation of capitalism is characterised not merely by economic or political crisis but by a catastrophe of the human essence" (Marcuse 2005b, p. 106). This dialectic approach to understanding the human subject and world history is a constant in Marcuse's thinking from the early 30s to the 70s, though talk of essences is less frequent in Marcuse's more mature writing. Dialectics play out at the level of the individual: "Judged in the light of their essence and idea, men and things exist as other than they are; consequently;

---

affinities with Heidegger's notion of *das Gestell* (See chapter five). The Heideggerian aspects of Marcuse's thinking have been explored by Wolin (2001) and in more writings, by Feenberg (e.g. 2005).

thought contradicts that which is (given), opposes its truth to that of the given reality" (ODM, p. 136). Concerning world history, seen from the viewpoint of modes of production, dialectics is also in play: "The established rationality becomes irrational when, in the course of its *internal* development, the potentialities of the system have outgrown its institutions" (ODM, p. 225 f., his emphasis). Yet, to Marcuse there is no necessity to this development. It must be a matter of free, human consciousness. "As historical process, the dialectical process involves consciousness: recognition and seizure of the liberating potentialities. Thus, it involves freedom" (ODM, p. 227).

More than three decades after writing his review of Marx's manuscript, at a 1966 Symposium held at the University of Notre Dame, Marcuse (1967b) returns to the question of the obsolescence of Marxism. He identifies five propositions, of which he considers the first four to have been corroborated by societal developments: social relationships are governed by exchange, rather than use-value; satisfaction of human needs is a by-product of production driven by profits; capitalism is subject to contradictions: between the social character of production and ownership of the means of production and between growing productivity of labour and its use for repression and destruction in the form of a cycle of wars, wasteful production and destruction of productive powers and, finally, the need for labouring classes to break this cycle by seizing the means of production. That is to say, at this late stage, Marcuse considers Marxism anything but obsolete. Later yet, in *Counterrevolution and Revolt*, Marcuse warns against a "mechanistic repetition of basic vocabulary" (1972, p. 34). The concepts used by a Marxist are themselves historical and must be applied anew to grasp the actual contradictions in society. Accordingly, Marcuse demonstrates in his writings a wide acquaintance with empirically informed analyses of work life and technologies. He also had intimate knowledge of bureaucratic and political modes of thought from his seven years of work for the US Office of War Information, the predecessor of the CIA. At the Office of Strategic Services, he had the task of analysing propaganda in Germany.

Marcuse suggested that the concept of "the working class" and its agency had lost traction as an analytical tool for thinking about the advent of a revolution. Genuine opposition had become "isolated from the masses and from the majority of organized labour" (1972, p. 57). The presumed source of opposition, the working class, had become integrated in the ideology of the majority, which was the focus of Marcuse's work, as suggested by the subtitle of his most popular book: Studies in the ideology of advanced industrial society. Accordingly, the concern for, and expectations towards, the "soul of the worker" is transformed. The strata of humans that are subject to the demands of the machine are vastly expanded, and the working class loses the meaning it had in Marx's analyses.

Rather, Marx's focus on the machine is what frequently reappears in Marcuse's thinking: "The enlarged universe of exploitation is a totality of machines – human, economic, political, military, education" (1972, p. 13).

Discussion of production and progress is another Marxist constant. Marcuse *did* join many others in scathing criticisms of the emergent consumer society – the economically necessary flipside of an enlarged productive force. As ODM is published, The Carousel of Progress is put on display at Progressland of the New York World's Fair. Designed and built by Walt Disney and General Electric, Progressland was an audio-animatronic celebration of the democratisation of consumption and domestication of progress that had characterised the second industrial revolution. Progress had moved into the home, and the spectator – to the tune of The Sherman Brothers' "There is a great big, beautiful tomorrow" – is transported to four different scenes of a typical, American home, with ever-new appliances.[2] Such an outlook, which saw an intimate relation between progress and technology, had been emphasised by historian Charles A. Beard in the 1920s, and already then reflected a widespread, American sentiment.[3] The close tie between consumption, technology and progress was an easy target for intellectuals. However, while Marcuse had a keen eye for the debilitating effects of consumption on the possibility of a critical, history-moving agent, he insisted: "'Consumer society' is a misnomer of the first order, for rarely has society so systematically been organized in the interests which control *production*" (1972, p. 23).

In what follows, the exposition of the place of technology in Marcuse's thought is framed by way of relatively coarse interpretive categories: the notion of instrumentalism, and the distinction between optimism and pessimism about technology. Regarding the latter distinction, we saw both tendencies feature in Marx's analysis of technology. The story of the development of technology was the story of increased alienation of human subjects and various forms of bodily, material and spiritual misery. Alongside this, one can discern a far more positive outlook, emphasising how technologies can at least offer the conditions for genuine progress – advancement, reward and advantages in different spheres of life.

---

[2] See Roderick (2016) and Weiner (1997) for analyses of the Carousel of Progress. Still running five decades later at the Walt Disney World Resort, the Carousel of Progress has mainly been subject of academic attention for the view of women that can be seen in its different reiterations over the years.

[3] See *e.g.* Beard (1927) for an original expression, and Marx (2010) and Nye (1996) for accounts of this sentiment.

The distinction between optimists and pessimists remains extremely pervasive.[4] While van der Laan (2016) marshals substantial evidence that the positive outlook on technology is dominant, this judgement relies on casting the net wider – historically and intellectually – than the immediate cultural and intellectual setting of Marcuse's philosophy of technology, and wider than philosophy of technology in the latter part of the 20th century.

The tenor of Marcuse's reflections on technology was certainly negative. This is only reinforced if one places too great an emphasis on his intellectual affiliation with members of the Institute for Social Research, where Adorno and Horkheimer had offered their famed criticisms of instrumental reason and enlightenment. Pessimistic views of technology reverberated with philosophical contemporaries of Marcuse's, such as Ellul and Mumford. The understanding that Marcuse was a pessimist is readily gleaned from large parts of ODM. At a late stage of his academic career, this is the work that propelled him into wider fame and made him a renowned figure among The New Left. His academic home, however, did not take up his reflections on technology to any great extent. As Habermas carried forward the intellectual movement of the Frankfurt school and its critical theory, the question of technology seemed largely relegated to the question of the proper bounds of a rational system with a logic independent of that of the lifeworld.[5] As is explored below, Marcuse's pessimism had a steady counterweight in optimistic strands in his thought, constantly searching for avenues of a qualitative change in our relationship with the productive apparatus of advanced, industrial society. One that would mean using technology as a means of liberation, not domination.

The first interpretive tool, instrumentalism, is also offered a key role in numerous discussions of technology, though often as a whipping boy. In this context, the concept of instrumentalism is best conveyed by prefixing "instrument" with "mere". As such, instrumentalism as a position is frequently contrasted

---

4 The presentations of philosophy of technology in Tiles & Oberdiek (1995), Dusek (2006) and van der Laan (2016) rely on the distinction. Thierer (2010) uses it to understand and categorise academic and popular responses to widespread internet use.

5 Andrew Feenberg has, in particular, been critical of this omission: "I base my [criticism] on the peculiar historical situation in which the most powerful modernity theory completely ignored the growing challenge to the technological underpinnings of modernity. [...] My critique of Habermas emphasizes two extraordinary lacunae in his theory – the failure to include technology and the absence of a theory of the bias of rationality. The role of design is at issue in both but absent from Habermas' theory. The exclusion of technology is indefensible" (2017, p. 44). A collection of essays published in celebration of the 50th anniversary of the publication of ODM offers the topic of technology scant attention (Maley, 2017). Below, we return to the issue of design as we discuss Marcuse's challenge to value sensitive design.

with positions that insist that we cannot view technologies as mere means to certain ends, set by a freely acting agent. In spite of their appearance as mere tools, one must realise that they, in certain ways, can embody values or somehow exhibit agency. A version of this thought is explored in chapter 4 on Langdon Winner.

3.2 Marcuse's pessimism: one-dimensional machine man and the happy consciousness

From Marcuse's early essays, such as his 1941 "Some Social Implications of Modern Technology", through his 1960 "From ontology and technology" (2011a) and to his *One Dimensional Man*, a pessimistic account of man's relation with technology clearly emerges. As I shall see, this is an imprecise formulation, as Marcuse did not consider man separate from technology, but only from technics. The distinction between technics and technology is not one that Marcuse maintained consistently, but one that I will suggest underlies his more positive outlook on technology in particular. The bare-boned structure of Marcuse's tale of pessimism, one I put more flesh on below, is as follows: *something* is spread, by *means* of something, *to* something.

A form of rationality informed by the workings of a machine, spreads to the human subject in spheres other than those traditionally associated with work and production. In doing so, it dominates other forms of rationality, most importantly ones that allow the human subject to take a reasoned and critical stance on external authorities. Further, it spreads to spheres of life that have otherwise been ruled by other norms of rationality (*e.g.* politics), or arguably, have been ruled by no form of rationality at all. The mechanisms by means of which this had been achieved in the affluent USA, where Marcuse wrote, are themselves shaped by the advent of new technologies, predominantly those used in mass advertisement and forms of behaviour analysis and modification. The end result of this process is that alienation, the driver of historical development, is utterly stunted in the happy consciousness.

Marcuse offers a grand historical narrative that ties the enlightenment to the spread of new technologies, which then "turn around" and thwart the rational, critical subject. He suggests: "In the course of the technological process a new rationality and new standards of individuality have spread over society, different from and even opposed to those which initiated the march of technology" (1998, p. 42). Marcuse suggests that the development of technologies that had continued into the 20th century was instigated by a class of citizens who held an ideal of being subject to no external constraints, but only to those derived from their rationality. Setting themselves beyond the immediate demands of the institutions of authority in surrounding society, these individuals would pursue self-interest on the premise that the self was rational, in some measure unlike norms and values of societal and religious institutions surrounding him. Kant offered perhaps the most famous expositions of this enlightened individual in his *Answer to the question: What is enlightenment?* where he pitted the courage of the reasoning individual against external norms.

Relying on ideas formulated by Veblen (1922) and empirical data from the work of the American Temporary National Committee, Marcuse positions technology as a threat to man's intellectual autonomy and ability to voice his own critical ideas.[6] To Marcuse, the liberalist societal framework required for the flourishing of the critical, rational individual had become one of renewed repression, now in the form of machinery utilised in the competition that dominates the capitalist mode of production. The rational and autonomous individual had become the efficient individual, whose "performance is motivated, guided and measured by standards external to him, standards pertaining to predetermined tasks and functions" (1998, p. 45).

These standards are informed by what Marcuse follows Veblen in calling a matter-of-factness derived from the machine process. While Marcuse's enlightened, 17th and 18th century middle-class citizen fought external norms with their own rationality and will – attitudes that Marcuse suggests were integral to the beginning of the "march of technology" – the machine process now appears as the embodiment of rationality: "In manipulating the machine, man learns that obedience to the directions is the only way to obtain desired results. Getting along is identical with adjustment to the apparatus. There is no room for autonomy" (1998, p. 46). Crucial to this process having taken place is the idea of spheres of life and their invasion by machine rationality in the form of "efficient compliance". The reader may be better acquainted with the very similar idea that informs Walzer's *Spheres of Justice* (Walzer, 1983) and, as mentioned, Habermas also worked with a version of this idea. Marcuse offers no clear definition of spheres, but lists: "libido…, offices, schools, assemblies and, finally, in the realm of relaxation and entertainment" (1998, p. 47 f). In ODM, the categorisation can be seen in terms of the structure of the book: subjectivity (the "unhappy consciousness" becoming happy), intersubjectivity ("discourse"), science, philosophy, and political life are the spheres where matter-of-factness leads to a heter-

---

[6] As explored by Eric Schatzberg (2018) and earlier, Leo Marx (1997), Veblen was a central figure in making the concept "technology" available and central for American social theory. Having, in the early 1900s, transformed the concept from a German use of *"Technik"*, Veblen placed the concept in the context of criticising some forms of capitalism.

onomous reproduction of the existing order, rather than a subject that projects its own critical plan, relying on its inherent reason.

For example, in extension of the use of the words "soul" and "alienation" that were appealed to in the introduction of this chapter, Marcuse took aim at ordinary language philosophy in its attempt to analyse this kind of language in a way that would, in Wittgenstein's terms, leave "everything as it is" and remain with description. To speak of soul carries a critical potential[7], and this aspect was largely absent when the concept was treated by philosophers like Ryle and Wittgenstein. They were content to remain with much simpler, supposedly everyday types of language, such as "the broom is in the corner". To Wittgenstein, the task of philosophy was therapeutic – "to give philosophy peace", and this, Marcuse considered an abject failure. The language with which ordinary people think, discuss and project possibilities is the language of "advertisements, movies, politicians and bestsellers" (ODM, p. 198). To gloss over how "the universe of thought and practice in which [people] live is a universe of manipulated contradictions" (ODM, p. 198) is for philosophy to become one-dimensional.

This process of the spread of matter-of-factness and machine behaviour is not experienced by the worker as an encroachment of something external upon the rationality of the individual. Adjusting and letting oneself be adjusted in different spheres of life has the clear appearance of being rational, or as Marcuse puts it summarily and dialectically in *One-Dimensional Man:* "The most vexing aspects of advanced industrial civilization: the rational character of its irrationality" (ODM, p. 11). Such contradictory statements are found predominantly in the later works of Marcuse and they should be seen as Marcuse's attempts at "jumpstarting" a dialectic process in society and subjectivity, one that would otherwise appear entirely arrested in the happy consciousness. Prescient of the extreme focus on privacy that has persisted with developments in informational technologies and forms of capitalism associated with it, Marcuse spoke of a private sphere being mobilised for mass production.[8] He saw in thinkers, as diverse as David Hume and William James, the understanding that social forces associated with large-scale enterprises that emphasise competitiveness would prevail. As a consequence, "individualism took on more of the overtones

---

[7] It is attested by the American title of the philosophically informed criticism of work: *Shop Class as Soulcraft: An Inquiry into the value of Work* (Crawford, 2009).
[8] Beniger (1986) argued that the technological developments described by Marx prepared the ground for the possibilities of control inherent in an information society. Zuboff's (2015) concept of surveillance capitalism highlights new avenues of capitalist production, as it encroaches on informational privacy with a view to production of knowledge from "raw material" – data.

of resignation" with individualism becoming "glorification of smallness, privacy and self-limitation" (1998, p. 60).

This is the picture of humans in industrial societies sketched out in 1941, and in many ways painted with more bite and irony in ODM:

> In this universe, technology also provides the great rationalization of the unfreedom of man and demonstrates the "technical" impossibility of being autonomous, of determining one's own life. For this unfreedom appears neither as irrational nor as political, but rather as submission to the technical apparatus which enlarges the comforts of life and increases the productivity of labor. Technological rationality thus protects rather than cancels the legitimacy of domination and the instrumentalist horizon of reason opens on a rationally totalitarian society. (ODM, p. 162)

With one-dimensionality, we see the human being, with its critical faculties, being devolved to a state of having little or no effective, autonomous critical faculty, subject to a multitude of external, psycho-social influences. These are not just designed and administered by businesses, but also by an amalgam of state institutions. The second-dimension of reason, the one critical of existing arrangements – the "facts" of democracy and freedom – and external voices of authority, had suffered erosion to a point where the "novel feature is the flattening out of the antagonism between culture and social reality through the obliteration of the oppositional, alien, and transcendent elements in the higher culture by virtue of which it constituted *another dimension* of reality. This liquidation of *two-dimensional* culture takes place not through the denial and rejection of 'cultural values', but through their wholesale incorporation into the established order, through their reproduction on a massive scale. In fact, they serve as instruments of social cohesion" (ODM, p. 60). Concerning the subject, Marcuse speaks of needs that are false by virtue of being "superimposed upon the individual by particular social interests in his repression: the needs which perpetuate toil, aggressiveness, misery, and injustice" (ODM, p. 7). Technological reality has largely erased the critical individual and its private sphere as "industrial psychology has long since ceased to be confined to the factory" (ODM, p. 12). In this state of play, the concept of alienation loses its grip, as there is little left of the productive and critical self that *can* be alienated in an overarching, mechanised system of production.

In addition to being subject to the spread of modes of mind associated with mechanisation, "people recognize themselves in their commodities; they find their soul in their automobile, hi-fi set, split-level home, kitchen equipment" (ODM, p. 11), rather than in production itself. Marx's tale of technologically mediated alienation would seem to have reached a depressing climax where the dynamics of alienation appear stunted by a human subject that is objectified by the works of its own machines – both their products and demands. This is not aptly described as a big bargain:[9] security and welfare for restrained criticism and acquiescence. As the subject is "violently defending [its] own servitude" (1967a, p. 80), there is in fact precious little that it *can* trade in terms of a critical perspective on the matters-of-fact or "a self of one's own".

We have outlined *what* was spread: a technological rationality vaguely understood as one that means conformity to external, machine-based demands, inspired by Veblen and ultimately, Marx; *to* what it was spread: the critical, human subject, with its different spheres of existence. In accounting for the mechanisms by which it was spread Marcuse was even less specific, but his astute criticism of the expressions of the advertisement industry suggests that he saw the application of techniques originally developed in the context of industrial and military organisations as the main culprit. That is to say, the human subject was exposed to social organisation inspired by automation and machine work not only in the sphere of work. This mode of organisation also increasingly came to the state and its institutions, and to those charged with marketing the glut of goods coming from post-WWII mechanised production: selling cars, wars, and political candidates by means of intimate knowledge of the human psyche. For purposes of a possible defence and renewal of his thought in the light of developments in cognitive and communication technologies, it is worth separating this empirically oriented Marcuse from the one who engaged with the philosophy of his day.

The empirically oriented Marcuse took over the term "organized capitalism" from Marxist Rudolf Hilferding "to describe the administrative-bureaucratic apparatus which organizes, manages, and stabilizes capitalist society" (Kellner, 1984, p. 233). Marcuse was familiar with Vance Packard's *The hidden persuaders* (1957). Having a media background himself, Packard made widely known how Ernest Dichter had carried out research in motivational theory and fused it with advertising research, relying on, *e. g.*, depth interview techniques to get consumers "musing absentmindedly about all the pleasures, joys, enthusiasms, agonies, nightmares, deceptions, apprehensions the product recalls to them" (Packard, 1957, p. 31).[10] However much such criticism of prevailing consumer cul-

---

[9] This term was used by Mumford in his *Authoritarian and Democratic Technics* (1964).
[10] While not wanting to here imply any sweeping condemnation, a contemporary Marcuse would likely have found Fogg's (2003) *Persuasive Design* interesting, along with the methods and goals of the originally UK state-sponsored *Behavioral Insight Team*, also known as the nudge unit. A recent source of empirical and theoretical backing for the idea of a besieged, minimised self in the context of work might come from Slaby's (2016) idea of mind invasion, which lets the idea of a social, embodied mind cut both ways: we use the environment to think and feel, but the environment also uses us, as it were. Consequently, they call for a political philos-

ture reverberated and reverberates, in "From Ontology to Technology", Marcuse insists: "Such an integration [of radical critique and effective opposition into the status quo] cannot be explained by the emergence of *mass culture*, the *organization man* or *The hidden persuaders* etc. These notions belong to a purely ideological interpretation that neglects the analysis of the most fundamental processes which undermine the base upon which a radical opposition might have developed" (2011a, p. 133). If these sociological, psychological, and economic analyses do not reveal the most fundamental processes that render the subject without the potential to negate and oppose the world around him, what does?

In answering this question, Marcuse, in an analysis that appears inspired by the thought of Heidegger, emphasises how the banning of appeals to final causes – a teleological structuring of observations and reality – had spread from post-newton scientific methods to society. Rather than finality, science seeks an "'order' based on calculability and predictability" (2011a, p. 140). The new science "abstracts itself" from the concrete individual and its "sensuous body" (2011a, p. 133). In a critical reading of Quine's scientifically informed philosophy of language and logic (1953), Marcuse registered how this science treats objects as "obsolete cultural postulates" (Quine 1953, p. 44, cited in Marcuse 2011a, p. 134). Gone are the dualisms in tension that drive dialectics. The natural world had since become a technical world and "technology has replaced ontology" (2011a, p. 134), where Marcuse takes ontology to consist of the Hegelian movement of synthesis of opposites. To Marcuse, humans in advanced industrial societies have, unlike humans in "pretechnological civilization" (2011a, p. 135), lost the ability to live in two dimensions; to view reality from vantage points different from the actual. Rather than facing an unforgiving nature – the original situation we saw Marx initially appeal to – technologically advanced man now faced "the very power of man" through which the technical world "has congealed into a second nature" (2011a, p. 136), more destructive and dangerous than pretechnological, original nature. A corollary to the disappearance of considerations of telos from science is what Marcuse suggests is the common ground between development in sciences and social life: the principle of efficiency. Marcuse sums up: "Consequently, technical reality is deprived of its logos, or, more precisely, that logos appears as deprived of reality, as a logical form without substance. Contemporary positivism, semantics, symbolic logic, and linguistic analysis define and filter the universe of discourse for the use of technicians" (2011a,

---

ophy of mind. See also Slaby & Mühlhoff (2018) for an analysis of Post-Fordism work. When moving beyond the workplace, aspects of the idea of the quantified self and its different measuring and motivational practices would likely have attracted Marcuse's interest.

p. 136). This concerns, not only objects, but also activities and concepts pertinent to workers, where actions are made fit for technicians through their analysis in terms of operations.

3.3 The missing technics in Marcuse's reception

So far, I have made a sketch of Marcuse's far-reaching and theoretically rich criticism of advanced, industrial society, culminating with *ODM*. Before we focus further on the role of technology in his criticism, it is worth reflecting briefly on the immediate reception of his thought. While enjoying immense popularity in wider circles, including social and political movements, the academic reception was unfavourable. Perhaps most critically, Marcuse's distinction between technics and technology has been widely neglected. Macintyre, in addition to attempting to argue that "almost all of Marcuse's key positions are false" (1970, p. 2), considered the development of Marcuse's thought to be set apart from "classical Marxism" (1970, p. 17). This way of approaching Marcuse made for a largely misguided presentation of his thought and might have led to oversight of the continuity of focus on production technologies in Marx and Marcuse.[11]

Among futurologists, Marcuse has widely been branded as a pessimist, and eventually, himself a purveyor of the one-dimensional intellectual sound bites that pass for genuine, oppositional thinking. Futurologists tend to focus on technology in their reflections on societal trends and predictions, and they have in Marcuse's writings largely seen the description of human subjects as powerless and impoverished in the face of increasingly complex and fast-paced technologies. An early proponent of this understanding was Toffler's influential *Future Shock* (1970): "…despite all the anti-technological rhetoric of the Elluls and Fromms, the Mumfords and Marcuses, it is precisely the super-industrial society, the most advanced technological society ever, that extends the range of freedom". Yet, the young mind is "…influenced by a stream of movies…fed by a prestigious line of authors from Kafka and Orwell to Whyte, Marcuse and Ellul [and] the fear of bureaucracy permeates their thought [...]. The fear of being swallowed up by this mechanized beast drives executives to orgies of self-examination and students to paroxysms of protest" (Toffler, 1970, p. 321). Throwing Ellul and Mar-

---

[11] Schatzberg also suggests Marcuse to be a "heterodox Marxist philosopher" (2018, p. 221). This line of interpretation of Marcuse has been the subject of consistent criticism. See in particular Kellner (1984, p. 400) and Gandesha (2004).

cuse in the same pot of strong anti-technological sentiment, with some caveats, remains a feature of futurology.[12]

While such appreciation of Marcuse's wider thought and his philosophy of technology are understandable in cases where the approach is based on a reading of ODM, the understanding of technology among those that were supposed to be his own – critical theorists – has perhaps been the most damaging.[13] As suggested, Habermas, the most influential thinker in the critical school amongst the generation following Marcuse's, has had relatively little to say about technology. Instead, he offered a linguistic development of the critical project. With his idea of a colonisation of the lifeworld, with its different spheres, by instrumental reason, he can be seen to have adopted a version of the idea of a certain spread of instrumental rationality that Marcuse also defended. In a 1968 paper dedicated to Marcuse, entitled *Technology and Science as Ideology*, Habermas initially lauds Marcuse for being the first to make the "political content of technical reason the analytical point of departure for a theory of advanced capitalist society" (1970, p. 85). However, in opposition to this, Habermas goes on to defend a universal, formal concept of technical rationality, which stands in opposition to Marcuse's narrative of technical rationality as an originally liberating force, but in advanced capitalism a rationality that "... protects rather than cancels the legitimacy of domination and the instrumentalist horizon of reason opens on a rationally totalitarian society" (ODM p. 162, cited in Habermas, 1970, p. 85). The very possibility of two-dimensional thought concerning technology would mean at least imagining a different kind of technological rationality. Habermas' argument against Marcuse's position is worth quoting at length:

> "[T]here are two kinds of mastery: a repressive and a liberating one" [ODM, p. X]. To this view it must be objected that modern science can be interpreted as a historically unique project only if at least one alternative project is thinkable. And, in addition, an alternative New Science would have to include the definition of a New Technology. This is a sobering consideration because technology, if based at all on a project, can only be traced back to a "project" of the human species as a whole, and not to one that could be historically surpassed. (1970, p. 87)

Habermas expresses agreement and sympathy with Marcuse's position on technology in what he calls its sociological aspects: the spread of a technical form of rationality through spheres that otherwise exhibit a form of rationality foreign to a technical, instrumentalist one. In the paper, he distinguishes spheres of

---

12 See *e.g.* Murphy (2016).
13 For the following two paragraphs, compare Feenberg (1999) and Gandesha (2004).

"'work' or purposive-rational action [by which] I understand either instrumental action [governed by technical rules] or rational choice", (Habermas, 1970, p. 95) which is colonising other spheres of institutional frameworks. These can be characterised by mythical, religious or metaphysical interpretations of reality, and have different norms of linguistic interaction. The colonisation takes place from above, in so far as the state and state-sponsored science and technology (with its own myths) assist in upholding the stability of capitalism, and from below, as rationality appropriate to the increasingly machine-based work spreads among humans. He develops his own version of the adaptation thought, according to which an active adaptation of nature to human needs has been eclipsed by passive adaptation, where various non-technical norms give way to technical ones.

These are thoughts of Marcuse's that Habermas took himself to be placing on a firmer footing. Yet, in the quote above, Habermas opposes Marcuse's position when Habermas suggests that technological rationality is an ahistorical and formal phenomenon, which is not itself amenable to historical development and possible sublation (*Aufhebung*) in a further stage of history. Relying on the thought of Arnold Gehlen, Habermas suggests that the history of technology is a history of "human species [having] taken the elementary components of the behavioral system of purposive-rational action, which is primarily rooted in the human organism, and projected them one after another onto the plane of technical instruments, thereby unburdening itself of the corresponding functions" (1970, p. 95). Whether or not we find such a biologically inspired account of technology and its development convincing, its character as a historical constant certainly sits poorly with Marcuse's dialectical outlook on man's essence and the possibility of a qualitatively different technology.

To understand Marcuse's contrasting position on the possibility of historical epochs, we return to his notion of "pre-technological man" and how he, in ODM, adds the idea of a post-technological society (ODM, p. 242). It would be uncharitable to interpret, say, the former to describe a presumed proto-human state, where humans are not yet cognizant of tool use. More charitably read, when speaking of technology, Marcuse likely has in mind the specific historical epoch that he suggested characterised advanced industrial societies, again, the subtitle of ODM, with an overarching, machine-like system that places humans – thinking, producing, consuming, communicating – in the service of profit seeking and continued economic growth. The mode of production under capitalism is the constant target of criticism in Marcuse's work, in which technologies played a central role in alienation. Habermas sums up Marcuse's position with clarity:

> At the stage of their scientific-technical development, then, the forces of production appear to enter a new constellation with the relations of production. Now they no longer function as the basis of a critique of prevailing legitimations in the interest of political enlightenment, but become instead the basis of legitimation. *This* is what Marcuse conceives as world-historically new. (Habermas 1970, p. 84, his emphasis)

Habermas' rejection of Marcuse's idea of developments in technology is based on a failure to make a distinction between science and technology. Habermas suggests that if "the peculiar fusion of technology and domination" can only be interpreted as a world project, then "social emancipation could not be conceived without a complementary revolutionary transformation of science and technology themselves" (1970, p. 85). Habermas' implicit reasoning is that social emancipation *can* be conceived but cannot be tied to a revolutionary transformation of technology. The idea of a revolutionary transformation in science and technology is met with a mix of incomprehension and rejection as a matter of "a secret hope", forms of religious mysticism, ideas of "a fraternal rather than an exploited nature", and, to Habermas, with the characteristic focus on language and communication: Habermas suggests that Marcuse would "impute subjectivity to animals and plants, even to minerals, and try to communicate with nature instead of merely processing her under conditions of severed communication" (Habermas, 1970, p. 86).

Fortunately, this rejection of Marcuse's position was premature, yet instructive. Marcuse's position is at odds with Habermas' assumption that a revolutionary transformation of science and technology cannot take place. In other words, he is taking issue with Habermas' suggestion that science and technology are at bottom ahistorical. While such a claim involves reflection on the relation between science and technology, it suffices to note how Marcuse, reasonably, in many instances separates the use of technologies from that of science, and emphasises the overall social character of technologies: "Pre-technological and technological modes of domination are fundamentally different – as different as slavery is from free-wage labour, paganism from Christianity, the city state from the nation" (ODM, p. 138). These are, as it were, distinct historical modes, one of which Marcuse characterises as "technological" or as that which characterises "advanced industrial society".[14]

---

[14] A world-historically new form of society with a radically different technological orientation than that which characterises industrial society and its capitalism, could be one that is characterised by an overarching concern for the natural environment, rather than exchange value. This was suggested by Marcuse (2005a), and has been discussed by Vogel (1996) and Feenberg (2005, chapter 6).

What likely causes some confusion among commentators is the failure to notice Marcuse's distinction between technics and technology. Only the former suggests an ahistorical form. This distinction can help us make sense of his claims about pre- and post-technological man and indeed, serve as the instrumentalist underpinnings of Marcuse's optimism in matters of technology. Unfortunately, Marcuse is not entirely consistent in his usage. While Schatzberg (2018) has offered a detailed and insightful study of the varied use of "technics" and "technology" as the former word migrated from Germany to North America and became "technology", he appears entirely dismissive of Marcuse. He casts Marcuse as a technophobic "European philosopher" (2018, p. 166), and apparently misses Marcuse's distinction when suggesting that "Marcuse's understanding of technology was explicitly instrumental" (2018, p. 224). In fact, the opposite is the case. Marcuse's concept of technology emphasised how capitalist values were intimately integrated with the design, use and spread of artefacts as well as machine-like modes of thought. "Technics" was the word used for the instrumental, "ahistorical" aspect of his conception of technology.

Yet, Schatzberg's account of the distinction remains of service. He casts Lewis Mumford as the true heir of Veblen's transformed concept of technology and, in 'Some Social Implications of Modern Technology', Marcuse claims inspiration from Mumford in upholding a distinction between "technics" and "technology".[15] The distinction, as offered by Marcuse, is relatively simple. Though advanced industrial society imbues artefacts with its values and modes of thought, technical artefacts – technics – can "promote authoritarianism as well as liberty, scarcity as well as abundance, the extension as well as the abolition of toil" (1998, p. 41). In so far as Marcuse's focus is overwhelmingly on the capitalist setting of technics, with its incentives to produce and consume that which machine-based, advanced industrial society offers its subjects, one might well lose sight of the aspect of Marcuse's thoughts on technology that distinguishes it from technics. This is why warnings against what we today would call technological

---

[15] We cannot here trace all the relevant parts of Schatzberg's detailed history of the concept of technology. He finds that "technology" carries a "...contradictory set of meanings [that] continues to dominate its academic use. Depending on how these meanings were deployed, the concept of technology could support either an instrumental or a cultural view. [Veblen] exemplified the use of technology as a liberating concept...]" (2018, p. 118). According to Schatzberg, the German "Technik" that Veblen transposed had both instrumentalist and cultural meanings, and "... Veblen developed his idea of technology into a sophisticated concept that drew from both the cultural and instrumental aspects of Technik" (2018, p. 130). In the work of Mumford that Marcuse cites – *Technics and Civilization* (1934) – an instrumentalist, German engineering concept of *Technik* is likely drawn on and the agency of humans in history maintained; also, the idea of the machine as a tool for exercising power over men is maintained.

instrumentalism in Marcuse's writings co-exist with the suggestion that technics is value-neutral. When arguing about the pervasive influence of capitalism, we read: "Technology, as a mode of production, as the totality of instruments, devices and contrivances which characterise the machine age is thus at the same time a mode of organising and perpetuating (or changing) social relationships, a manifestation of prevalent thought and behaviour patterns, an instrument of control or domination" (1998, p. 41), and later, in "From Ontology to Technology": "One should therefore reject the notion of technical neutrality, which offers a perspective on techniques beyond good and evil and which appears as objectivity itself, susceptible to social usage in all its forms. Indeed, a machine, a technical instrument, can be considered as neutral, as pure matter. But the machine, the instrument, does not exist outside an ensemble, a technological totality," (2011a, p. 136). Such passages emphasise how artefacts, as a matter of fact but not of possibility, are at home in capitalist society, and in this setting, infused with a focus on exchange value. Yet, in ODM, in discussion of Marx's "handmill quip", Marcuse also suggests that "the social mode of production, *not technics*, is the basic historical factor. [...] The Machine is indifferent towards the social uses it is put to" (ODM, p. 158, my emphasis). If we take Marcuse to uphold his distinction consistently, we can see it at work when Marcuse says that the truth of the neutrality of technics becomes political, in so far as it suggests that technology is neutral. "In my opinion, the neutrality of technology ... is a political concept. ..... technicity requires domination" (2011a, p. 137). Only when read as a claim about technics under technological capitalism can we make sense of such claims. In contrast with Habermas' position, they point to the possibility of a different technology and form the basis of Marcuse's optimism.

3.4 Marcuse the optimist: the art of living and a new logos of technics

On the one hand, Marcuse vividly describes a beleaguered modern subject, exposed to a host of sophisticated methods of manipulation and social engineering and further made docile by the pleasant feeling of consumption. In short, the happy consciousness with no prospect of qualitative change in outlook, making pertinent the question raised in ODM: "[H]ow can the administered individuals – who have made their mutilation into their own liberties and satisfactions, and thus reproduce it on an enlarged scale – liberate themselves from themselves as well as from their masters? How is it even thinkable that the vicious circle be broken?" (ODM, p. 255). On the other hand, Marcuse is anything but blind to the potential of technology in alleviating human suffering and stunted development. In *An Essay on Liberation*, this is emphasised: "science and technology are the great vehicles of liberation" (1969, p. 12), and in One-Dimensional Man: "*Technics*, as a universe of instrumentalities, may increase the weakness as well as the power of man" (ODM, p. 240, my emphasis).[16]

In so far as economical and political forces use technics to shape and re-engineer man, Marcuse does not see the potential of a change in the historical mode of production. Again, "escalation of commodity production and productive exploitation join and permeate all dimensions of private and public existence" (1969, p. 17). As humans adapt to these repressive states of affairs, a change is needed in both the infrastructure of society and man, in order to break the "voluntary servitude". Ultimately, such a change will come from the ability of human beings to experience things differently through what he calls a new sensibility, and with a new logos informing technics. Under the aegis of capitalism, the "logos of technics has been made into the logos of continued servitude". Rather, the logos – understood as "law, rule, order by virtue of knowledge" – of technics should be what Marcuse calls pacified existence, opening up "a universe of qualitatively different relations between man and man, and man and nature" (ODM, pp. 163, 171, 239). In this way, Marcuse's continuation of Marx's idea of a revolution and a new stage of civilisational development invites us to consider carefully and critically how technology is perceived, talked about, and the way that use of technologies might influence our attempts to use our imagination.

Will the light gradually dawn, or will there be a bright spark, a historical break offering a leap to a new stage, characterised by a different logos? When Marcuse points to the former, he seems to think that sufficient quantitative change – however insignificant – might eventually add up to a qualitative one. Death by a thousand cuts, typically appealed to in connection with technologically driven erosion of basic rights, delivered by a diffused agency, could also happen to the logos of technics under capitalism and further spur subjects into action. In *An Essay on Liberation*, he discusses how initiatives ranging "[f]rom the harmless drive for better zoning regulations… to… decommercialization of nature, total urban reconstruction…" (1969, p. 35) might eventually gain sufficient momentum to critically weaken the technological mode of production and lead to "a collapse of work discipline, slowdown, spread of disobedience to rules and regulations, wildcat strikes, boycotts, sabotage, gratuitous acts of non-compliance" (1969, p. 86).

---

16 Of course, in *An Essay on Liberation*, Marcuse should have written "technics", for consistency.

Another possible factor in the advent of a revolution is the idea of everyday experience of contradictions – the overall irrationality of the apparently rational – that wears at the moral fibre of the subject. At both the outset and conclusion of ODM, Marcuse does much to offer descriptions of everyday experience of production and consumption that aim to expose contradiction and futility. Perhaps best known is his characterisation of the phenomenon of car ownership: "In a way, I feel cheated. I believe that the car is not what it could be, that better could be made for less money. But the other guy has to live too… We have it much better than before. The tension between appearance and reality melts away and both merge in a rather pleasant feeling" (ODM, p. 230). This expresses the hope that to the extent that people experience work and consumption as decreasingly meaningful, they will opt for qualitative change of their role in capitalism and their mode of participation in its technics. Also, Marcuse saw in dispersed political movements across the globe signs of both bureaucratic management and corporate capitalism being strained under pressure from protest. In these movements, initiated not by workers or "kept intellectuals", but by those on the fringe, Marcuse saw different manifestations of what he called the "the great refusal", which is intimately coupled with the ability to "recognize the mark of social repression, even in the most sublime manifestations of technical progress" (1969, p. 11).

Marcuse calls for a return to utopian thought, which in spite of its perceived lack of scientific character, will be a tool for critical, multidimensional thinking. After all, "utopian possibilities are inherent in the technical and technological forces of advanced capitalism and socialism" (1969, p. 14). Conceiving of utopia is the beginning of thinking about a revolution being instigated by a "bright spark". Marcuse offers no one way of conceiving utopia, no one way of fostering the ability to recognise repression and fostering "the awareness of the transcendent possibilities of freedom [that] must become a driving power in the consciousness and imagination which prepare the soil for this revolution" (1969, p. 31). His optimistic thought in particular – his investigation of prospects for change – appears unfocused as it explores different avenues. As Habermas would see use of tools as a constant in species, Marcuse at one point tries to have an organic foundation of morality serve as the guideline for a qualitative change, where he would emphasise an "erotic drive to counter aggressiveness, to create and preserve 'even greater unities' of life" (1969, p. 19). This would be the foundation for solidarity among human beings. Yet, Marcuse also recognises that the human organism responds to its environment and changes accordingly; patterns of response become "ingrown", and this ingrown, second nature of hardened patterns will also be subject to revolution. Biology, conceived as "the process and the dimension in which inclinations, behavior patterns, and aspirations become vital needs which, if not satisfied, would cause dysfunction of the organism" (1969, p. 20), is no firm foundation for Marcuse nor Habermas, but is itself subject to change and possible *Aufhebung*. Specifically, Marcuse suggests that the need for "possessing, consuming, handling and constantly renewing the gadgets, devices, instruments, engines, offered to and imposed on the people" (1969, p. 20f) has become a biological need in this enlarged sense. As he will say in *Counterrevolt and Revolution*, nature, too, awaits revolution, and by this he meant both human nature and the environment of humans. The soul of the worker is subject to a "socially engineered arrest of consciousness" (1969, p. 25) and the instinctual structure of the worker is shaped by vested interests.

In *Counterrevolution and Revolt* and *The Aesthetic Dimension*, written after the failure of the 1968 revolution, Marcuse justifies looking to aesthetics at a time when the prospects for a wholesale political change looked bleak again: "In a situation where the miserable reality can be changed through radical political praxis, the concern with aesthetics demands justification. It would be senseless to deny the element of despair inherent in this concern" (1978, p. 1). Marcuse is here presenting too narrow a view of his engagement with aesthetics and technology. Analysing different forms of art was a constant throughout Marcuse's writings. Rather than seeing this late, more strongly thematised preoccupation with art as conceding defeat, we should say that Marcuse sees in art a continued concern for both "the soul of the worker" – human consciousness in advanced industrial society – and the preconditions for a radically different society:

> Freedom indeed depends largely on technical progress, on the advancement of science. But this fact easily obscures the essential precondition: in order to become vehicles of freedom, science and technology have to change their present direction and goals; they would have to be reconstructed in accord with a new sensibility – the demands of the life instincts. Then one could speak of a technology of liberation, product of the scientific imagination free to project the forms of human universe without exploitation and toil. (1969, p. 28)

To Marcuse, this sensibility is a central and overlapping concern of both art and Marxism in the form of critical theory, here expressed in his 1937 "Philosophy and Critical Theory": In "...every act of cognition the individual must once again re-enact the 'production of the world'" (2009, p. 111). To see what is not yet present, Marcuse insists on the importance of fantasy; not, however, unrestrained fantasy, and not one based on universal laws of essence, but on "technical limits in the strictest sense. They are prescribed by the level of technological development" (2009, p. 114). It is in combining contemporary technology with a non-degraded imagination that we stand the best chance of answering

Kant's question, "What may I hope?" That is to say, it is the best form of assistance to a Habermas to see what he couldn't: A "new technology" as something that can surpass the present. Marcuse can offer few specifics for such utopian visions, but they would place technology in a different mode of production. Technology would serve life, and technics would become informed by what Marcuse calls an aesthetic ethos, where the aesthetic becomes a factor in the technics of production.

Relying on Kant's third critique, Marcuse emphasises how senses are productive and creative and have a share in producing images of freedom. Marcuse, like Kant, sees imagination restrained by sensibility and reason, but to reiterate, Marcuse takes reason and sensibility to have been shaped and repressed historically: "The objects which the senses confront and apprehend are the products of a specific stage of civilisation and of a specific society, and the senses in turn are geared to their objects" (1969, p. 43). Thus, the freeing of imagination for projecting new social moralities and new institutions of freedom, has been, and remains, central for qualitative change. A qualitative change that will have to be communicated and discussed with "old words" that have their ordinary home in one-dimensional society and might be in need of a reversal of meaning. In such a setting, Marcuse suggests that art can take on the role of a Kantian regulative idea, presenting humans in a non-alienated state of being, exhibiting qualities that are distinct from those that prevail under advanced capitalism – beauty, tenderness, playfulness.[17]

Miles (2012) argues that there is continuity in Marcuse's preoccupation with art that stretches from his intellectual work immediately following his own, minor participation in the failed German revolution, to the writings that are informed by the political pessimism following the 1960s. In the aftermath of the failed revolution and before studying under Heidegger, Marcuse studied the artist novel for his doctorate, and in *An essay on Liberation*, he considers literature to be the primary form of art. An overarching theme in the novels of *e.g.* Mann and Goethe was the overcoming of alienation experienced in a bourgeoisie environment where "the artist must overcome this twoness: he must be able to configure a type of life that can bind together what has been torn asunder, that pulls together the contradictions between spirit and sensuality, art and life, artists' values and those of the surrounding world" (Marcuse, *The German artist novel*, p. 78, cited in Miles, 2012, p. 37). An integral part of this pulling together was the emergence of a new sensibility. Yet, art is a double-edged sword. It runs

---

[17] Again, this would seem to render beauty a non-historic constant, in contrast with Marcuse's overall dialectic outlook. I shall not pursue this further at present.

the risk of affirming the culture of which it is a part, by being itself an act of production and subsequent commercialisation. Art can relegate the vision of a different technological constitution to *mere* fantasy.

As already indicated, Marcuse's later thought can appear unfocused as he thinks practically and theoretically about the possibilities of qualitative change in technology – a new overall framing of technics.[18] Yet, he is consistently continuing the dialectical outlook of Marx's philosophy and its focus on production. He continues both strands of Marx's thinking. One encapsulated by the idea of small quantitative changes – discontent and increased experience of meaninglessness – summing up to an eventual major upheaval for the better. Another strand emphasises the use of imagination as a driver for projecting different possibilities that have the ability to move a sufficient number of people into action. Here, the Marxist call for workers to unite and act becomes an emphasis on the need for practically everyone – whether engaged in productive activities or not – to have their imagination refreshed by literary and other modes of art that can project such possibilities. This would allow people to see through and beyond what Marcuse frequently calls "the technological veil" (e.g. ODM, p. 35).

Marcuse's overarching concern for our mental life and our possibilities of expression in a deeply technological environment remains mirrored in countless, more contemporary discussions. While Marcuse would be concerned with the very possibility of critical expression and saying something new with "old words" in advanced industrial society, robotic researcher Sherry Turkle expresses similar concerns as she reflects on the changing nature of the interactions both children and adults have with robots. This is revealed in the recorded responses children and adults have had during and after interaction with relational artefacts – from text-based Eliza in the mid-1960s, over the 1997 Tamagotchi fad to robotic pets like the Furby decades later. Turkle reflects: "These children are learning to have expectations of emotional attachments to robots in the same way that we have expectations about our emotional attachments to people. In the process, the very meaning of the word emotional is changing. [...] Ultimately, the question is not whether children will love their robotic pets more than their animal pets, but rather, what loving will come to mean" (Turkle, 2011a, pp. 68, 74). Turkle describes the different psychological benchmarks – such as "being alive" – for authenticity as a moving target, historically, as we have interacted with different kinds of machines through the decades and evolved in our responses to them. Rather than being consumed with the question of robots' abil-

---

[18] I have not explored Marcuse's reliance on Freud and his notion of surplus repression in a society with potentially little scarcity.

ities in terms of intelligence and ability to present functional equivalences of *e.g.* emotions, she takes the crucial question to be what *we* become as we interact with robots in various spheres of life.

Before ending in aporia and anecdote, Turkle's reflections draw on psychology, theology and biology. I point to Turkle's reflections as they help us put Marcuse's struggle to attain a critical stance on technology in perspective. He made clear how technics, originating on the production floor, had spread to different spheres of life and had a debilitating influence on the human subject. To make this case, however, Marcuse saw the need for a benchmark for human subjectivity. Being critical of the influence technologies had on human subjectivity, he naturally sought the benchmark elsewhere – biology, psychology and art. Since Marcuse wrote, this theme has been explored in a number of arenas such as those explored by Turkle. Though at times it *can* appear like grasping for straws, looking to art, psychology and biology, as Marcuse did, seem reasonable and promising avenues to pursue with the aim of giving sufficient attention and depth to the answers to the questions that technology presented for Marcuse and that remain with us.

3.5 Marcuse's challenge to value sensitive design in education

While I have suggested that Marcuse was often empirically informed in many of his discussions, his thought, and the presentation of it here, moves at a high level of abstraction. I want to now point to a specific design where Marcuse's ideas can present a challenge, both at a concrete level of interpretation of empirical data and to the systematisation of design processes that in part recognise and try to implement Marcuse's insights. While Marcuse appears unfocused in his search for an intellectual and moral counterpoint to what he perceived as one-dimensional man under the sway of technology, I suggest he motivated and offered the outlines of what has become known as value sensitive design. Below, we explore one case of value sensitive design, carried out in an educational context.

When Nissenbaum (2001) called for engineering activism in software design and Friedman, Kahn and Boring (2006) spoke of "frontloading ethics" as key to understanding value sensitive design, they were reiterating an idea that had also found an expression in Marcuse.[19] The driving idea behind value sensitive

---

19 Recent overviews of the school of design are found in Friedman, Hendry & Boring (2017) and

design is that achieving a design that takes into account the ways technologies influence humans and human societies requires the integration of modes of knowledge that are often kept separate by virtue of the institutional anchoring in higher education. Rather than have philosophers and sociologists carry out an after-the-fact assessment of the impact of any given technology, their insights should play a role in the design process before the technology is offered to the public. Accordingly, value sensitive design operates with a tripartite division of modes of knowledge that have roles in a design process and iteratively inform each other. First, conceptual knowledge of *e.g.* "trust" or "privacy" (currently the most discussed designed-for value) is required if you want to design for one of these values. Second, empirical knowledge is required to ascertain the values that various stakeholders – different users as well as external stakeholders – actually hold, and further investigate if these values are in fact supported as the technology is used. Finally, technical knowledge is needed in order to realise and embody the values in the relevant, technical artefact or system. This involves a translation of values into specific design requirements and is most clearly something that requires the different kinds of knowledge to be integrated in the design of an artefact, such as a piece of software or a design for learning.

This crucial aspect has been explored by van de Poel (2013). Translating from a general value to a more specific norm and then a design requirement, is called a specification, while translating from the specific to the general is a "for the sake of" relation. He illustrates this by using the example of chicken husbandry systems, which involve the values of animal welfare, human wellbeing and environmental sustainability and knowledge drawn from a branch of biology, ethology, as well as other sciences. The first value, animal welfare, is translated into norms concerning living space, litter, perches and presence of laying nests. This can be further specified into a design requirement in terms of square footage available. The result of such a process is a value hierarchy, where different values pertaining to a practice are clarified and, ideally, implemented in the design.

Marcuse was by no means the first to do so, but he very clearly points to the possibility of value sensitive design towards the end of ODM:

> ...the historical achievement of science and technology has rendered possible the *translation of values into technical tasks* – the materialization of values. Consequently, what is at stake is the redefinition of values in *technical terms*, as elements in the technological

---

Friedman & Hendry (2019). Though "moral imagination" features in the title of the latter, I suggest the central task of "eliciting values" from stakeholders would benefit from an approach inspired by Marcuse's.

process. The new ends, as technical ends, would then operate in the project and in the construction of the machinery, and not only in its utilization. (ODM, p. 236)

Marcuse not only offers a clear motivation for value sensitive design. In earlier writings, he makes the suggestion that what is problematic is the *lack* of this kind of technological rationality. In the sense of materialism just pointed to, we are not material enough: "The oppressive features of technological society are not due to excessive materialism and technicism. On the contrary, it seems that the causes of the trouble are rather in the arrest of materialism and technological rationality, that is to say, in the restraints imposed on the materialization of values" (2001, p. 57). While value sensitive design as a movement originated in software design, it is by no means restricted to this application, and the methods developed have more recently been applied to questions concerning the use of robots in healthcare. A constant theme throughout its development and arenas of application remains the actualisation of values.

With the technical character of repression and one-dimensionality, Marcuse in places emphasises the importance and promise of educating the youth in technical matters. Alongside such guarded optimism, his concerns for education are predictable, in light of the themes of this chapter: the needs of education are dictated by external stakeholders who have an interest in upholding status quo and manufacturing of consent. Education is included in the "totality of machines" (1972, p. 13), and the forms of education that cater for skills of immediate use in productive activities are given priority. Indeed, higher education itself is a matter of production: "Higher Education is called upon to study the 'detailed needs' of the established society so that the colleges know 'what kinds of graduate students to produce'" (1972, p. 28).

Helping people learn is also a matter of design – teachers and related professionals design for learning. [20] If one were to combine an astute awareness of values in education with a value sensitive design process, this would both hold promise and face challenges. A challenge that is well recognised in the field of value sensitive design is getting potential and actual users to express their values. Accordingly, a range of empirical methods – ranging from those of ethnography over interview to *e.g.* rapid prototyping and testing – have been adopted to help address the empirical aspects of the question. At a general level, a challenge inspired by Marcuse would be whether values that somehow subvert or challenge the status *quo* would at all find expression among those in the educational system. The school was, after all, identified as an avenue of one-dimen-

---

[20] For an exploration and analysis of this claim, see Dohn and Hansen (2018).

sionality, and perhaps most clearly a place where socialisation takes place. Further, in so far as expressions of values that run counter to the status quo *are* expressed, one may worry that "restraints are imposed" on the kind of values they are thought to be expressions *of*. That is to say, Marcuse would challenge a value sensitive design process both from above – what values are being designed for? – and from below: how do we do justice to the expressions of the users as we turn them into something of sufficient generality to count as a value?

There are a few documented cases of value sensitive design processes being carried out in education, and one of the documented examples of using value sensitive design in education can be seen to strengthen the worries we have identified. RAPUNSEL was a game developed specifically for teaching young girls to program computers and was described as a "test bed for how to embody values in a complex, real-world system" (Flanagan, Howe, & Nissenbaum, 2008, p. 333). The process had three principal investigators representing the philosophical, empirical and technical investigations and forms of knowledge. The values included those laid out in the definition of the project, primarily gender equity; those discovered during the process of the design, such as those associated with different player points of view in a game and reward systems; and those held, consciously or not, by the designers, such as diversity. Finally, the values of the users – girls testing different versions of the evolving game design – were explored. One value that was discovered among users was subsumed under the heading of "subversion". For example, one of the young girls would ask if it was possible to make their programmable game character "run off and die?" (2008, p. 338).

One would need more knowledge of the context to interpret such statements with greater accuracy, but it can be seen to suggest a small act of refusal to play the game at all – to not want to meet the expectations of an educational system that focuses on the skills and knowledge that serve industrial interests and affords status and compensation by virtue of putting such skills to use. One-dimensionality means that the goals and attitudes of the individual are themselves moulded and produced by technical means, with a view to preservation of the status *quo* and "positive thinking". Attitudes that seem counter-productive are, if not somehow amenable to productive use, ignored or undermined. To Marcuse, an important avenue for identifying and fostering two-dimensional thought is the act of subversion. He therefore considered it to be of utmost importance that educational systems recognise their political character. Marcuse primarily saw subversive potential in art, but also in fringe social movements of his day and potentially, in education: "Self-liberation is self-education but as such it presupposes education by others. In a society where the unequal access to knowledge and information is part of the social structure, the distinction and the antagonism between the educators and those to be educated are inevitable" (1972, p. 47). However, rather than antagonism and refusal, the objection of the young girl was interpreted and translated by the designers into more general values of autonomy, freedom and creativity, and made part of the design for learning to code.

We cannot be certain of the adequacy of this translation and the strength of our challenge to it. Yet, Marcuse's challenge to value sensitive design becomes that of conducting what he would call a metaphysical analysis of values, in the sense that some of them must be seen as containing potential – an essence – that seeks to be unfolded. There is a tendency in value sensitive design to see the question of values as predominantly settled by empirical work, which runs counter to Marcuse's insistence on what we called a teleological structuring of observations and reality. Feenberg has expressed this well:

> Modern reason flattens out the difference between the essential potentialities of things and merely subjective desires. It declares its "neutrality" over against the essences which govern the earlier technai. Arbitrarily chosen values are placed on the same plane as essences and no ontological or normative privilege attaches to the latter. (Feenberg, 2005, p. 87)

Value sensitive design has taken on the key task of translating values into design requirements and carefully interpreting the values that users and other stakeholders express. It now faces the challenge to entertain a critical discussion of the values that are materialised in technologies in various spheres, as well as the challenge of listening attentively to expressions of such criticism without immediately absorbing the criticism for the very purposes that are being criticised. Education is a craft, one among more *technai*, that has its inherent goals. Potentialities and values should be judged in that light. One recent suggestion is that the purpose of education – what makes an education *good* – runs along three dimensions: qualification, in the form of fostering skills, such as those needed for a job market; socialisation, understood as the acquisition of norms and values in the surrounding society, such as a democratic mindset in may Western contexts; and finally, the goal of education is subjectification, briefly put, understood as the opposite of socialisation (Biesta, 2010). In his exposition of subjectification, Biesta draws on ideas from Kant that were also highlighted in our exposition of the fate of the modern subject according to Marcuse. Subjectification means learning to be intellectually self-reliant and exhibiting a fundamental orientation towards freedom. There is much to suggest that Marcuse would highlight the deficit of the materialisation of subjectification in educational technologies, and he would likely resist the idea that this value should be considered on par with the values of convenience, diversity, entertainment or equity in the design of education.

4 Langdon Winner: Tools without handles

4.1 A strange idea and ritual forswearings

In his *Autonomous Technology: Technics-out-of-Control as a Theme in Political Thought* (1977), Winner explores the importance of technology for political processes and argument. The overarching theme from Marx that Winner treats is the appearance of a technologically embodied alien will that confronts the worker and, indeed, anyone involved with technology at the level of complexity that characterises much of everyday technological existence. In connection with alienation, Marx spoke both of the will of the capitalists as well as the will of capital itself, with its technological embodiment in a system of factories and machines. Winner's study seeks to further our understanding of this apparent distribution of agency between humans and technology. Probably the most remarkable case of alienation is that which takes place between human subjects and their own technical creations, and the title of Winner's 1977 study is reminiscent of some of Marx's characterisations of alienation between humans and the capitalist way of producing as a "…consolidation of what we ourselves produce into a material power above us, growing out of our control, thwarting our expectations, bringing to naught our calculations" (MECW 5, p. 47).

Winner is prominent among several more recent theorists who have emphasised the political properties of technologies. To Lessig (1999), code is law; to Feenberg, technology is legislative, and he asked: "If technology is so powerful, why don't we apply the same democratic standards to it we apply to other political institutions?" (1999, p. 131). Winner concurs and laments that there has been only a late realisation of the flipside of Plato's understanding of statecraft as a *technē*: "Evidently, it did not occur to Plato or to anyone else for a very long time that the analogy could at some point qualify in reverse, that *technē* itself might become a *politeia*, that technical forms of life might in themselves give powerful and authoritative shape to human affairs. If that ever did occur, what would the response of political theory be?" (1983, p. 97f.). Winner suggests that most of us suffer from what he calls technological somnambulism, and his exploration of the political qualities of technology and the grounds of autonomous technology – imperatives and reverse adaptation – can serve to gain a sufficient awareness. Finally, Winner suggests a few avenues of action that one can pursue as part of technological politics.

Marx's work was critical in the sense that he sought to understand and expose what he took to be the ailments and injustices of his contemporary society, and he is famed for his emphasis on drastic social change as the cure for capitalism. During his authorship, he seemed to become increasingly sceptical of the potential of human agency in this matter. Nevertheless, whether social change was going to be brought about primarily through human agency or as a consequence of increased systemic tensions, an ultimate crisis and subsequent revolution was to offer humans a social reality that would allow for flourishing to a far greater extent than what had been possible in the industrial society Marx described. There are several challenges in developing Marx's thinking and making it workable. The ones that shall concern us in this chapter centre on the idea of limitations in human agency in the face of some very general aspects of the way that technologies operate in their social environment, and the way these aspects can give shape to reason-giving in politics.

Based on famed quips as well as his more thorough analyses, Marx has been strongly associated with technological determinism.[1] Langdon Winner has undergone the same fate.[2] As we saw, to Marx this was partially a descriptive, or methodological matter: if you want to describe and understand a society, past or present, look at its collection of technologies. In the past, a few historians have been taken by technological determinism, and have frequently partitioned history according to technologies and delineated the stages by various technological revolutions.[3] In Marx's writings, the question of technological determinism also takes on a normative aspect. Here, determinism is predominantly a matter of how the use of a technology allows the capitalist to settle arrangements concerning production in a way that is to his immediate advantage. The actions flowing from one human will, extended and embodied through technology, is

---

[1] See *e.g.* the collection *Does Technology drive history?* (Marx & Smith, 1994) for an overview and, in particular, Bimber (1990), reprinted in the collection.
[2] Wyatt (2008) opens her survey of technological determinism with an account of the formative experience of reading Langdon Winner's "Do artefacts have politics?".
[3] A highly appraised example of technological determinism at work is found in Mokyr's *The Lever of Riches: Technological Creativity and Economic Progress* (1990). Historian Lynn White subscribed to a version of technological determinism, and one of the clearest, and also most widely questioned examples is his famous characterisation of the stirrup found in his *Medieval Technology and Social Change*. "Few inventions have been so simple as the stirrup, but few have had so catalytic an influence on history. The requirements of the new mode of warfare which it made possible found expression in a new form of Western European society dominated by an aristocracy of warriors endowed with land so that they might fight in a new and highly specialised way. 'The Man on Horseback', as we have known him during the past millennium, was made possible by the stirrup..." (1962, p. 38). Arendt suggested that "[t]ools and instruments are so intensely worldly objects that we can classify whole civilisations using them as criteria" (Arendt, 1958, p. 144)

the limitation of another human will and its possibilities of action and realisation of the human subject.

Technological determinism, conceived with full generality, is an extremely unspecific idea: technology within one domain influences some other domain. For instance, technologies of communication might influence human physiology[4]; as we shall see, the political power of a class of citizens might be determined not only, or primarily, through the ballot, but by the infrastructural design of the cities where they dwell. The insistence on difference of domain of technology and the domain of influence is motivated by the following observation: technologies are designed with the view to purposefully bring about a change in states of affairs within a certain domain, say, transport. For the thesis of determinism to be interesting, what is determined should not be what the determinant in the first place is intended, or widely recognised, to determine. To wit, in philosophy, "determinism" is perhaps most clearly associated with philosophy of mind, where determinism suggests that the phenomenon of free will is in fact determined by physical facts, which are taken to exhibit law-like, unfree, behaviour. Technological determinism will mostly concern matters where human agency is thought to be more unrestrained from technology. To say that automotive technologies determine our possibilities and habits of transport is largely obvious and uninteresting as a position of technological determinism. To say that the self-same technologies determine, say, sexual behaviour by virtue of the possibilities of the freedom and privacy they afford, and in time, determine sexual morals, is more surprising and interesting as a claim about determinism.[5]

I have used "influence" to describe the relation between the technology and the relevant domain, the meaning of which is sufficiently vague and unspecific to include what different thinkers have meant by "determinism". The meaning can be specified by locating it on two spectra. One spectrum concerns what

---

[4] This brand of technological determinism has become increasingly widespread with the strengthened interest in neurological explanations of a wide range of phenomena. It has been pursued by Small (a neuroscientist) & Vorgan in the popular science book *Ibrain: Surviving the technological alteration of the modern mind* (2008). In addition to espousing this version of technological determinism, the authors will frequently speak of technology as autonomous with phrases such as "technology's unstoppable march forward". The possible neurological effect on the hippocampus of widespread use of GPS technologies have been explored by *e.g.* Konishi & Bohbot (2014). From a post-phenomenological perspective, use of GPS navigation has been argued to determine our mode of relating to our environment, making it "disembodied" (Besmer, 2014).

[5] See *e.g.* Jeansonne (2006, p. 116 ff.) for an account of this response in America in the early 20th century. Similar concerns are widely raised with the projected advent of connected and autonomous vehicles. See *e.g.* Cohen & Hopkins (2019).

can be called the strength of the relation: at one end, some thinkers will speak of "the consequences of technology *x*" or "technology *x* causing so and so". Appealing to a form of logical consequence and causation suggests a strong brand of determinism. At the other end of the spectrum, "influence" is a concept that allows for a relation between the determiner and determinant that is quite weak. In between, one finds talk of technologies structuring, persuading (Fogg, 2003), making something possible, legislating (Lessig), offering a script to a transformed, combined actor (Akrich & Latour, 1992; Latour, 1999), different concepts of affordance (Gibson, 1979; Norman, 1998), and limiting (MacKenzie, 1984) when describing the relation between technologies and a domain. The other spectrum can be partitioned into what we may call levels micro-, meso- and macro-analyses, and they are meant to capture the difference between, for example, saying that the imperatives (Winner) or scripts (Latour) are associated with and direct my use of a certain tool for writing; that business and administration are shaped by technologies for composing and storing texts, and that societal, historical trends can be discerned through analysis of *e.g.* information technologies (e.g. Castells' "Network society" (2010) or Rainie & Wellman's (2012) networked individualism).[6] Not everything is captured by strength and level of analysis. There are qualitative and possible moral differences between being faced with a technology that tries to persuade and one that issues imperatives. Yet, these different cases of determinism remain united in insisting on technologies as an avenue of influence on human behaviour, society and culture.

The theses of technological autonomy and determinism are often conflated, and Winner has contributed to our understanding of both. "Determinism" at times gets used in connection with the point of view that there is a set, law-like course for the development of technology in history, and that the development in some other way is beyond our control. We leave this aspect out of our understanding of determinism, and reserve "autonomy" for the suggested "out-of-control" feature of technology. As we will use the term, technological determinism does not concern the question of what propels technological development, and if it indeed advances in a predetermined, possibly law-like manner. One can be a technological determinist in some respects or other, as when Plato claimed that the technology of writing would adversely affect people's memory, but still hold that the development of technologies is firmly under

---

6 Rainie & Wellman place their mode of determinism on the first spectrum by offering a comparison of the influence of information technologies with that of an operating system on a personal computer: use of new communication networks giving us a *new social operating system*. Concerning the second spectrum, they begin their book by an illustrative tale of a couple drawing on help from their network, but soon move to other levels than this microlevel.

the control of humans. The most fascinating and daunting thesis is the combination of the two theses: in some way, technology appears to be an autonomous agent, largely out of human control, and technology determines a range of key domains, such as economics, provision for a range of key, human needs or power relations in politics and elsewhere.[7]

Marx's writings displayed two kinds of answer to the question of what drives technology. Typically, the suggestion is that technology features as an extension of somebody's will and agency, as when the capitalist pits his will against the worker through technical means. However, in Marx's writings, we also see a view expressed that technology *itself* is a force that, in a sense, acts independently of human agency. In his 1977 work, Langdon Winner explored different facets of the idea that there are "tools without handles". Given that a handle is a necessary prerequisite for control of tools, Winner's coinage neatly conveys the gist of the thesis of autonomous technology. Whether convinced of the thesis of autonomous technology or not, expressions and endorsements of the thesis are ubiquitous in everyday language, in film and in literature. Informal conversation frequently contains the claim that "one cannot stop" the development of a given technology. Under the label of animism, Winner offered a survey that illustrates how widespread the thesis of autonomous technology was in the seventies. He identified prominent literary examples such as E. M. Forster's *The Machine Stops*, Samuel Butler's *Erewhon* and Mary Shelley's *Frankenstein*. In different ways, these works imbue technology with a life of its own. Creation myths of various religions have frequently depicted humans as artefacts that have turned against their maker. A central theme in animism as a literary phenomenon is the transfer of human life, will and capabilities to technological artefacts and the ensuing perfection of those capabilities in their new medium. The transfer leaves the creator impoverished, and possibly even unaware of this impoverishment. Winner adds Marx to the list of technological animists, in whose writings the organised system of machines is at times cast as a "mechanical monster... [with] giant limbs [and] countless working organs" (MECW 35, p. 384). Finally, one of Winner's inspirators, Jacques Ellul, spoke plainly of the

---

7 My usage of "determinism" thus departs from what is found in some prominent discussions, such as Wyatt (2008), and some others recorded there. She writes: "One of the problems with technological determinism is that it leaves no space for human choice or intervention and, moreover, absolves us from responsibility for the technologies we make and use" (2008, p. 169). Understanding determinism this way cannot make sense of Winner's analysis of Robert Moses, to be explored below, and raises the topic that Winner mainly discusses under the heading of "autonomy." My usage is mirrored by the two chapters on determinism and autonomy found in the philosophy of technology textbook, Dusek (2006).

doings of *technique* – a system of technologies – as if it were an agent like any other, ascribing to it anthropomorphic features such as a will to continued existence.

Winner also cites a range of prominent scientists – John K. Galbraith, physicist Werner Heisenberg and biologist René Dobus – who have all claimed to see a certain thrust in technological development that escapes the firm grasp of man. Dubos expressed it: "Technology cannot theoretically escape from human control, but in practice it is proceeding on an essentially independent course" (Dubos, 1968, cited in AT, p. 14). Finally, Winner noticed how expressions of the thesis are found in philosophy. To Winner, Heidegger offered what appeared to be a very clear expression of the thesis of autonomous technology: "But technological advance will move faster and faster and can never be stopped. In all areas of his existence, man will be encircled ever more tightly by the forces of technology. These forces... have moved long since beyond [man's] will and have outgrown his capacity for decision" (Heidegger, 1966, cited in AT, p. 14).

Winner points to a poignant case of moral implications of the thesis of autonomous technology. German armament minister Albert Speer appealed to the thesis during his defence at the Nuremberg trials, and the idea of autonomous technology features prominently in his *Spandau Diaries* (cf. Kitchen, 2015). Heisenberg, in conversation with Carl Friedrich von Weizsäcker, upon Otto Hahn's haunted realisation of the potential of his discovery of Uranium fission, also appealed to the thesis: "The word 'guilt' does not really apply... Otto Hahn and all of us have merely played our role in the development of modern science"[8] (Cited in AT, p. 69). Speer's appeal could not exonerate him and subsequent thoughts and actions of the scientific inner circle at Site Y12 at Los Alamos suggest that its members were not convinced of the thesis of autonomous technology. Nevertheless, appealing to technology-run-amok would have been as understandable to Speer's audience as it was among the key scientists at Los Alamos, and the appeal has only gained in resonance since then.

It is the tension between the widespread resonance of the thesis of technology-out-of-control held together with its ultimate untenability that Winner explores in his 1977 work. As Winner puts it: "How can we account for the fact that so many intelligent persons have embraced an idea so strange and unlikely?" (AT, p. 19). Winner's answer runs along two lines. Firstly, while acutely aware

---

[8] We may, for present purposes, replace Heisenberg's reference to "science" with "technology". Particularly in the chapters on Dewey and Latour, we shall treat the relationship between the two in more detail.

that the idea *is* strange, he sets out to present the idea with more credibility than the mere, but ever-present, mention of the idea in and of itself offers. Winner's second line of answer to his question can be summarised as follows: begin with the notion of a god of the gaps. This is the idea that the existence of God is posited as a consequence of vast ignorance in the face of one's natural environment. Supposedly, as the gaps in our knowledge of nature lessen and our capacity to manipulate it increases, our propensity to posit the existence of God equally diminishes. In the case of technology, Winner suggests that the reverse process has taken place. The existence of a technological system imbued with agency and a life of its own is posited in response to decreased transparency of technological systems. We simply don't understand and command our technology the way a simple "hammer – nail" or "problem – design – use" conception of technology would suggest. Our response to this situation is the widespread conviction that we are faced with a technological system with a life and will of its own, in spite of the fact that the origin of this system clearly is human.

Since Winner's writing, intelligent persons across academia have struggled to come to terms with both determinism and autonomy. For example, in her discussion of authorship and originality, Fitzpatrick draws on Lessig's (1999) notion of values and laws embedded in electronic communication networks. She finds some of these values to be at odds with those that scholars in the humanities profess to work by. Yet, she also reports a "need to perform the ritual of forswearing technological determinism: "I'm not arguing that the technologies with which we work determine social, intellectual, or institutional structures within which we use them. Computers do not make us think differently" (2011, p. 4). Historians are particularly critical of both theses. Here is Williams, former MIT dean:

> As a historian, I winced to hear my MIT staff colleagues express undemocratic capitulation to technological determinism. As a manager, however, I had to agree. [...] It is easy to refute the logic of determinism, but the everyday experience of having to conform to "the technology", "the software" or "the computer" cannot be refuted by logic. (Williams, 2003, p. 117)

When historian of technology David Nye discusses technological autonomy, he does much to emphasise cases where technologies are *not* introduced into society on the background of a case of collective decision-making, such as Japan's long-standing rejection of guns and the careful evaluation of technologies carried out by the Amish. Yet, without subscribing to the thesis of autonomous technology, and discussing it under the heading of "determinism", Nye interjects concerning commercial technologies such as smartphones: "Belief in determinism paradoxically seems to require a 'free market'" (2006, p. 18). These are the kind of paradoxes of freedom that Marcuse made much of. Finally, scholars in Science and Technology Studies have been reluctant to ascribe too great an emphasis on technologies in determining other phenomena, working rather from the assumption that technologies are socially shaped by different groups of users and non-users, markets, states and other actors.[9]

While the two theses *are* logically separate, one of the features of Winner's thesis of autonomous technology is the idea that technology presents us with imperatives. We therefore begin our account with Winner's famed example of determinism in one of his later works. We will then return to the question of why so many have been swayed by the thesis of autonomous technology. The chapter then continues by drawing a line from Winner's discussion of a literary expression of autonomous technology – Mary Shelley's Frankenstein – to contemporary discussions of our relationship with artificial agents. The chapter concludes with an exposition of Winner's "epistemological Luddism" – one of his proposed tactics in the face of the perceived limits on human agency and freedom that technology presents.

4.2 Forms of determinism

Winner remains best known for placing urban planner Robert Moses' New York highway bridges in the context of seeking an understanding of the interplay of politics and technology. This had already been done by Robert Caro, in his 1974 biography of Moses, and Winner uses, among others, the example of New

---

9 A formative expression of this was found in Pinch & Bijker (1987). Based on a study of the design of the bicycle, they proposed a model of the development of technologies far more complex than a linear one beginning with a design and ending with a user. Different groups of both users and non-users will shape the design in various ways, according to their values and interests. Taking their cue from the strong programme in the sociology of science, they were critical of what they called "whig history of technology", according to which we have the technologies we have, because they are better or more efficient in achieving their purpose. More recently, Ihde (2008) has relied on a comparison with the intentional fallacy – what he calls the designer fallacy – to make a similar point. Feenberg's (1995) analysis of the plasticity of the French Minitel system makes the same point: the intentions of the designers did not win the day in eventual use of this communication device, which turned into a platform for adult chat services, among other things. Winner's much cited 1980 article, to be discussed below, was the opening chapter of the first edition of *The Social Shaping of Technology* (Mackenzie & Wajcman, 1985). This is a central collection in the STS community of scholars, where Winner's kind of determinism has been countered in a number of studies.

York State highway bridges to shed light on the question that also makes up the title of an influential article of his: "Do artefacts have politics?", originally published in 1980. One's exercise of power is frequently an exercise of technologies. What Winner initially focuses on is the question of whether technologies *themselves* have political properties and in virtue of that, determine something. In his discussion, Winner alternates between saying that things have political properties (such as being just) and that things have politics. The latter more clearly suggests an active agency (someone pursues a politics with a certain agenda) and might, therefore, immediately make the thesis sound like a category mistake: people have politics, things don't. The latter are not agents, and therefore not moral agents.[10] Winner suggests two ways in which technologies can have politics, where one of them entails the claim that the politics reside in the things. First, there are "instances in which the invention, design, or arrangement of a specific technical device or system becomes a way of settling an issue in the affairs of a particular community" (1986b, p. 22). Secondly, Winner points to what he calls "inherently political technologies", where it is not obvious that anyone has designed a technology with the intention of settling matters in any particular way. These are the cases where we more naturally ascribe agency to things.

Winner offers an example from the first category that lies in clear extension of Marx's analysis of the plight of the worker. At Cyrus McCormick's reaper manufacturing plant in Chicago, costly pneumatic moulding machines were intro-

---

10 Some have, in a manner reminiscent of Gilbert Ryle's notion of a category mistake, thought that the argument I here point to ultimately wins the day. For instance, in discussion of technology and agency, Peterson & Spahn (2011) take Verbeek (2005) to task for making the category mistake. Such quick objections rely on a view of linguistic meaning that I suggest overlooks relevant aspects of the functioning of language. The Aristotelian-inspired notion of focal meaning is of relevance here (cf. Owen, 1986). To take the classic example, it would be misguided to say that calling my diet healthy is a category mistake, with reference to the fact that health is something that is said of an organism, not of vegetables. Cabbage is rightly called healthy in so far as it contributes to the health of my organism, just like urine may be called healthy in so far as it is indicative of a healthy organism. In such ways, there are quite legitimate uses of words that are systematically related, rendering such very quick, linguistic objections to the notion of artefacts having politics unsuccessful. City structures may well be unjust in the sense that they contribute to an unjust allocation of goods, and in so far as they so contribute, they are quite naturally described as agents in a way that is derived from the agency ascribed to human beings. A different defence of the language used would be appealing to the idea of an intentional stance (Dennett, 1971). If technology systems indeed are very complex and provide us with imperatives, then that would invite treating them as a rational agent with beliefs and purposes and moving from the design to the intentional stance (cf. Vermaas, Carrara, Borgo, & Garbacz, 2013). Finally, as we explore in chapter 8 on Latour, we may just expand the concept of an agent beyond its ordinary application.

duced in the mid-1880's with no improvement in terms of product quality or in terms of reduced costs. Rather, the moulding machines were introduced in order to be able to employ unskilled labour in the production process, offering Cyrus McCormick II an upper hand in the power struggle with the National Union of Iron Molders. Once McCormick had won a round in this ongoing battle, use of the machines was abandoned.[11] Technologies serve to settle matters of power and distribution of goods differently than through the usual avenues of power and contestation. In offering another example from the first category, Winner turns to the distribution of access to recreational areas from the city of New York. He describes Robert Moses as someone whose intentions, as shaped by political and racial proclivities, live on in the structures of New York City. Overpass bridges on Long Island parkways were designed with relatively low clearance in order to favour the social layers where car ownership was widespread. They would enjoy free access to Robert Moses' Jones Beach, an attractive recreational area, while low-income groups – to a great extent consisting of racial minorities – would be barred through technological means: these groups had to rely on public transport, and twelve-foot tall buses were unable to handle the low overpasses. In such ways "[m]any of [Moses'] monumental structures of concrete and steel embody a systematic social inequality, a way of engineering relationships among people that, after a time, became just another part of the landscape" (1986b, p. 23).[12] In this way, before any actual use of the pneumatic moulding machines or parkway overpasses, these technologies were imbued, by a

---

[11] It may be a coincidence, but in 2008 in Denmark, at a time when tensions over pay were running high between government and care personnel at the nation's care homes, the relevant government minister seemed particularly keen to attend and bring attention to trial runs of robotic technologies at care facilities. Thinking systematically about some of the ethical issues in such scenarios has developed into care centred, value sensitive design (van Wynsberghe, 2016).
[12] In an American context, the urban design of the most populous city has attracted the most scholarly attention. Joerges (1999) is sceptical of the case Winner makes against Moses' motives as related by Caro's highly critical 1974 biography. For example, access to Jones Beach had long been possible by means of ordinary roads, and Joerges reports that planners and engineers frequently provide better explanations of the rationale behind the low overpasses than the one Caro and Winner suggest. Further, the original plan for "little Jones beach" did include bus drop-off zones. Nevertheless, although Winner's example is in the best case a highly stylised version of the truth, its lesson remains useful when analysing the technological structures around us. Joerges suggests we see Winner's example as a parable in the sense of it being a fictitious story that is true to life. Winner's account of McCormick II's moulding machines – an example lending itself to the same conclusion, that things can be imbued with political intentions – is largely ignored by commentators. Relying on the New York State Department of Transportation database of bridge clearances, Campanella (2017) registers lower mean clearance on Moses' overpasses, when compared with those existing structures he modelled his design on.

human agent, with political qualities in addition to their immediate purposes to do with production and transport.[13]

To illustrate the second, less conspiratory way in which technologies may have political qualities, Winner relies on an analysis of the mechanical tomato harvester. Designed at the University of California in the late 1940s, the harvester, to a great extent, replaced the practice of handpicking. Introduction of the costly machine is likely to have led to a drastic restructuring of patterns of farm ownership, with consolidations taking place in the tomato industry. The number of tomato growers was reduced to less than a sixth over approximately ten years, and it is estimated that about 32,000 jobs were lost. Eventually, the California Rural Legal Assistance took action and made the case in court that the university had wrongly been spending tax monies that favoured a narrow range of private interests while putting workers and small-scale farming at a disadvantage. Subsequent studies of the events exonerate the developers of having had any malignant – political or other – intentions towards the small-scale farmers. The university argued that if successful, the charges "would require elimination of all research with any potential practical application" (Winner, 1986b, p. 27).[14] Winner concurs and suggests that rather than seeing malignant intentions, we should see the development as "an ongoing social process in which scientific knowledge, technological invention, and corporate profit reinforce each other in deeply entrenched patterns, patterns that bear the unmistakable stamp of political and economic power" (Winner, 1986b, p. 27).

While such formulations may smack of a technology out-of-control – with talk of there being a stamp of political power without any human subject having made the stamp – Winner insists that there are choices to be made when faced with a new technology: The choices broadly fall into two categories: firstly, there

---

[13] Strangely, Ihde refers to Winner's discussion of Moses in support of the position that the designer fallacy – uses and consequences of technologies that are unexpected to the designer – "may well be the rule rather than the exception" (2008, p. 54). Langdon Winner is arguing exactly the opposite in his analysis of Moses' bridges, and in fact, Ihde further strengthens Winner's case, while weakening his own, by pointing out how Moses' technologically mediated intentions were overruled by different politics and intentions. According to the Eisenhower Interstate development, bridges were required to have sufficient clearance for the transport of ballistic missiles. I remain sceptical of Ihde's claim and suggest that the intentions and values of the designer being embodied in a given artefact is the background assumption from which there are interesting departures. Assessing how widespread the designer fallacy is would be an enormous empirical task, not undertaken here. Neither shall we discuss the base of Ihde's analogous argument, the intentional fallacy in theories of literature, nor the nature of the analogy between the base, and the target, design of technologies and their use.

[14] Winner cites *University of California Clip Sheet* 54:36, May 1, 1979.

is a simple yes/no question. In our last case, should we, or should we not, introduce mechanised harvesting into the organisation of a part of society? Secondly, once the decision is made to introduce a piece of equipment, significant questions remain concerning *how* a given technology should be configured. For instance, one can have mechanical tomato harvesters with or without electronic sorters, and there are reasons to think that the decision on this matter deeply influences the distribution of wealth and power.

This account would seem to leave decision-making and technological agency firmly with *human* agents. Technologies are imbued with political qualities by virtue of human choice. However, we should firstly note that we frequently make some of these choices with insufficient care, awareness or information. Secondly, once introduced and widely adopted, technologies tend to become less and less flexible in their configuration. To challenge an insistence on the importance of human volition in matters of technology and make good the idea of *inherently* political technologies, Winner points to a discussion of authority brought forward by Engels. Engels invited his opponents, a group of convinced anarchists, to consider the post-revolutionary society: "Supposing, to adopt entirely the point of view of the anti-authoritarian, that the land and the instruments of labour had become the collective property of the workers who use them. Will authority have disappeared, or will it have only changed its form?" (Engels "On authority", cited in Winner, 1986b, p. 30). Engels' answer was clear: operating ships, railroads and having factory production require authoritarian structures with superiors and subordinates no matter who owns the technologies: "If man, by dint of his knowledge and inventive genius, has subdued forces of nature, the latter avenge themselves upon him by subjecting, in so far as he employs them, to a veritable despotism independent of all social organization" (Engels "On authority", cited in Winner, 1986b, p. 30).

Engels' corrective to a technologically naive idea of post-revolution society is the suggestion that some technologies *require* certain political and social arrangements for their functioning. Winner offers a moderation of this position in terms of *strong compatibility* between a given technology and socio-political arrangements. For example, many have argued that decentralised energy production is strongly compatible with a democratic, egalitarian society, rather than an authoritarian one.[15] Further, Winner points to a distinction concerning

---

15 Mumford made the claim in "Authoritarian and democratic technics" (1964). In 1980, Winner ominously suggested: "In my best estimation, however, the social consequences of building renewable energy systems will surely depend on the specific configurations of both hardware and the social institutions created to bring that energy to us. It may be that we will find ways to turn this silk purse into a sow's ear" (1986, p. 39). As wind energy has come to mean big, centralised

the compatibility of technologies with politically significant structures. The compatibility may exist *within* a certain technology, as when the functioning of a railway transport system is seen to be compatible with the existence of authoritarian, centralised power structures, while impossible to be run by small-scale businesses. Or, as in the case with solar energy, the claim may be that the compatibility is external to the technology: supposedly, decentralised energy supports the attempts of communities to manage their own affairs, and thus, will foster skills and virtues that transfer to the tasks of maintaining democratic institutions more generally, but as such, these virtues are unrelated to any requirements of running the technology.

In this way, a range of transport and production systems apparently require, or expressed a little weaker, are strongly compatible with a given social arrangement. A measure of secrecy and surveillance seems to be required by utilisation of nuclear power, at least in its prevalent, historic configurations; family businesses were unlikely to ever, in necessary unison, operate rail transport across the North American continent. Winner resists talking about any hard, deterministic laws, but maintains that "[t]he available evidence tends to show that many large, sophisticated technological systems are in fact highly compatible with centralized, hierarchical managerial control" (1986b, p. 35). Exactly *what* the requirements of any given technological system are, is something that needs to be settled by careful empirical investigation. As some of Winner's cases suggest, some technologies are fairly flexible regarding their design, and their requirements will have less force. However, Winner finds that appeal to overtly political values is frequently trumped by competing political values presented under the guise of appeals to technological necessity *á la* "liberty and privacy yes, but that is no way to run an transport system". When such modes of reasoning are accepted and technical reasoning eclipses other kinds of reasoning involving moral and political concepts, Winner finds that technologies become political.

4.3 Technology: Whose control, what mastery?

Plato may have been right that a ship at sea necessitates a clearly defined and adhered-to power structure. However, no such requirements emanate from a ship anchored in a harbour, about to be decommissioned. This scenario indicates

---

business, it seems to have spurred on a state of deficit in democratic participation, a deficit that has otherwise traditionally been associated with strongly centralised energy sources. See *e.g.* Aitken (2010) and the critical work of investigative journalist Peter S. Hjort (2012), who has closely followed the sizeable wind industry and its questionable practices in Denmark.

the choice that may well appear to remain firmly within our reach: whether to have a technology or not. Winner's initial characterisation of the introduction of the tomato harvester and David Nye's mention of the introduction of new products suggested otherwise, and Winner summarised his thoughts by speaking of "... an ongoing social process in which scientific knowledge, technological invention, and corporate profit reinforce each other in deeply entrenched patterns". Such patterns seem to restrict the freedom of deciding the first question, whether or not to have a technology, and combined with inflexibility in the design of the technologies (the second avenue of human choice), this offers a picture of technology-out-of-control that Winner sought to address in his 1977 work. Again, denying this freedom flies in the face of both common sense and much historical scholarship, but at the same time attests to a widespread experience.

To frame the discussion of autonomy, Winner points to a strong streak in Western self-understanding that stresses dominance and power. He sees in Francis Bacon a defining expression of a world view that continues to shape our conception of technology and science. Bacon, in his *Novum Organum*, held that the new science should equip humans with new discoveries and powers. Obeying nature would lead to discovery of her secrets, which in turn would furnish men with increased powers. In contrast with the politicians, scientists offer lasting power and control, and a benchmark for Western science became a matter of what one could do, as much as what one could explain or how elegant one's explanation was: "In the last analysis, the popular proof of science is technology. This is why we consider Bacon prophetic..." (AT, p. 25).

On this background, the thesis and experience of what appears to be autonomous technology is a sore point that challenges the crux of the Baconian narrative. It also challenges the thesis that enjoyed some popularity in the 20th century, that a certain technologically adept elite, rather than a democratically elected body, is the genuine centre of power. The prevalence of the Baconian, voluntarist self-understanding, coupled with equally prevalent language of autonomous technology, lends an air of paradox to a human self-understanding as *Homo Faber*. In short, the idea that man is best characterised as a free and deliberate yielder of tools, in conjunction with the idea that tools yield both themselves and humans, frequently thrive in close proximity. The challenge is attested to by another significant strand in Western political thought. Alongside the Baconian story that emphasises power and control, one finds a distinctly un-Baconian countertradition that focuses on the unpredictability of intervention in worldly states of affairs. Thinkers as diverse as Marcus Aurelius, Sartre and Arendt have in different ways emphasised the lack of control and predictability in the sphere of action. Such emphasis frequently appeals to the notion of undesirable consequences. In the writings of Machiavelli, *Fortuna* powerfully sweeps aside the ambitions and endeavours of man, who is to resist by means of *virtú*. According to Arendt, human capacity for action is only dimly perceived in science, where action is a matter of "releasing of processes" (Arendt, 1958, p. 323), understood as a chain reaction of largely unknown character. Currently, technology assessment is claimed to help reduce the number of unforeseen and uncontrollable consequences of the introduction of any given technology, yet remains challenged by Collingridge's dilemma of control, originally suggested in *The Social Control of Technology:* "When change is easy, the need for it cannot be foreseen; when the need for change is apparent, change has become expensive, difficult and time-consuming" (1980, p. 11).[16]

Such a corrective to the Baconian narrative also challenges those 20th century philosophers of technology that see in technological developments a flaw of human nature put on display. For example, Lewis Mumford saw in what he called authoritarian megatechnics human ignorance combined with power hunger at work.[17] Horkheimer and Adorno restricted their criticism to Western man, seeing in him a diseased faculty of reason that was born from the urge to dominate, which they thought had ultimately reduced reason to a purely instrumental faculty. Turning from the nature of man to his place in creation, others yet have in the book of Genesis seen a particularly Judeo-Christian view of man's relation to nature that underscores domination. Such criticisms face severe challenges on several accounts. It seems an unlikely interpretation of the everyday actions of engineers and scientists that they should *really* be driven by a deep-seated urge for power. Even if such understandings were fundamentally correct and the sweeping historical claims could be made precise and credible, the thesis of autonomous technology suggests that the avenue of technology would be a questionable avenue to pursue for purposes of domination and release of power urges. Someone bent on power should not choose an instrument that is itself overpowering and out of control. Winner explores an instructive picture of this conundrum in the 19th century treatments of the notions of slave and master. Aristotle described a slave as a tool, and it was around the time that slavery was becoming widely abolished that Hegel, Marx and Nietzsche in different ways pointed to irony and paradox in the relationship between slave and master.

---

[16] While Winner in 1977 was generally sceptical of attempts at remedying our ignorance of technological systems, he went on to suggest the idea of "design politics", which will have to somehow negotiate the dilemma. See his "Political ergonomics" (1995).

[17] Mumford distinguished between authoritarian megatechnics and democratic polytechnics. He did not think that man essentially exercised such vices, that they were part of his essence. Rather, modern man is held by a myth that he is essentially a toolmaker, and that this is best expressed in megatechnical monstrosities, rather than small-scale, democratic tools.

In Hegel's master-slave dialectic, the slave gains the upper hand in so far as he, unlike the master, objectifies himself when working on nature, an activity that in turn renders the master dependent on the slave. In Marx, there are similarities to this dynamic in the revolt of the working masses. Such a story is recapitulated in numerous depictions of technology.[18]

Winner identifies three common assumptions at work when reflecting on the nature of our relation to technology. Firstly, that humans know best what they themselves have made. Secondly, that what is human-made is under humans' firm control and, thirdly, that technology is a neutral instrument in the sense that the responsibility for its associated benefits or harms rests solely with its user. We have already discussed the third assumption, and the first two – knowing and doing – are interconnected in the case of artefacts, as well as systems. Winner traces the first assumption to Aristotle's characterisation of *technē* as the combination of experience of facts and an understanding of underlying causes of the facts, exercised by an individual. Winner locates the assumption most clearly in Hobbes and Plato. When the latter wished to offer examples of episteme, he would utilise imagery from the practical arts, as in the discussion of statecraft mentioned above. Hobbes' *Leviathan* was possible through perfect knowledge. Against such a notion, Winner joins others in speaking of the urban barbarian, who has comprehension of the workings of almost none of the technical aspects of his milieu. What is left is a group of specialists, "left to trade on each other's ignorance" (AT, p. 284). This is what Winner calls manifest social complexity, where a range of interconnected, highly specialised activities take place without anyone having a grasp of the nature of the interconnected whole. An additional factor is when the overt nature of the complexity becomes concealed. I order a ticket on a computer, whose functioning is hidden from me. My order involves a range of professionals with whom I have no interaction and would not even be able to identify accurately should I try. The price is often personalised by algorithms, the character and interplay of which I do not understand. Faced with both manifest and concealed complexity, our cognitive situation is not unlike that of a newborn baby, but without the dramatic advance in its understanding of its immediate surroundings. As such modes of understanding are lacking, we are increasingly inclined to speak of autonomous technology.[19]

---

18 The etymology of "robot" (the Czech "Robota") is "compulsory labour" and entered English language from a play by Karel Čapek (1921), *R. U. R. (Rossum's Universal Robots)*. The play features slave robots rising in revolt against their human master, and the scenario motivated Asimov's three laws of robotics.

19 The notion of concealed complexity plays a role in Latour's philosophy (chapter 8) and has been given a renewed expression with the idea of a black box society, informed by algorithms

Winner suggests that, to many, the assumption of control appears borne out by common sense. Common sense in this case sets out with the fact that technologies are designed and constructed with certain intended ends, and thus essentially an extension of the human will. For example, Winner is likely to have had some more or less basic understanding of and control over the workings of an electric typewriter, which he presumably used to write his book. He might well have been able to do minor repairs on it if necessary. Today, computer manufacturers and sellers are increasingly shutting down repair departments, as the knowledge required for doing most of the repairing to a personal computer, as well as its software, is vast and complex. The majority of users of word processors are even more chanceless when technologies break down and remain largely ignorant of their workings. Indeed, grand old man of philosophy of technology, Carl Mitcham, has offered a passionate defence for a simpler writing software, one that would offer the user more mastery and transparency (Mitcham, 2009). A similar analysis can be made of our ubiquitous transport and energy technologies. With increased sophistication of the technologies with which we surround ourselves, most simply do not master these technologies in the sense that we do not have a perspicuous overview of their inner workings and cannot alter them according to our needs and wants.

4.4 The mechanics of autonomous technology – imperatives and reverse adaptation

Rejecting the two assumptions of transparency and mastery suggests a picture of our cognitive situation being comparable to the one I suggested have led some to posit a god of the gaps. To lessen the gap, Winner offers two concepts that can strengthen our understanding: imperatives and reverse adaptation. As we explored in our account of Marx, the thesis of autonomous technology would gain prominence as historians and sociologists became inspired by thermodynamics in their account of societal development. Not only had historians and sociologists, since the 19th century, offered key importance to discoveries in physics when accounting for societal change – they had also explained society and technology in terms of thermodynamics. As a consequence, they would naturally ascribe a certain dynamism and inevitability to technological developments. So-

---

that lack transparency, even for individual members of the teams that create them (Pasquale, 2015). As decisions in a range of spheres, from health to finance, are increasingly automated, algorithmic transparency continues to be a much discussed topic.

ciety would be seen as passively undergoing various "-isations" (industrialisation, modernisation) modelled on irreversible, physical processes. Technology has since then been ascribed momentum, acceleration and force, and the language of David Landes' 1969 *The unbound Prometheus* was typical: "It was the Industrial revolution that initiated a cumulative, self-sustaining advance in technology whose repercussions would be felt in all aspects of economic life" (Cited in AT, p. 50).

Wanting to make voluntarism in matters of technology cohabit with the thesis of autonomous technology without the air of paradox, Winner seeks to offer a more refined account of the thesis of autonomous technology than he finds on offer in physics-inspired sociology. To achieve this, Winner draws on Jacques Ellul in positing the existence of *the ensemble* and, as we explore below, joins more recent theorists of technology in relying on a model from biology when explaining technological change.[20] The ensemble is an aggregate of technologies. It is not the case that particular technologies – certain weapons or genetically modified foods – cannot be altered, or as the case was with Japan, successfully denied for a period of time. At such a level of analysis, human effort makes a distinct impression on the course of events. However, the ensemble of techniques takes on properties that challenge human control. Winner suggests: "... the autonomist assumption, that is, that society and culture are things in themselves and must be studied as such, is the most important premise in all of sociology. In this regard, Ellul is distinctive only in the particular source he identifies at the heart of the condition of autonomy, *la technique*. He is also distinctive in his desire to put the collective process against the pretensions of the individual" (AT, p. 63).

While critical of Ellul, Winner recognises in Ellul's autonomist assumption a crucial thesis. The linchpin of Winner's construal of the thesis of autonomous technology and the challenge it presents to human control is the notion of a technological imperative that gradually trumps other imperatives. Winner agrees

---

20 Winner traces the nature of what he calls the autonomist assumption to Durkheim's *Rules of Sociological Method:* "Society is not a mere sum of individuals. Rather, the system formed by their association represents a specific reality which has its own characteristics" (Cited in AT, p. 62). For example, committing suicide is typically seen as a profound issue with human volition at its centre, but Durkheim could also analyse the rate of suicide as a socio-religiously determined fact. In his methodology, Durkheim insisted that "...[t]he voluntary character of a practice or an institution should never be assumed beforehand" (cited in AT, p. 67). In relying on biology in understanding technology, Winner is placed in the company of range of thinkers from Ernst Kapp to Ray Kurzweil, who sees "technological evolution as a continuation of biological evolution" (Kurzweil, 2005, p. 7).

with Ellul that what characterises Western civilisation from about the 18th century and onwards is not the emergence of widespread technological determinism as such. Technologies have determined humans in various ways for much longer, and other things have determined humans and presented imperatives as well. Rather, it is the predominance of technological determinism over other spheres that potentially determine the thoughts and actions of man. An idea that we shall return to in later chapters[21] is that in previous times, the impact of technologies was restrained by other influences. In ancient Greece, "… the rejection of technique was a deliberate, positive activity involving self-mastery, recognition of destiny, and the application of a given conception of life. Only the most modest techniques were permitted – those which would respond directly to material needs in such a way that these needs did not get the upper hand" (Ellul, cited in AT, p. 119). Ellul also saw severe technological restraint in the medieval monasteries. Here, the religious sphere was an overarching determinant. While Ellul's account of the technical capabilities and the outlook of ancient Greeks as well as medieval monastics might not survive careful scrutiny, Winner insists that the outlook of such cultures was far more multifaceted than ours, and locates the seed of our current technologically centred culture with the receding of competing determinants. The combined fading of Christian taboos on tampering with the presumed natural order of things and a weakening of authoritarian social structures, such as peasant communes or guilds, made social structures and public consciousness more plastic.[22] Combined with an atomistic conception of the individual, the road was paved for a more singularly technological orientation. This leads to a wholesale avoidance of bigger questions and "[u]ltimately, it is precisely a well-trained technical narrowness that lies at the foundations of the phenomena of unintentionality and technological drift…" (AT, p. 129).

How do imperatives more precisely issue from technology? While Winner follows Ellul in emphasising totalities and their properties, Winner's more refined conception of technology can assist us in locating the imperatives. The imperatives do not require ascription of agency, but simply issue from the requirements for a piece of technology to function. Winner defines the concept of technology as consisting of *apparatuses:* physical objects employed as tools, such as weapons, computers, phones and lawn mowers; *techniques:* the skills, methods, procedures and routines that people engage in to achieve tasks; *organisations* that signify "all varieties of technical (rational-productive) social arrangements" (AT,

---

21 Heidegger, in particular, proposes something similar.
22 14–19th century guilds have weighed in forcefully against new technologies. Cf. Desmet & Parente (2014).

p. 12). Fundamental to Winner's construal of technological imperatives is the claim that "[t]echnologies are structures whose conditions of operation demand the restructuring of their environment" (AT, p. 100). Rather than seeing this as an addition to his definition, it is a way of locating imperatives at different levels, along the second spectrum, suggested above. A car, one-laptop-per-child or a research organisation all place demands on their material and social environment. Attempts at technology transfer can make the requirements particularly clear.[23]

Thus, along with deciding a means to an end – ends within transport or education – comes the task of providing a set of means to the mean, and a technology will have a tendency to refashion its environment in accordance with its requirements. On this background, Winner can claim that the technological imperative "contains a logic that accounts for much of the way change occurs in modern society. [...] If you desire X and if you have chosen the appropriate means to X, then you must supply all of the conditions for the means to operate. To put it differently, one must provide not only the means, but also *the entire set of means to the means*" (AT, p. 101). Means interlock and are interdependent and they must mutually adjust. Making a decision means aligning a whole system of apparatuses and techniques. The instrumental and economic conditions are but one source of technological imperatives. As technologies develop, their availability become perceived as a necessity of life, and supplying them becomes something akin to a moral, and frequently, a political imperative. For example, making internet connectivity widely available is increasingly seen as something like the satisfaction of a human need, to the extent that work, education, socialising and leisure *require* connectivity. In sum, Winner finds that the set logic of imperatives issued from what he, like Galbraith, calls the industrial system makes society increasingly inertial, inflexible and "unresponsive to any other ends than its own survival and growth" (AT, p. 105).[24]

In speaking about environment and adaptation, Winner relies on a biological model in his theory of autonomous technology. While one might think that technologies need to adjust to their environment as well as the goals they serve, Winner suggests that reverse adaptation is widely taking place. This simply is "the adjustment of human ends to match the character of the available means"

---

23 Since Winner wrote, Tiles & Oberdiek (1995) and Selinger (2009) have discussed transfer of technology in relation to the demands technologies make on their social and material environment.
24 It seems to me a plausible suggestion that technical imperatives, arising from financial technologies and cross-border production lines among other technological systems, have, for a long time, largely trumped a political imperative to have the United Kingdom leave the European Union.

(AT, p. 229). In the theory of natural selection, adaptation is a central explanative term for a change in an organism that enhances its chance of surviving in its given environment. If the organism, rather than adapt itself, adapts the environment, we have reverse adaptation.[25] Similarly with technological systems: rather than the technological system adjusting to the needs and requirements of its environment – nature and societies of humans – the system adjusts its environment. This also means that imperatives do not necessarily emanate from a technologically informed elite; the political-cum-technological thrust is equally offered by the imperatives of networks of interdependent technologies. Such a process has accelerated as technologies form more and more complex wholes, with each part being crucial for the functioning of others. As we already noted, such states of affairs offer the disciplines of planning and technology assessment crucial importance, but Winner takes it that the necessary concomitant of this practice – ends – are themselves under the influence of technology as a whole: "Under the logic that takes one from size, interconnection, and interdependence to control and planning, it can happen that such things as ends, needs, and purposes come to be dysfunctional to the system" (AT, p. 241). Winner remarks that from the understanding that a key component of rationality is a means-ends structure with independence between the two, the technological system as a whole takes on irrational features: "[r]everse-adapted systems represent the most flagrant violation of rationality" (AT, p. 242).

There is evidence to the effect that technologies in aggregate start determining avenues that might otherwise be taken to be determined by human will and decision making. Firstly, markets are controlled by means of vertical integration, where the planning unit seeks to influence more and more steps of the value chain. Markets are further controlled by means of large-scale state contracts where amounts and prices are set over a long period. Winner concludes: "that the market [should be] an effective means for controlling large-scale systems is known to be a nostalgic, off beat, or fantastic utopian proposal with little to do with reality" (AT, p. 243). Secondly, political processes and institutions are another obvious avenue of fixing ends, and here Winner suggests that "one need only review the historical success of the railroads, oil companies, food and drug producers, and public utilities in controlling the political agencies that supposedly determine what they do and how" (AT, p. 244).[26] Thirdly, in what appears

---

[25] There are scattered references to this explanation in the biological sciences before and after Winner wrote. The concept served a key role in the analysis of electricity grids offered in Kellow (1996), but it seems otherwise largely neglected.

[26] Tiles & Oberdiek (1995, pp. 130–138) offer an instructive account of the success of the car as a transport technology in the US, one that supports Winner's sweeping claim.

as a summary of the first two points, Winner finds that technological systems tend to seek a mission to their capabilities once their original rationale is exhausted.

This leads Winner to revise the notion of a technocracy. There may indeed be a group of individuals who appear to become equipped with greater powers by virtue of the technical insight.[27] However, rather than necessarily relying on sophisticated training or insight, what characterises this group of people is that they simply find themselves more directly faced with technological imperatives, and as a consequence, they end up making "the kinds of decisions that any intelligent person in a position of power and authority would be required to make when confronted with accurate information on the condition of the technological order at a particular point in time" (AT, p. 258). The decisions are less a result of free deliberation on, and implementation of, political or other values and ends than they are a result of coping with the necessities of technical configurations. Technocracy does in fact not require any particular technological ideology to have taken over the hearts and minds of decision-makers: "...it can be said that those who best serve the progress of technological politics are those who espouse more traditional political ideologies but are no longer able to make them work" (AT, p. 277).

Technocracy becomes a word not for the capture of power by some at the loss of others, but for the loss of control suffered by a society as a whole. To Winner, this is the tale of a process where original ends of any given technological system are increasingly lost sight of, while procurement of the means takes centre stage in the political discourse: "Decisions made in the context of technological politics... carry an aura of indelible pragmatic necessity. Any refusal to support needed growth of crucial systems can bring disaster. The alternatives range from utterly bad service, at a minimum, to a lower standard of living, social chaos, and at the far extreme, the prospect of lapsing into a more primitive form of civilized life" (AT, p. 259). Winner finds footprints of technological imperatives and reverse-adapted social ends in all sorts of more or less mundane settings to do with law, foreign policy, state budgets, research organisations and

---

[27] Veblen seized on the idea, and it continues to thrive in expositions of Marx: "It is true, of course, that the particular forms of the social organization of modern industrial work are often incompatible with the development of individuality and freedom. They involve a division of labour which concentrates expertise and control in a select group of engineers and managers, and condemns the vast majority of workers to operations and tasks from which all aspects of skill and knowledge, and opportunities to exercise initiative and independence, have been deliberately and systematically eliminated" (Sayers, 1998, p. 64).

subsidies.[28] Unlike the truly central, technocratic figure of Robert Moses, the technocracy of autonomous technology is a decentralised form of government: "The social history of modern technology shows a tendency – perhaps better termed a strategy – to reduce the number of centers at which action is initiated and control is exercised" (1986a, p. 93).

With the concepts of technological imperatives issuing from means, and reverse adaptation altering the ends, Winner has still not made a strong case, empirically, but speaks of patterns. Imperatives of all sorts can be, and are, offered resistance with lesser or greater success. Systems can become obsolete with no adaptation of their environment seeming possible to ensure their survival in the form of new ends. Nevertheless, with his central concepts, he has offered what he set out to achieve: a useful tool for those wanting to awake from their technological somnambulism to explore how avenues, considered to be subject to the control of political processes, to a greater extent are controlled and mastered by technological ones.

4.5 Caring for monsters

> "I'm an engineer, and I used to just build out my ideas and hope they would mostly speak for themselves…" (Mark Zuckerberg, 2019)

In passages of *Capital* inspired by Feuerbach, Marx emphasised human responsibility for the regrettable states of affairs under unbridled capitalism. In both religion and a system of factory-based production, humans face something they themselves have created. Elsewhere he would describe the factory – and indeed, capitalism itself – in terms of monstrosity, exploring the analogy by talking of limbs and organs of the factory (for example, the central power source of the factory is the heart) and underscoring how human labour is utterly dwarfed by this monster. By urging us to carefully consider the lesson of the animism of Mary Shelley's *Frankenstein,* Winner continues and refines these strands of thought in Marx.

---

28 A mundane setting is the work life for researchers in the humanities at the University of Southern Denmark. With the university having purchased a super-computer, the *Abacus 2.0*, in 2015, researchers were called to several meetings where they were strongly encouraged to align their research interests with the possibilities this computer offers. So far, the reverse adaptation appears largely to have failed. The imperatives were not of sufficient strength to an obstinate faculty.

Human relationship with technologies is a dominant theme in myth, literature and popular culture. The myth of Prometheus and Icarus, Swift's *Gulliver's Travels*, Goethe's *Faust* and Mary Shelley's *Frankenstein* seem to uniformly tell cautionary tales of technology-driven hubris and unexpected consequences of their use. Not unlike concerns for the effect on our brain of widespread use of GPS, Plato told a story of the invention of reading and writing and its effect on memory and wisdom. In his *Phaedrus*, he has the Egyptian god, Theuth, visit Thamus, king of Thebes, offering up various technologies, and receiving a reply suggesting scepticism concerning the blessings of technologies. Langdon Winner discusses several of these myths and stories. In a contemporary setting, the most interesting is his discussion of Mary Shelley's *Frankenstein*, and it is a theme he has returned to in later writings (2017a).

Since Winner offered his analysis of *Frankenstein*, discussions of autonomous technologies have largely shifted from the level of the ensemble to individual artefacts. From autonomous weapon systems to fiancial services, machines are increasingly performing roles in ways that give them human-like qualities, including different levels of autonomy. Conceptual and practical work is being done on imbuing machines with what we might call a sense of ethics, through discussion of the nature and design of artificial moral agents.[29] While discussion among engineers, scientists and philosophers are likely well ahead when compared to actual and projected capabilities of robots and forms of artificial intelligence, the question of autonomous machines has taken on a new urgency in the academic community and among men and women in the relevant industries. Also in this context does Winner's analysis of Shelley's Frankenstein deserve a rereading. The tale is typically thought to hold lessons either by virtue of the lofty ambitions of Victor Frankenstein, or the agency of his monster. In contrast, Winner highlights how the monster voices the importance of seeing autonomous technologies – from systems to artefacts – as patients, rather than agents, in questions of ethics. One way this has recently entered moral debate is the question of robot rights.[30]

---

[29] A lot of work is focused on what is called explicit, ethical agents, with algorithms being envisaged that are supposed to capture the reasoning that goes on in deontology and consequentialism, respectively. See *e.g.* Anderson, Anderson and Armen (2005).

[30] We cannot here discuss the relation between moral agents and moral patients. Rather than relying on a version of the second spectrum suggested above, Floridi and Sanders (2004) bring their method of abstraction to the question of the relation between moral agents and moral patients. David Gunkel (2018) has framed the discussion of whether robots *can* (the ontological question, as also presented by Moor – see below) and *should* have rights (the ethical question) in terms of a matrix of four positions. In subscribing to what he calls a relational turn in ethics,

Part fact, part fiction, Victor Frankenstein was Shelley's amalgam of a range of contemporary scientists. Smitten with the thirst for knowledge and with a thorough interest in electricity, Frankenstein achieves a remarkable feat in bio-engineering, assembling something human-like from body parts. The creature exhibits sentience, animation, intelligence and emotion, and by virtue of these features, Frankenstein's monster raises a range of issues currently discussed in branches of AI and robo-ethics: the distinction between the artificial and the real, the human and inhuman, and not least, technological responsibility. Concerning the latter, the tale is frequently interpreted as one that "warns of the manifold dangers which accompany the promise and progress of science and technology" (van der Laan, 2016, p. 173). Van der Laan, like many others, sees in Mary Shelley's Frankenstein the themes of technological hubris and unintended consequences on display. However, it is the idea of responsibility to treat our creations as moral patients that Winner explores, and he reads Shelley as addressing the responsibility that engineers have towards *any* creation of theirs – sentient, intelligent or not. While the difficult question in branches of AI and robo-ethics is taken to be a matter of placing human creations, such as robots, on the right side of a line dividing humans, and possibly animals, from other creations,[31] Winner sees in the tale of Frankenstein's monster the grounds for moral consideration and care for technologies in the fact that technologies have to interact with their social and material environment.

While numerous, early adaptations depict the monster as largely speechless, Winner recounts how Shelley gives it a voice that speaks on behalf of autonomous, complex machines and systems. Subsequent to his technological achievement, Frankenstein, terrified at his own success, utterly loses his nerve and takes flight from his creation. The being appears benign, but very powerful and largely at a loss in a social world it knows nothing of and cannot navigate without assistance from its creator. It slowly and under tragic circumstances gains an understanding of its environment and the circumstances of its creation, and after some years have passed, it is able to present its case for due care and concern to its creator. In a dialogue set on the icy slopes of the Alps, the monster emphasises Frankenstein's duties as creator, and the dire consequences of neglecting them: "His stern admonition to Victor is to recognise that the invention of something powerful, ingenious, even marvellous cannot be the end of the work at hand" (Winner, 2017a). It reasons with Frankenstein and expresses its wish for

---

he gives priority to data from actual human-robot interaction, while finding the ontological question less important.

31 For the framing of the discussion in terms of an ontological line, see *e.g.* Moor (2011).

a place in the community of humans, but it lacks the care and help of its creator. Though Frankenstein is swayed by both the reasoning and the threats issuing from his monster, Frankenstein neglects his duties, the care is denied, and a spectacular tragedy ensues.[32] To Winner, our lack of care for, and sometimes determined ignorance of, our autonomy-exhibiting, imperative-issuing creations are comparable to those of Frankenstein's writ large: "Technology…allows us to ignore our own works. It is license to forget" (AT, p. 315). In the hands of Winner, Marx's idea of technological monsters, exhibiting some kind of autonomy, has become something that by virtue of their complexity and social interaction with human communities – whether as an artificial being like a robot or a complex system of technologies – leaves room for a key moral role of caring for these technologies. While not framing the question as one of robot rights, but one of care, Shelley, and Winner in particular, should be seen to endorse the position that while autonomous technologies cannot have rights, they *should* on account of what they ultimately do to us.

40 years later, Winner surveys contemporary discussions of technology and sees Frankenstein's attitude repeated in the discussion of artificial intelligence, automation and the future job market:

> Studies of and speculation about issues of this kind has inspired the creation of a collection of new research centers at leading universities. Among them are the Cambridge Center for the Study of Existential Risk and The Future of Life Institute at MIT. Taken together the shelf of books on AI and Robots, the systematic studies of the future of automation and employment, and the excited warnings about artificial devices superseding human beings as the key actors on the stage of world history are, in my view, a contemporary realization of the prescient concerns and warnings at the heart of Mary Shelley's book – concerns and warnings about the headlong flight from responsibility. (Winner, 2017a, par. 44)

Winner suggests our culture generally overvalues the aspects of technology that emphasise innovation and creation, something Winner has explored in more recent writings.[33] Other researchers have, in Winner's account of Frankenstein's monster, seen an emphasis on the moral importance of maintenance and the work of the service technician, such as those taking care of photo-copiers: "[M]achines and their users need understanding, help, explanation, negotiation,

---

32 The subtitle of Mary Shelley's book *A Modern Prometheus*, suggests that her errand may well have been a critical corrective to the vision of god defying, civilised, technology-yielding humanity offered by the tradition in which her husband's play *Prometheus Unbound* was placed.
33 In *The Cult of Innovation: Its Colorful Myths and Rituals* (2017b), Winner surveys everyday language and points to what he calls gadgetology, elitism and optimism as key features of our cultural infatuation with innovation. Also, he takes aim at the widespread use of Schumpeter's idea of creative destruction.

and translation for the machines to function in the world, and this is what the technicians really do" (Orr, 2000, p. 150).[34]

With use of Winner's analytical tools, we may begin to increase our knowledge of autonomous technology and Winner can deduct a range of desiderata for technologies: the design process should be of a participatory nature; technologies should be intelligible for ordinary users; they should be flexible and not foster dependencies.[35] Yet, these principles are utopian and we frequently find that the "the real field is already taken" (AT, p. 328) by informational and other infrastructures and intensely marketed devices. We live and have our being with artefacts and systems created not in our lifetime and of which relatively little is known. There are no unintended consequences of the decisions by the vast majority of technology users, because there are no decisions and actions that the consequences could meaningfully be said to flow from. Asking whether we should have grid electrification, cars, the internet and other such technologies simply does not represent a live option. And this gives less occasion for thinking about *how* we should have these technologies – the second avenue of decision-making with respect to technology.

Finding ourselves in a crowded space with few intellectual and material resources for new designs, Winner points to more drastic means for achieving the relevant techno-political "white-boxing": epistemological Luddism. Compared to reverse adaptation, epistemological Luddism as an idea has been more widely adopted.[36] Traditionally, Luddism is mostly understood to denote a violent anti-technological form of action and sentiment, originating among textile workers in the Midlands and Northern England. Winner's Luddism is not destructive as such but serves an immediate epistemological goal. The idea is to make complex systems "unworkable in order to provide the opportunity to learn what they are doing for or to mankind" (AT, p. 300). Of course, this would seem to imply a kind of destruction, but in Winner's case, "making something unworkable" should be understood to concern a smaller group of users. The drift of Winner's idea is turning off your internet router or social network software, not the inter-

---

[34] See also Russell & Vinsel (2016), *Hail the Maintainers*, for an overview of scholars who explore how maintenance work is a severely undervalued aspect of the phenomenon of technology.

[35] There is a great overlap with Illich's concept of convivial technology (cf. Hansen 2018).

[36] Shying away from suggesting the real thing, Frishmann & Selinger (2017) open their study of surveillance, privacy and human behaviour with an invitation to the thought experiment of *imagining* human existence without "The frightful five" – Amazon, Apple, Facebook, Alphabet and Microsoft. Epistemological Luddism informs the analysis of such phenomena as digital detox (artefact level) and highway removal (system level) found in Lachney & Dotson (2018).

net or Facebook itself. There will be a point where the epistemological Luddism becomes genuine Luddism. In the case of networked technologies, however, this will take the kind of coordinated, large-scale activities, the impossibility of which motivates epistemological Luddism in the first place. Ordinary consumers do not have the choice, say, to turn off the grid and rethink electrification or most networked information technologies. It is very difficult for any individual or group of individuals to make a difference in these matters, and to ignore this fact in any kind of user design or general technological reflection is to put a blind eye towards reality – "real technologies do not permit such wholesale tampering [i.e. tearing down]" (AT, p. 329). However, ordinary consumers can on occasion be cut off from the grid or can at times decide to leave artefacts in disrepair, and this can serve as an opportunity to learn about the hidden complexity, technological imperatives and possible goal adaptation of a given technology.

Winner is suggesting an intended extrication of oneself from technological systems and apparatuses as a method of inquiry of fundamental importance, leaving us wiser about the nature of our involvement with any given technology and its interconnection with others. Epistemological Luddism becomes a way of "recovering the buried substance on which our civilization rests. Once unearthed, that substance could again be scrutinized, criticized and judged" (AT, p. 330). Emphasising the epistemological aspects, meticulous data-gathering is of central importance. Winner suggests that the discomforts experienced as a result of his method of Luddism are key. Epistemological Luddism will allow us to get a clearer view of the way technologies shape our relationships, communication, needs and habits – our form of life. And while not necessarily designing anything new from scratch, there will at times be a genuine question whether, and in what way, the device should be turned on again or the system of technologies joined again.

5 Martin Heidegger: thinking beyond technology

5.1 Heidegger's Mysticism

To Heidegger, the forgetfulness of Being is the source of a range of ailments that plague Western culture as a whole and its individuals. It shows pre-eminently in our relationship with, and character of, modern technology. While the subject of metaphysics is often taken to be closely related to the topics of language or religion, one of the novelties of Heidegger's thinking consists of seeing metaphysics as the key to understanding the character of technology in modern Western culture. Accordingly, to frame Heidegger's account of technology, this chapter will set out by presenting an account of his metaphysics, and then go on to present more familiar concepts of *Gestell* and "dwelling" on that background. Heidegger thought that Greek conceptions of technology had a normative structure foreign to ours, and one from which we should learn again. To bring this into focus, we shall follow his engagement with ancient Greek philosophy and its concepts.

Two towering figures of 20th-century European philosophy, Heidegger and Wittgenstein, shared a pull towards mysticism as well as frequent reflection on the use of tools. Wittgenstein was drawing on his training as an engineer when authoring the *Tractatus Logico-Philosophicus* and concluded the work by insisting that "…that there is indeed the inexpressible. This shows itself; it is the mystical" (1922, §6.522). In his later works he would, among other things, rely on comparisons of tools and words in order to shape and convey his philosophy of language. Heidegger, with comparatively little technical background, continues to exert, by far, the greatest influence on the philosophy of technology of the two. In *Being and Time,* Heidegger reacted against affording primacy to a cognitive attitude that takes a distanced, observational stance towards the world. Heidegger would rather have us give priority to seeing the world as something humans engage with and take care of, and consequently, he initiated his analysis of human existence with a description of being in a workshop. According to the author of *Being and Time,* our most immediate and ubiquitous encounter with the world is by way of *Zeug* – equipment that exists in often nested relations of in-order-to. For example, for a hammer to exist is for there to be the activity of driving in nails; thereby two pieces of wood are joined in order to make the frame for a wall in a house that protects a family against the elements and marks a certain social standing. This is how we primarily approach the world and what a world *is*, rather than, say, a range of material objects with a range of properties that make up the world as it is anyway. The concrete human being, *Dasein*, is fundamentally concerned about itself, others and things, making "care" (*Sorge*) the very being of Dasein. A world is pervaded by a certain mood (e.g. boredom), a medium in which things are disclosed.

In Heidegger's later thought, Being itself, rather than the being-interpreting human, *Dasein*, takes centre stage. Integral to this turn was a combination of mysticism and metaphysics, the interest in which was likely sparked by Heidegger's early studies of medieval theology, including the logic and ontology of Duns Scotus and Thomas von Erfurt and the mysticism of Meister Eckhart. Currently, the term "mysticism" has a tendency to assume a negative meaning close to "obscurantism". I here intend to use "mysticism" in a neutral sense, which focuses not on (a lack of) proper methods in acquiring and communicating knowledge, but according to which one insists on there being something, or some kind of insight, one cannot speak of – at least not in the way that we ordinarily refer to things by means of garden-variety, subject-predicate sentences. In different ways mystics, both Heidegger and Wittgenstein were sceptical regarding the expressive powers of language, and reflections on the nature of language were what led them to their respective mysticisms. Wittgenstein's early work can be read as a carefully structured argument that is meant to bring into perspective features about language and reality that cannot, for principled reasons, be spoken about. Compared to this, Heidegger appeared far more permissive. According to him, the unspeakable can be approached and delineated from the outside through rational thought, *Denken*. Meanwhile, the poet, exemplifying another way of thinking that Heidegger at one point called "meditative", is able to place himself more directly in view of Being and somehow convey this perspective and its contents.

Heidegger's thought on technology is not restricted to his few writings that are explicitly dedicated to technology. Not just in his lecture entitled "The Question Concerning Technology" but also in "The Thing", "Discourse on Thinking", "Building, Dwelling, Thinking" and other writings, he offers technology a central role in the drama of our relationship with Being. Reading "The Question Concerning Technology" as a self-sufficient piece on the nature of technology will make it nearly impossible to follow several strands of Heidegger's reasoning contained therein. To Heidegger, the history of Being is a story[1] of human forgetful-

---

[1] As Heidegger warns in the lectures entitled *Time and Being*, his conception of time and history is elusive and difficult to understand. We should not here think of history as simply a series of events, selected, explained and categorised. German distinguishes history (*Historie*) in this sense, and *Geschichte*. Regarding the latter, Heidegger follows and explores the etymology of something being sent, while he elsewhere, in *Discourse on Thinking*, speaks of history as a mode of knowing. The history of Being is what sends, or destines, these and other overarching

ness of Being. This forgetfulness is particularly aggravated through a particular conception of, dealing with, and thinking informed by, technology. Heidegger had sufficient cause for his dismay about Western culture when intellectually grappling with Being in the 1930's and 40's. Remarkably, when seeking a full understanding of cultural ailments, metaphysics is the culprit, according to Heidegger. It is this grand narrative involving Being, technology and metaphysics, that we shall explore in the present chapter.

While Heidegger's early and far more systematically inclined philosophy was more overtly centred on instrumentality and tool use, it is strands of thought from his later years that continue to attract by far the most attention in matters of reflecting on technology. This attention is initially somewhat surprising, as his later discussion of technology is couched in parlance and has a style that has lacked sympathy from large parts of the philosophical community and proves challenging to approach, even to those who are otherwise sympathetic to Heidegger's way of doing philosophy. Part and parcel of Heidegger's thinking was a confrontation with ways of thinking inherent in the language[2] handed down through the ages. The consequent contortionist and, at times, downright odd German written by Heidegger is no less strange in its various translations. Heidegger would insist that German and Greek are ideally suited to doing philosophy, while English is disadvantaged on account of its fewer grammatical possibilities, and its less transparent and looser tie between everyday and philosophical vocabulary. Mainly in response to Heidegger's perceived preten-

---

epochs as well as what remains hidden and forgotten. "The age of the World Picture" has it that "metaphysics grounds an age" (1977a, p. 115), determining what actions and thoughts are appropriate within each epoch. For example, viewing everything around you as created by God should not be seen as an additional (metaphysical) fact next to others, but something that shapes your view of property, progress and social institutions, eroticism, money and much more. While Marx shared Hegel's teleological account of history, Heidegger turned them both on their head in rejecting their shared view of a potential being realised through history. To Heidegger, the one overarching feature of history is that of increased forgetfulness of Being.

2 The following passage from "Building, Dwelling, Thinking" points both to our cultural and personal, existential ailment, as well as Heidegger's philosophical method of appealing to often forgotten meanings of linguistic constructions. "Man acts as though *he* were the shaper and master of language, while in fact *language* remains the master of man. Perhaps it is before all else man's subversion of *this* relation of dominance that drives his nature into alienation... Among all the appeals that we human beings, on our part, can help to be voiced, language is the highest and everywhere the first" (1971a, p. 144).

tious abuse of language, there has always been a strong current of highly critical – and often downright dismissive – commentary on Heidegger's work.[3]

On this background, a presentation of Heidegger faces challenges on several counts. Most fundamentally, as we shall see, the very genre of philosophy is being contested. The relevance of carefully structured, clearly presented and often empirically informed arguments is being questioned when it comes to expressing what is fundamental and what, according to Heidegger, truly matters, Being. Famously, and in its extreme, from *Contributions to Philosophy – from Enowning:* "Making itself intelligible is suicide for philosophy" (1999, p. 307). Heidegger would emphasise that philosophy is always underway. It is a process, in Heidegger's case, focused on the task of becoming aware of, and making perspicuous, the historical event of what he calls unconcealment, which in turn is closely related to the concepts of truth and Being. Consequently, his later thought frequently engages with the history of philosophy, but artists, their works and their thought also shape Heidegger's thinking. When we present Heidegger as someone who takes a potentially clear, accessible and rationally assessable position on technology, we do it on the assumption that while it is impossible to make Heidegger speak English, it is not impossible for English – with its contemporary philosophical concepts and their historical baggage – to address the question of Being. The exposition will revolve around Heidegger's writings after his U-turn and will only occasionally be looking back at his early, far more stringent work that culminated in *Being and Time*. Later Heidegger's thought on technology was part of his construal of (German) history and its direction, and its dramatic pre-WWII turns and twists. As some remarks of Heidegger suggest, and some interpreters emphasise, Heidegger may have been a naive, political-cum-philosophical megalomaniac with a romantic penchant for simple,

---

[3] The *locus classicus* is arguably Carnap's famed analysis of Heidegger's *Was ist Metaphysik?*, 'Überwindung der Metaphysik durch logische Analyse der Sprache' (1932). Simon Blackburn's (2000) review of a translation of Heidegger's posthumously published *Beitrage zur Philosophie (Vom Ereignis)* continues the tradition, and perhaps most vehement is Edwards' *Heidegger's Confusions*, who prefaces his book on Heidegger with an expression of his intent to "stem this tide of unreason" (2004, p. 9). When claiming not to understand, Heidegger's commentators are usually bragging. Gilbert Ryle's less critical confession of incomprehension in his review of Heidegger's early work makes for a rare and welcome exception. In the present chapter we explore elements of Heidegger's views on the potential of art. In addition to Nietzsche's overarching influence, many of Heidegger's contemporaries would use aesthetic categories to understand war, politics and history. This common approach has left plenty of work behind for understanding Heidegger's complex relationship with the political powers and thinkers related to Nazi-Germany. Zimmerman (1990) and Blok (2017) emphasise Heidegger's inspiration from Ernst Jünger and his notion of a *Gestalt*.

pre-industrial life. For present purposes, these often disturbing political aspects will be left to one side.

5.2 Being

To avoid the misunderstandings that grammar and typography at times invite, and to help get his points across, Heidegger would write "Being" ("*Sein*") in various ways, to address the focal point of his later philosophy. He would use the old spelling, "*Seyn*", to convey something ancient and forgotten, and to suggest the ineffability of Being, we find typographic varieties of "*Sein*". I shall capitalise "Being" when addressing the central topic of Heidegger's later philosophy. This also serves to affect a contrast with *a being*, such as the computer in front of me, as well as the study of metaphysics (see below), a general study of what all beings share – being. To further approach this focal point of Heidegger's philosophy, we begin by exploring a concept that traditionally is closely related to Being: truth.

To offer an exposition of Heidegger's use of "truth", we set out with a position, currently known as sortalism: to be is to be an F.[4] A sortal tells us what any given thing is, as opposed to what it is like or what it is doing. Simply put, sortalism suggests that when we speak of existence or being – of what there is – we always speak of some *kind* of thing. Though it is also common parlance in much analytical philosophy to speak of objects, sortalism entails that we never encounter – or indeed, speak meaningfully of – objects as such, but only things that have criteria of identity and can clearly be counted through knowledge of what F stands for. "Object" may grammatically appear as a sortal (there is a book / there is an object) but is rightly considered to be a shorthand for proper sortals like "rock", "book", "electron" and other kinds of things. Thus, the question "how many objects are there in my room?" fails to raise a meaningful question, in so far as we have little idea what to count (electrons? tables? table legs? etc). On the contrary "how many books are there in the room?" is a fine question of existence. Having a firm grasp of the concept of a book allows one to begin individuating them, recognising some as the same as earlier and do a count. "Book" is a sortal, and the world consists of such things as books, electrons, Higgs particles (most probably), tables etc. If one counts correctly or gets the right reading from a particle accelerator, one may go on to make a true statement

---

[4] See Wright & Hale (2001, p. 387 ff). In Hansen (2012; 2010), I offer an exposition of the importance of sortals for both metaphysics, such as the question of Being, and ontology.

about reality. The truth of the statement is a matter of language – consisting of elements such as sortals, singular terms like names and definite descriptions, quantifiers and other predicates – being used to describe what the world is made of.

Heidegger, working in the phenomenological tradition, emphasises the way things appear. Like sortals are considered a requirement for being an object in large parts of what is referred to as the analytical tradition in philosophy, phenomenology emphasises that things always appear in one way or another, here expressed in his *1957 Introduction to metaphysics:* "Being means appearing. Appearing is not something subsequent that sometimes happens to being. Appearing is the very essence of being" (1974, p. 101). Being a hammer (its *"wesen"*) consists of a certain activity. When Heidegger expresses himself in a slogan-like fashion, he says that he offers verbs priority over nouns. To understand what one might think of as the essence or nature of a thing, we should home in on the activity and process implied in *"wesen"*. It is found in the English use of "-works", as in "water-works" and "fire-works", and is frequently translated as "presences". Though "water-works" functions as a noun, it is linguistically conspicuous that it names a dynamic process in time and space. Heidegger expands this usage as much as branches of analytical philosophy do sortals and objects: to Heidegger, the world, time, truth and more *works*, and as we shall explore, the linchpin for his understanding of technology is that it designates "… the way in which everything presences" (QCT, p. 17).

Drawing on analytical metaphysics, we have now offered the background for what Heidegger calls the *un*hidden nature of truth, which would take the shape of a correspondence theory of truth. Such a theory typically operates with a distinction between truth-bearers and truth-makers. Truth-bearers are frequently taken to be propositions, and these can be made true by truth-makers (typically, objects and facts play this role). Whatever relation bearers and makers have, the two notions are to a great extent mutually explanatory. To be a fact is to be understood in terms of true propositions and *vice versa*. On this understanding, the world comes ready-made into facts and objects, and increasingly, philosophers are happy to leave the job of cutting nature at its joints – to say what the facts are – to our best scientists. These philosophers are naturalists of various kinds and have a recent originator in the works of Quine.

We clearly need to know, and agree with others on, the meaning of the relevant *F* in order to count and communicate properly. This usually works unproblematically, but Quine and others taught us to think hard about what underlies the assumption, that we, in fact, know the meaning of the relevant sortal. He famously invited us to consider a rabbit-observing field linguist, in the process of acquiring a new language, purely based on the available empirical evidence.[5] The field linguist naturally assumes that the repeated utterance of "Gavagai!" of the native speakers in the presence of a rabbit, is meant to refer to the furry biological whole that *we* speak of by means of the concept "rabbit". However, other interpretational possibilities are available, such as "undetached rabbit-part", "temporal rabbit-stage", "fast" and the like. These more or less bizarre interpretative possibilities bring into focus the shared understanding that is always at work in the background, when we use words to pick out elements of the world. Truth as correspondence rests on agreement in interpretation, in various traditions called a horizon, a world view or a conceptual scheme: "The understanding of being already moves in a *horizon* that is everywhere *illuminated*…" (Heidegger, 1982, p. 284). It allows for a commonly intelligible, inhabitable world in which one can manoeuvre. Both the use-centred, non-linguistic approach to the world, as well as the narrower relation to the world by means of propositions, make up our relation to the world we inhabit.

While Quine's thesis of the inscrutability of reference did throw a spanner in the works of those attempting a certain style of observation-based theory of meaning, it might initially seem wholly uninteresting for someone interested in metaphysics – conceived as the question of the existence of not any particular kind of thing, but a general study of existence. Something is left out when we interpret everyday, as well as scientific, statements regarding what exists, but this would seem to have no bearing on the question of what there is. Heidegger, however, makes much of the background on the basis of which we successfully refer to things and things appear to us. So in the *Origin of the Work of Art:* "in order to understand and verify the correctness (truth) of a proposition one really should go back to something that is already evident, and that this presupposition is indeed unavoidable" (1971b, p. 50). While in agreement that there is a rightful purpose for a notion of truth as correspondence, or as he calls it "correctness", truth to Heidegger, such as that entailed by a correspondence theory, expresses neglect of everything that is *not* brought to attention. This is what leads him to revive a Greek version of the concept of truth, *a-lêtheia*, the unconcealed. It plays on the co-occurrent events of presenting what is the case and hiding something. According to this picture, truth as correspondence amounts to taking something out of hiding into the light, while something remains hidden. Bringing forth the unity of the biological whole at the same time neglects other aspects of what there is. Truth is a simultaneous concealing and unveiling.

---

[5] See Quine (1960).

We have made initial use of a prop from analytical philosophy of language and logic in our presentation of Heidegger's philosophy of Being.[6] Expectedly, significant caveats must be made. Most importantly, while the radical interpreter and we can readily switch between possible interpretations and thereby freely conceal and unveil various (aspects of) objects, this is not so with the different horizons. As suggested in Heidegger's *Discourse on Thinking* (1966), they are transcendental. They amount to the practically embedded language use in which our thinking has its being and shapes the presentation of any fact and action whatsoever – the scaffolding "from which something becomes understandable as something" (1996, p. 193). This language is not my doing, but something I take over from my environment and its history, with more or less reflection. In the parlance of Heidegger's earlier thinking, as a language user, I am thrown into circumstances not of my doing – it is my facticity. In his technology lecture, Heidegger discusses the inscrutability of reference and maintains that no "committee of researchers" (QCT, p. 23) ever decides on the horizon where revealing and concealing takes place and an intelligible world, a clearing, emerges. Thus, what respectively remains hidden – outside the clearing – and what is presented for our consideration and how it is presented, is not in the first instance of our doing or willing. In contrast, and to allow for *some kind* of volition in human cognition, when Heidegger uses the word "truth" in connection with uncovering and achieving a clearing where beings appear, he draws our attention to cognates of the German *Wahrheit: wahren* and *verwahren* suggest active preservation. In matters of philosophy, this means we must listen carefully to lost meanings. Again, in "Building, Dwelling, Thinking": "That we retain a concern for care in speaking is all to the good, but it is of no help to us as long as language still serves us even then only as a means of expression" (1971a, p. 144).

Beings can be discovered within our horizon, and there is much we *can* do to make discoveries of beings within our horizon: we can travel, take wine tasting lessons, build observatories, labs and particle accelerators in order to settle what things – mountains, bouquets, fundamental particles – there are. This is an exploration of beings. We may also seek to bring out formal features of beings as they appear within a horizon. The Aristotelian project of studying being *qua* being is one such study that seeks to bring out universal features of any being. This study might explore part-whole relationships of beings (mereology)

---

[6] We here follow the approach of Young (2001) in drawing on W.V.O. Quine in exposition of Heidegger's thought. In his presentation of the themes we are currently investigating, Wrathall (2011) utilises the work of Quine's student, Davidson. Wrathall finds that Heidegger and Davidson share the view that there is no clear boundary between knowing a language and "knowing our way around the world generally" (Davidson, 1986, p. 443).

or the different way things can be dependent on other things for their existence. Temporality is a universal feature that played a key role in Heidegger's early philosophy. If we call this study of the universal features of beings the study of being (lower case "b"), one can at least imagine a study of something that is concealed by a given horizon and name it "Being". This study would have a subject matter that lies beyond Aristotle's categories, his metaphysics and other formal studies of beings. Integral to such an undertaking is the notion that world-determining horizons are historical and changing *and* have features similar to transcendental or otherwise formal laws of thinking. What remains concealed by virtue of our horizon is Being. Thus, things (beings) would be different or would have different aspects where we, *per impossibile*, inhabit different horizons, and the key subject, Being, lies beyond the horizon: where beings and being originate – the originating region (*Herkunftsbereich*) or the generative ground.

To sum up our distinctions and our typological means of talking about them: we have studies of beings (small "b"); we have a study of being, which is the formal features that are shared by all beings, and finally, there is Being (capital "B"). In *Discourse on Thinking*, Heidegger speaks of that-which-regions as "the hidden nature of truth" (1966, p. 83), and for present purposes, we take "that-which-regions" to be another of Heidegger's ways of getting at the inexpressible, at Being. We *seem* to speak freely of Being, but we are not uttering any truths in the prevalent sense of correspondence with things. Truth in this latter sense is a disclosure, whereas Being falls beyond the area that is revealed by us – it is in the region of unintelligibility.

We may display our cognitive relation with Being by way of a picture that Wittgenstein used in connection with his own, quite differently motivated mysticism:

For the field of sight has not a form like this:

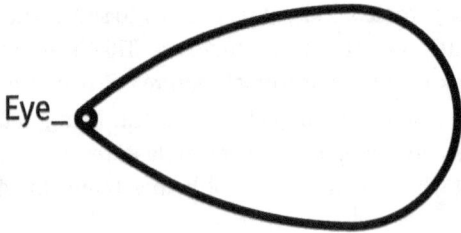

(Wittgenstein, 1922, §5.6331)

Within the field of sight – the linguistically and practically mastered clearing – there is the familiar and also yet to be discovered world of beings (such as bouquets and fundamental particles). In Wittgenstein's picture, they would appear in the visual field, but the field of sight includes neither the eye nor what is *not* in the field of sight. That is why the representation of the field of sight is misleading. A study of being, of universal features of beings, would be equal to a study of formal features of the human visual field, such as its two- or three-dimensionality, colour or temporality. These features are not seen but can be explored through systematic reflection on, and investigation of, features of seen beings. Next, as mentioned, our language *appears* to be in fine working order when attempting to go beyond the visual field and speak about Being as that which lies *beyond* universal features of beings – we have, after all, given it a name and placed it on a depiction of our visual field as lying beyond its horizon. Aware that Wittgenstein offers us a misguided representation, the depiction of the visual field can help us resist thinking about that which lies beyond, Being, as a matter of correspondence to beings.

By means of the typographical and linguistic props previously mentioned, Heidegger emphasises that the appearance *is* misleading. When seeking out Being, we are in the business of untruth, not of falsity, as this implies intelligibility, but of the unintelligible, yet something we need to convey somehow. This is the task of meditative thinking. Intelligibility and unconcealing, and *inter alia*, beings and the conditions for their intelligibility, being, is grounded in Being. Being in its fullness is what remains concealed in our unconcealing. Heidegger's *Discourse on Thinking*, his very probing discussion featuring "the scientist", "the scholar" and "the teacher", also raises the point of misleading topographical analogies in talking about what is beyond our horizon, here addressed as "that-which-regions". Should one imagine placing Being in our visual field, one could offer a depiction of a hendecachoron (a four-dimensional shape) making an appearance in our three spatial dimensions. Any representation *we* see in three dimensions is a simultaneous hiding and revealing, and never a revealing of the geometrical shape with its full number of sides.[7] Still, our relation with Being is disanalogous to our relation to a geometrical form like a hendecachoron: while we can calculate and make various projections to make aspects of four-dimensional objects appear in a three-dimensional space, the relationship between Being and beings cannot unproblematically be described in terms too firmly fixed *within* the horizon. For instance, Heidegger is reluctant to say that Being *causes* being (cf. QCT, p. 44). Rather, he chooses to speak vaguely of it

---

[7] Lanier has sparked interest in the shape in wider circles (Lanier & Sequin, 2007). The geometrical comparison is apt in that Heidegger, in "What are poets for", also speaks of reality as having a number of sides hidden by any transcendental horizon (cf. 1971d, p. 124).

as sent and granted in an event (*Ereignis*) of simultaneous showing and concealing. To Heidegger, the ground or source of this granting is what matters. It grounds our intelligible existence and is what is truly worth asking about; it is "real" (QCT, passim) and it is what is worth thinking about.

Unlike early Wittgenstein, whose official line was silence regarding that of which one cannot speak, Heidegger insisted that there are those who can get near Being through language: artists and poets. Hölderlin, in particular, attracted his attention and was the subject of several of Heidegger's lectures in the 1930s. Poets potentially achieve what we might call a horizon-transcending use of language – *Dichten* in contrast to *Denken*. Also, one can cognitively approach Being through horizon-bound, systematic philosophy – but less fully so: here one only approaches Being negatively, as a something wholly other I-know-not-what, but in a more thorough way that can assure that the poets are getting at something.[8]

A central theme in later Heidegger's concern with Being is that of widespread forgetfulness. We suffer as individuals and as a culture from the oblivion of Being, and what underlies this forgetfulness is, somewhat surprisingly, metaphysics, conceived in a certain, narrow way. Aristotelian, Cartesian or Kantian metaphysics as such make for valuable and legitimate studies. After all, metaphysicists do manage to capture and express the way Being is revealed in a given epoch. To Heidegger, the problem with the discipline is that in its reflection on universal features of beings – the features they have purely by virtue of existing – metaphysics has a strong tendency to neglect not just what the disclosure simultaneously hides, but also *that* it hides something. It wrongfully works under the impression that the universal features of beings, being, is all there is to *any* question of being. It remains with truth understood as an unveiling, and is forgetful that the unveiling always reveals a subset of the full attributes of Being, and thus, it forgets that there *is* that which remains hidden: "To metaphysics, the essence of truth always appears only in the already derivative form of cognitive knowledge and the truth of propositions that formulate such knowl-

---

[8] Thus, to Heidegger, the height of philosophy – but not of thinking – might well have been Wittgenstein's *Tractatus:* it did, after all, argue for the existence of something one cannot speak about, and the overall structure of the work, is to my mind, best understood as having the shape of answering the question: "What must be the case for there to be true or false representations of the world?" While Wittgenstein remains known for his call for silence in matters one cannot speak off, Wittgenstein notoriously *did* go on to recite Indian poetry to scientifically minded members of the Vienna Circle, who in their characteristic "brain-racking" manner wished to discuss the *Tractatus*. Wittgenstein and the members of the Vienna Circle seemed to have very different views of the significance of that of which one cannot speak.

edge" (Heidegger, 1998a, p. 280) and "revealing as such" – that is, metaphysics "drives out every other possibility of revealing" (QCT, p. 27). This, in turn, leaves us blind to the mystery of Being, to reality in its fullness. It hinders an appreciation that being is granted by Being and this, in turn, is described by Heidegger as the essence of nihilism. Rather than seeing depth and origin, we see only our own horizon and what lies within and remain increasingly unaware that it is a horizon. The forgetfulness and universalising features of such metaphysics is a manner of thinking and relating to the world that also characterises our relationship with technology.

5.3 Metaphysics and technology

To jog our collective, linguistic memory, Heidegger's technology lecture draws attention to possible meanings of key concepts and he initially introduces a distinction between modern and ancient technology to illustrate these concepts. The examples and descriptions of technologies initially seem naïve and hackneyed: Heidegger contrasts use of the hydroelectric plant with the old windmill and the peasant farmer with the "mechanized food industry" (QCT, p. 15). But rather than focus on the actual, concrete technologies, Heidegger wants us to consider the way they are approached and shape our thinking. To tease this out, he traces a largely forgotten meaning of "causality" and its cognates and contrasts it with the current one. He initially notices the obvious fact that we frequently use technology to achieve some effect or other. We make something happen and we produce (*her-stellen*[9]) something. To be an effect entails the existence of a cause, and it is this concept that serves as the linchpin for Heidegger's analysis of our current horizon, which he calls *Gestell*. There is no entirely happy translation. "Enframing" is widely used, and "scaffolding" is closest to the German word. However, a mode of revealing is not anyone's doing. Though far removed from "frame", "scaffolding" and cognates, "mould" or "cast", suggested by translator and Heidegger commentator Eldred (2009), is preferable, as it suggests something already given and as giving shape to matter, though shaped by humans. We shall leave the German expression untranslated. Heidegger introduces the concept by drawing an analogy with a mountain range. The German prefix "ge-" is used to express the linking togeth-

---

9 With the hyphenation of the German word for production, Heidegger achieves a play between two meanings that are intertwined in Heidegger's thinking: To produce ("bring forth") involves both making and representing.

er of particular items, such as the mountain range – *Ge-birg*. The *Gestell* thus becomes the name for the way Being currently reveals itself. A now dominating aggregate of things produced (*her-stellt*) in a certain way and most importantly, with a certain mentality.

Heidegger's "conceptual revival" takes its beginning by reminding us of the Aristotelian four-fold analysis of "cause", according to which an end or a purpose is a cause – *causa finalis*. This is one of the four kinds of causes, the others being *causa materialis*, *causa formalis* and a kind of causality, *causa efficiens*, that entirely dominates our current horizon. The Latin etymology of "cause" points to the verb "to fall" and "means that which brings it about that something turns out as a result in such and such a way" (QCT, p. 7). To Heidegger, the Greek "*aition*" suggests "that to which something is indebted" (QCT, p. 7), rather than "cause". Relying on this, Heidegger describes the sacrificial chalice as owing its existence to the silver (matter) as well as the silver having a certain shape (form). It owes its existence to the silversmith and finally, it owes its existence as a sacrificial vessel to its purpose in a religious ritual. Thus, the silversmith as such cannot bring about the existence of the silver chalice: "... what is decisive about *technē* does not lie at all in making and manipulating or in the using of means, but rather in the aforementioned revealing. It is as revealing, and not as manufacturing, that *technē* is a bringing-forth" (QCT, p. 13). Heidegger finds that the best linguistic rendering of what the four causes combined achieve, is to *occasion* the silver chalice, and the occasion is the bringing forth [her-vor-bringen] from the non-present to the present. That is, the silversmith cannot do it of his own accord, but "considers carefully and gathers together" (QCT, p. 8) the elements and brings forth something that is already there in the material, the design, its social texture and surrounding institutions.[10]

To the Greeks, this bringing forth, or *poēisis*, was a more wide-ranging kind of occasion than that in which the silversmith takes part. There is *poēisis* in nature (*phusis*) as well as in the aided bringing forth, *techné*, of handicraft, poetry and artistry. The Greek word for "to bring forth or produce" is *tiktō* and *techné* belongs to the verb's root, *tec*. The natural *poēisis* happens of its own accord as when an acorn becomes an oak, while the *poēisis* in *techné* is also owed to what we today call the artist, craftsman, or thinker. The occasion of bringing

---

[10] Hölderlin, in particular, emphasised that artistic creativity was a matter of drawing out what was already there in the material, and Heidegger reminds us that the cabinetmaker responds "to such things as the shapes slumbering within the wood" (1968, p.53f) in a way that no industrial worker achieves. Heidegger here relies on his understanding of "logos", usually translated "reason", as being derived from "legein" – to harvest or gather. As we shall see below, gathering is also something things achieve.

5.3 Metaphysics and technology

forth is a revealing, and we should now be able to see how the issues of truth and Being introduced in the previous section play a role in Heidegger's assessment of technology. What makes technology possible, what lies at the bottom of it, is revealing that which does not bring itself forth, be it chalices, poems, oratories or paintings.[11] What we today tend to consider an aspect of fine arts - helping bring a dance, a painting or a sculpture into being – was considered part of a wider range of activities by the Greeks. They conceived of both natural and artificial activities as *poēisis*.

Heidegger thought this background would offer Greek conceptions of technology a normative structure foreign to ours. According to Heidegger, the Greek thinking would run along these lines: A tree appears as the result of an acorn and its inherent powers. Similarly, the world as a whole owes its existence to an art "world acorn"[12], with the acorn being concealed, mysterious and overwhelming (cf. 1971b, p. 68). To the Greeks, looking at nature as the result of a "world acorn" coming into presence would imbue the former with a sacred hue. Artificial *poēisis*, *technē*, becomes loaded with a certain respect and awe for this self-expression of the divine in nature *and* the activity of *technē* is itself viewed as something akin to natural bringing forth. Conservation, care and letting be, become the order of the day. *Technē* can in its nature not consign itself entirely to letting be, and as a consequence, technological activity is seen as an aide to what was about to arrive in any case. Characteristically, in *What is Called thinking*, Heidegger marshals linguistic evidence, here in connection with "chre", from which he unearths an understanding of "use": "Proper use does not debase what is being used – on the contrary, use is determined and defined by leaving the used thing in its essential nature. But leaving it that way does not mean carelessness, much less neglect. On the contrary: only proper use brings the thing to its essential nature and keeps it there. So understood, use itself is the summons which demands that a thing be admitted to its own essence and nature, and that the use keep to it" (1968, p. 187).

Heidegger thinks these moods associated with a preeminent sense of use – awe, aiding, letting be – makes for an important contrast with the revealing carried out in *Gestell* and modern technology. Here, we foremost see a challenge, in

---

11 As a natural consequence of the view that *technē* is a revealing, Heidegger points to the fact that the physical sciences are deeply technological, and he suggests an inversion of the relation between technology and science, the latter being an application of the former. This theme has been central in some of Don Ihde's writings, and will be explored in the chapters on Dewey and in particular, Latour.
12 This is not Heidegger's expression, but one offered by Young (2001) in his exposition of Heidegger.

the shape of demands that a constantly available resource – a "standing-reserve" – be present. The contrast is perhaps clearest in Heidegger's example of the Rhine River as an object of poetry in one of Hölderlin's works and as an object of stored power when one places a hydroelectric plant in the river or when the tourist industry considers it an important driver in the development of the regional experience economy. *Dasein* is at the centre of this way of revealing, but it can become, as Heidegger emphasises, itself brought forth as a standing-reserve – a human resource. Whether he knows it or not, the old-fashioned lumberjack is "made subordinate to the orderability of cellulose, which for its part is challenged forth by the need for paper, which is then delivered to newspapers and illustrated magazines. The latter, in their turn, set public opinion to swallowing what is printed, so that a set configuration of opinion becomes available on demand" (QCT, p. 18). To Heidegger, what stands at the centre of current revealing, of world disclosure, what currently holds sway, is that to be is to be a resource – *Bestand*. Not only energy stored in the shape of coal is considered as a resource, but everything – cars, marriages, university degrees, songs, books – appears ready-to-hand, fit for productive activity.

This is not a way of revealing that is distinctive of modern technological practice and thinking. Most cultures have seen trees as firewood or construction materials, the countryside as construction sites and have been producers in all sorts of ways. To wit, use of tools is exactly what is at the centre of the initial analysis of everyday existence found in *Being and Time*. Thus, to get at the distinctly modern, technological epoch-defining world disclosure, the *Gestell*, we need a further distinguishing feature. The phrasing is reminiscent of one of the formulations of Kant's categorical imperative. The modern unconcealing has things appear only as a resource, and not also as a thing in its own right: "…what is unconcealed no longer concerns man even as object, but does so, rather, exclusively as a resource" (QCT, p. 26 f), or at greater length in *What are Poets for?:* "Only in modern times does [the hidden nature of technology] begin to unfold as a destiny of the truth of all beings as a whole; until now, its scattered appearances and attempts had remained incorporated within the embracing structure of the realm of culture and civilization" (1971d, p. 109).

It is in this way that metaphysics lies at the bottom of the modern malaise. As explored above, metaphysics has the tendency to neglect that producing *is* a revealing that leaves Being concealed. Today's fine artists might work in a modern car factory to support their part expressive, part responsive artistic activities, their *poēisis*. An artist giving up their aspiration and spending their days stamping out metal bits for cogs in some wheel, seeing nothing but cog-shaped metal in any lump of metal, is, writ large, the *Gestell*.

5.4 On being a thing and building for dwelling

Moral philosophers have a fairly firm grasp of what it means to respect rational agents as an end in their own right, and not purely as a means. What does the equivalent mean when it concerns things? What does it mean that everything shows up "completely unautonomous" and with "objectlessness" (QCT, pp. 17, 19) and not also a thing in its own right? To have everything show up not as a "gigantic gasoline station" (1966, p. 50), not purely in the light of the needs and designs of *Dasein*, but as things in their own right? "Thing" or "object" here emerges as an art normative concept in metaphysics. When beings are utterly heteronomous, they are not even things, but pure resources. To understand this, we need to continue our exploration of Heidegger's view of metaphysics, here in the shape of his concept of a thing from his "The Thing". It is not just of Being that we are forgetful: "The thingness of the thing remains concealed, forgotten" (1971c, p. 168), and we remain unable to be confronted by the thing even in our thinking.

Many are convinced by externalism about the semantic content of natural kind terms. One aspect of this idea is that we, in suitable circumstances, find it acceptable to defer to experts when it comes to knowing the true meaning of "mountain", "gold", "tiger" or the like. We use the words meaningfully and knowingly to refer to things, but in doing so, we rely on their linguistic labour, as it were. Now, Heidegger asks of us to accept a similar division of linguistic labour, with artists – mainly poets on account of their language use – assuming the role of being the experts on a range of metaphysical terms, such as "thing" and "world". The overarching motivation is that the *Gestell* also wreaks havoc on the essence of human beings. Being under the sway of the *Gestell*, we need artists to help us regain sight of the things around us, and to become what we truly are: beings that exist not for the sake of the gross domestic product, or more generally, not to challenge forth beings, but to "enter into the highest dignity of his essence. The dignity lies in keeping watch over the unconcealment..." (QCT, p. 32). As Heidegger phrases it, we are to become shepherds of Being, even as times are destitute and man is consumed by producing a standing-reserve of beings and becoming such beings themselves. In short, poets help us remember what truly matters: "The world's destiny is heralded in poetry" (1998b, p. 258), and we need thinking that listens to poetic language.

Leaving aside difficulties of placing "untouched nature" in Heidegger's conceptual landscape, it seems clear that some objects have their criteria of identity – they are the sorts of things they are – independently of human practices, while some rely on *Dasein* to be what they are, to have their "what-ness". Were astronauts to encounter an accurately chair-shaped mass on Mars (but no Martians), they would be inclined to say that they had encountered something that *looked like* a chair, rather than saying that they had in fact encountered a chair. This is linguistic evidence of the quite reasonable position that essential to being a chair is to be able to feature as a part of human (or the like) practices. Clearly, some objects will not in that way depend on Dasein.[13] They are what they are independently of our needs and doings. However, when *das Gestell* holds sway, "What is unconcealed no longer concerns man even as object" (QCT, p. 26 f). For an object to concern man as an object, means for it to have elements of autonomy, or own-ness. Thus, the Rhine River can show up as energy not yet reigned in, or it can appear as an object of contemplation, in the background of other pursuits and with its natural surroundings and elements – trees, water composition and colour, and banks. In the way we shall expound below, *Gestell* takes this latter own-ness away from things.

The revealing characterised as *Gestell* is the particularly modern trait that Heidegger singles out. To reiterate, everything presents itself the way a petrol station does – ready for transformation and consumption – and we do not encounter things in themselves. Rather, they are warped around us – ever ready-to-hand – according to our "in-order-to" way of being and revealing. What do we miss and how do we escape our predicament? The first question will be difficult to convey to anyone in a culture where *the Gestell* holds sway, and the second question might suggest a solution that only involves more of the same – a technological fix, as it were. To remain with the geometrical analogy, it would be like trying to draw a picture to a two-dimensional man, conveying to him basic features of his world and a world beyond his life on paper. Heidegger offers a linguistic excavation, unearthing traces of a different revealing.

Addressing the first question, we return to the concept of *poēisis*. When *Gestell* holds sway "...it drives out every other possibility of revealing. Above all, [*Gestell*] conceals that revealing which, in the sense of *poēisis*, lets what presences come forth into appearance" (QCT, p. 27). Let us recall that Heidegger's sense of *poēisis* is more inclusive than the one exclusively concerned with what we today call fine arts, and he extends the richer sense of coming into being that we normally create with the creation of, say, a statue to quite ordinary things:

---

[13] I shall here refrain from the intricate discussion of *which* things have this status. The geographical objects that interest Heidegger, such as mountains and rivers, are also in other strands of philosophy taken as paradigmatic examples of things that have their essence independently of human practices (cf. Searle, 1995). However, formal ontologists argue persuasively that mountains are anything but straightforward cases of independently existing objects. See *e.g.* Smith & Mark (2003), which in more ways is echoed by Latour's (2013) discussion of the ontological status of a mountain.

"The jug and the bench, the footbridge and the plow... tree and pond, too, brook and hill are things each in their own way" (1971c, p. 180). To Heidegger, by way of his famed grammatical inventions, this becomes a matter of the thing thinging when it comes forth into appearance. What, then, does the thing do as it autonomously things away? What is it that the *Gestell* keeps us from seeing and acting on appropriately? To Heidegger, answering this question serves as the entry point for an understanding of man. It is of man's essence that he dwells poetically in the fourfold. When, in turn, giving an explication of the fourfold, Heidegger's concept of a thing is central. This is the background for Heidegger's description of the significance of building houses, addressed to engineers and architects in bombed-out Darmstadt, in "Building, Dwelling, Thinking":

> The making of such things is building. Its nature consists in this, that it corresponds to the character of these things... The edifices guard the fourfold. They are things that in their own way preserve the fourfold. To preserve the fourfold, to save the earth, to receive the sky, to await the divinities, to escort mortals – this fourfold preserving is the simple nature, the presenting, of dwelling. (1971a, p. 156)

Dwelling is more than having a shelter. Mortals are in the fourfold by virtue of their dwelling, the basic character of which is to safeguard the unfolding of the fourfold: "... dwelling itself is always a staying with things. Dwelling, as preserving, keeps the fourfold in that with which mortals stay: in things... But things themselves secure the fourfold *only when* they themselves *as* things are let be in their presencing" (1971a, p. 149). The meaning of "thing" as a gathering of individuals is preserved in Nordic languages, and Heidegger relies on this sense of coming together when he says that a thing gathers the fourfold.[14]

In *The Thing*, Heidegger carefully considers the jug. When not addressed as the philosophical tradition (according to Heidegger) has done, "as an unknown X to which perceptible properties are attached" (1971a, p. 151), it becomes the focal point of a range of ways that its environment interconnects. It has a

---

14 As Roger White made me aware, an early, possibly the first, written, unequivocal use of "thing", simply to denote an inanimate object, was the use of the word in Shakespeare's *Coriolanus*, as in the description of Coriolanus capturing Corioli in Act 2, scene 2, reducing Macbeth from a man of blood to a thing of blood:
> from face to foot
> He was a thing of blood, whose every motion
> Was timed with dying cries; Alone he ent'red
> The mortal gate of th' city, which he painted
> With shunless destiny; aidless came off,
> And with a sudden re-enforcement struck
> Corioli like a planet. (Shakespeare, 2009, p. 45 f.)

given immediate purpose, but more importantly to Heidegger, being a thing consists of gathering the presence of the fourfold unity of earth, sky, mortals and divinities: "The potter makes the earthen jug out of earth that he has specially chosen and prepared for it. The jug consists of that earth" (1971c, p. 165). When pouring out the drink, the earth is gathered in that it comes from the springs and streams of the Earth. The sky is gathered in so far as the warmth of the Sun is needed for the creation of the drink. Mortals are gathered to celebrate, mourn, be refreshed and share the joy of drinking[15], and it is in the honour of the gods that a drink is being had. Thus, the jug mingles and assembles the fourfold.

The notion of the fourfold is introduced in Heidegger's first post-WW2 lecture called "Insight into that which is". That man dwells among things in an environment of earth, sky, other humans and gods is, with the possible exception of the latter, not of itself novel or particularly informative. What sets Heidegger's account apart, in addition to this dwelling being essential to man, is the poetic language being used in his description of this. Heidegger attempts:

> Earth is the building bearer, nourishing with its fruits, tending water and rock, plant and animal... The sky is the sun's path, the course of the moon, the glitter of the stars, the year's seasons, the light and dusk of day, the gloom and glow of night, the clemency and inclemency of the weather, the drifting clouds and blue depth of the ether.... The divinities are the beckoning messengers of the godhead. Out of the hidden sway of the divinities the god emerges as what he is, which removes him from any comparison with beings that are present... The mortals are human beings. They are called mortals because they can die. To die means to be capable of death as death. Only man dies. The animal perishes. It has death neither ahead of itself nor behind it. ... We now call mortals mortals – not because their earthly life comes to an end, but because they are capable of death as death. Mortals are who they are, as mortals, present in the shelter of Being. They are the presencing relation to Being as Being. Metaphysics, by contrast, thinks of man as animal, as a living being... This simple oneness of the four we call the fourfold. Mortals are in the fourfold by dwelling. But the basic character of dwelling is to spare, to preserve. Mortals dwell in the way they preserve the fourfold in its essential being, its presencing. Accordingly, the preserving that dwells is fourfold. (1971a, p. 147f)

Doing damage to the essence of a thing is not primarily a matter of causing havoc around thinly populated fjords, turning vast areas of untouched forest into farmland or building vast dams in order to harness energy from the natural environment. To Heidegger, saving the world would not be a matter of launching a daring mission on RIBs to foster an awareness of our reliance on fossil fuels and its

---

15 And thus, also remembering their mortality. In "What are Poets for?", Heidegger uses the word "technique" in connection with what he calls death evasion.

5.4 On being a thing and building for dwelling — 117

inherent risks or engaging in projects of rewilding. Rather, it is a matter of not being able to see the havoc potentially caused by oil rigs and hydropower dams for what it is, namely stopping someone or something from becoming what it is.[16]

Heidegger speaks of the use of technology suggested by dwelling both as something passive and active: "Building in the sense of preserving and nurturing is not making anything. Shipbuilding and temple-building, on the other hand, do, in a certain way, make their own works. Here building, in contrast with cultivating, is a constructing. Both modes of building – building as cultivating... and as the raising up of edifices... – are comprised within genuine building, that is, dwelling" (1971a, p. 145). Taking bringing forth and caring for the fourfold – active and passive relations respectively – as the guiding light for the production of buildings, Heidegger offers some immediate pointers for, in the first instance, architecture, but also for the uptake of technology more generally. Thus, one way to systematise Heidegger's understanding of a poetic way of being with technology is along a matrix offered by Young (2001, p. 106):

	Earth	Sky	Gods	Mortals
Passive caring for (architecture example)	2	3		1
Active caring for (architecture example)				
Passive caring for (other examples)				
Active caring for (other examples)		2		

We shall not attempt a completion of the matrix at present but shall draw attention to a few examples.[17]

1) A central theme in Heidegger's thinking is one's relationship with death, and one possibility of caring is having architectural practices that assist people in owning their own death. So, one can passively care for mortals by not hiding death away from other elements of the design of a city, as it is widespread practice in many societies, but actively building knowledge and awareness into the plan of a house. *Building, Dwelling, Thinking* concludes with the description of a Black Forest farmhouse. Such houses would frequently feature a *Totenbrett*

---

16 In addition to those already noted, an influence on Heidegger was Rilke's notion of *Ding-werdung*, thing-becoming, coined in response to Cézanne's paintings of everyday things. Letting the thing be was a *Leitmotiv* in both Rilke's and Cézanne's account of the task of the artist.
17 Sharr (2007) traces the influence of Heidegger on a range of architects and seeks to explicate the relevance of Heidegger for practicing architecture.

or a *Totenbaum*, a log placed outside the house, serving as a coffin rest for those of the household who had died. As Heidegger will say, this should not be understood as a call for the mass production of Black Forest farmhouses, but rather, a call to carefully consider how our construction should flow from a dwelling.

2) In German and other languages, the equivalent of "soil" (*Erde*) is used to describe both soil and the planet Earth. To Heidegger, it is the literal as well as metaphorical ground of man's existence. Mortals can passively care for the earth by simply letting its features be. One can place a construction so it does not significantly alter the features of a landscape, but seeks to let it be. This could simply be a matter of not placing a house on a ridge, but on a slope, with a roof that "works with the environment" in order to withstand its elements, such as heavy snowfall or torrential rain. Active caring for the Earth could be done by actively restoring streams to what their original course was, allowing for far greater biodiversity and helping, as it were, the stream become what it was meant to be (and in this case, what it once was).

3) Like "earth", "sky" (*Himmel*) has both celestial and planetary connotations as well as those to do with the weather and changing seasons. Caring for the sky *could* be reflected in the way both natural light and artificial light feature in our built environment and allow for the celestial bodies to frame our dwelling, rather than carefully designed imitations of sunrays, placed at our demand, such as can be seen in domestic click-and-grow smart gardens. Heidegger insisted that the seasons and its challenges and joys should be equally accepted with grace.

Caring for the gods raises a host of topics that we shall not explore at present. The kind of construction and tool use that flows from the concept of dwelling cannot be derived in any singular, formal fashion. While it should be clear that Heidegger has a lot in common with various brands of ecological thinking, his thinking rather makes for a possible metaphysical underpinning of such programmes and agendas. A responsive attunement and mood is the basis upon which action might be taken, or indeed, further awaiting, listening and letting be is done. To *save* the Earth, *receive* the sky, and *await* the divinities is a radically different kind of comportment than what characterises the *Gestell*.

5.5 What to do? How to think?

As we also saw in the Marxist tradition, humans seem faced with a technological complex and mental landscape leaving them impoverished and disempowered. In this case, the *malaise* has its origin in the way a world is revealed to, and by, us, rather than a range of devices with certain features. As designing and building things with a purpose is one of the human activities *par excellence*, the *Gestell* is not easily overcome, and in "The Thing", Heidegger reiterates aspects of his mysticism: "... the inexplicable and unfathomable character of the world's worlding lies in this, that causes and grounds remain unsuitable for the world's worlding. As soon as human cognition here calls for an explanation, it fails to transcend the world's nature, and falls short of it. The human will to explain just does not reach to the simpleness of the simple onefold of worlding. The united four are already strangled in their essential nature when we think of them only as separate realities" (1971c, p. 177 f). While Marx, Winner and Marcuse had a range of suggestive answers and explanations in relation to the question that headlines this section, it would seem that Heidegger leaves us in a place where – if he is right – neither doing or, indeed, much of our mental activity is of any avail where the *Gestell* reigns. Our thinking is not the powerhouse that Descartes and the stoics envisaged: "There is nothing entirely in our power except our thoughts" (Descartes, 2006, p. 23). Indeed, Heidegger will speak of fate (cf. QCT, p. 28) when it comes to the *Gestell*. It reigns and holds sway, and as is well known, at one point he famously proclaimed that "only a god save us".

However, the fate of the *Gestell* is "never a fate that compels" (QCT, p. 25). Heidegger insists it is not a fate in the sense of something inevitable, and he leaves us with a pointer beyond both Luddism, forms of *status quo* and the hopeful listening to poets. Seeing things *qua* their potential for being useful for humans and their designs is by no means unique to the *Gestell*. The threat of technology taking away the own-ness of things is found wherever technology is, and it is very much a central feature of man's everyday existence. In "The Turning", Heidegger suggests that a possible reform, a change from *Gestell*, "in no way means that technology, whose essence lies in [Gestell], will be done away with." Rather than try to master technology, Heidegger has it that "modern man must first and above all find his way back into the full breadth of the space proper to his essence" (1977b, pp. 38, 39). To assist with this finding one's way, Heidegger points out that what characterises the *Gestell* is that, unlike under other horizons, there is no counter to the technological way of seeing the world – to the "unconditional self-assertion" (1971d, p. 109) where man only "encounters himself" (QCT, p. 27). It is not technological artefacts and systems themselves that are problematic: "There is no demonry in technology" (QCT, p. 28), and it was only for a brief and overtly political period that Heidegger called for a widescale abolition of advanced, industrialised forms of life in favour of a rural, less urbanised and geographically contentious Germany.

So, again, what is the problem with technology under the *Gestell*, and what is the way out? To answer, we quote again parts of the passage from *What are*

Poets for?: "[U]ntil now, its [the hidden nature of technology] scattered appearances and attempts had remained incorporated within the embracing structure of the realm of culture and civilisation". Other horizons had something ours lack, which allowed them to counterbalance, or incorporate, the constant threat of technology becoming "totalitarian" – of shutting out other modes of revealing. They enjoyed occasions where they could be transported out of the realm of everyday existence. Under this *aegis*, Heidegger offers various answers to the question. The festival, the artwork, the holiday and the poem are all ways out of the everyday existence and the metaphysical, totalitarian aspects of the *Gestell*. During the festival, we exactly stop working and are able to see our surroundings in a different way. Of course, the holiday or the festival itself must be authentic, and not appropriated purely for being refreshed for work. A holiday should not be mere cessation of work. Rather, it should be an entrance into wonder – a release from the ordinary in order that we may marvel *that* there is a world (cf. Zimmerman, 1990, p. 153). Indeed, though Heidegger saw Greek philosophy as having set Western culture on a wrong track, it also espoused a conception of philosophy as starting in wonder *that* things are. At the festival in the temple, amphitheatre, or stadium, the Greeks had an opportunity to come to their senses, be transported away, ecstatic, set apart from their everyday, purposeful caring. We should listen – ever so slowly and carefully – to the poet, who reaches further than the *Gestell* allows. For instance, "Rilke has in his own way poetically experienced and endured the unconcealedness of beings which was shaped by that completion [of Western metaphysics]" (1971d, p. 95), and generally concerning the poet, Heidegger suggests:

> Not only does the holy, as the track to the godhead… remain concealed; even the track to the holy… seems to be effaced. That is, unless there are still some mortals capable of seeing the threat of the unhealable, the unholy, *as* such. They would have to discern the danger that is assailing man. The danger consists in the threat that assaults man's nature in his relation to Being itself, and not in accidental perils. This danger is *the* danger. It conceals itself in the abyss that underlies all beings. To see this danger and point it out, there must be mortals who reach sooner into the abyss. (1971d, p. 115)

Poets are more directly in the draft of Being and able to express this situation and instil a sense of reverence and awe for the *poēisis* of things. The play, the artwork, metaphysics based on wonder and ultimately, the God, in different ways allow for a time-out from everyday, purpose-driven and -shaped existence, allowing the human to enter a mood – and inter alia, a world – where the radiance of ordinary things as they are given to us shine forth. In short, we need a holy day. Poets such as Hölderlin allow us to survey what later Heidegger took to be pervasive moods, the awareness of which is crucial in becoming receptive to something other than the *Gestell*.

This is for us an opportunity to become metaphysicists in a non-pejorative sense: not trying to calculate and accurately represent formal aspects of things, but wondering *that* there are things, and renouncing our active willing concerning them. Releasement or equanimity (*Gelassenheit*) towards the *poēisis* of things, rather than willing and challenging. A certain steadfast, waiting, meditative thinking, a hoping and encouraging, rather than brain-racking over things. Above, we emphasised that no mental activity on our part will be of avail, as long as this is marked by ordering things according to a status as a standing-reserve in the all-encompassing *Gestell*. Rather, receptivity, listening, pondering and waiting is what we can do, and indeed, these aspects of thinking are what Heidegger points to as a way out of the *Gestell*.

6 Albert Borgmann local technologies

> Technological devices are extremely shallow... We must recover man as a being of absolute depth and learn to realize that if we increasingly surround him with shallow things, he will become shallow also. The depth of the world and the depth of man depend on one another. Perhaps an order will arise from the depth of things.
> (Borgmann, 1973, p. 35)

6.1 Technology: force and character

The intimate connection between the things with which we surround ourselves and the human character is a constant in Borgmann's thinking. In his 2006 *Real American Ethics*, he expresses it in terms of what he calls the Churchill principle. In a 1943 address on rebuilding the House of Commons, Churchill reminded Members of Parliament: "We shape our buildings, and afterwards our buildings shape us" (2006a, p. 5). Buildings, the way they sustain dwelling and the artefacts that surround this dwelling are central to Borgmann's work. With his notion of dwelling in the fourfold, and of a thing that gathers its environment, Heidegger had offered a framework for an analysis of things that contrasted with one that revolved around the notion of the *Gestell*. Practical insight and recommendations are rare with Heidegger. Remarks about pens, planes, farms, bridges and mugs are scattered in his writings and remain suggestive and placed in the scheme of thinking about the history of Being. It is in the writings of fellow countryman Borgmann that we witness a sustained attempt to make central aspects of Heidegger's thinking more workable. In place of the *Gestell*, Borgmann speaks of a pattern of technology use – the device paradigm – that shapes our mode of engagement with the surrounding world. To make this pattern visible, and to give it persuasive force, Borgmann entertains what he calls deictic discourse that points to what contrasts with devices: focal things. Borgmann does give poetry a role in this use of language but predominantly relies on accounts of what he calls practical people, past and present.

One of Heidegger's avenues for thinking critically about technology relied on the concept of culture. Here, he saw a possible counterweight to the *Gestell*, and it is primarily this line of thought that Albert Borgmann has developed. Cultural phenomena such as celebrations (religious and those surrounding sports), holidays, the meal and the potentially orienting qualities of such things and practices, play a pivotal role in Borgmann's analysis of technologies. Borgmann suggests their role is that of a cultural counterforce to the more pervasive pattern of use of devices, to be explored below. While inspired by Heidegger, Borgmann does not claim to be elaborating the Heideggerian philosophy of Being. The nature of the relation between Heidegger and Borgmann, and their different styles of philosophy come out perhaps most clearly by noting the different ways in which the hearth features in their thinking. To later Heidegger, the receptive, listening attitude is seen clearly in Antigone. In staying by the hearth, she stays with the homely, while remembering and sheltering. In sum, she exhibits the way of the hearth[1]. In Borgmann's writings, the hearth is the oft-cited example of a focal thing and as such, subject to a more practically oriented analysis, in terms of its requirements and its structuring effects on the daily lives of its users, particularly when compared with more recent technologies like central heating – an example of a device. While Heidegger in his more enigmatic moments maintained that only a god could save a culture in the sway of the *Gestell*, Borgmann discusses possibilities of, and obstacles to, a reform of the device paradigm and the kind of politics it would require.

That is not to say that religion does not concern Borgmann. Particularly in *Power Failure* (2003) he puts to use concepts and ideas developed in his 1984 *Technology and the Character of Contemporary Life* in order to argue that technology has a debilitating effect on religion, and that religions, in turn, contain practices and things that can serve to structure and make meaningful everyday lives: bread and wine, celebrations, the cross and the oriented and orienting architecture of churches. In later writings yet, Borgmann sounds decidedly like Heidegger as he reflects on the significance of the wilderness. The wilderness is a place where one can encounter the sacred and "…it engages us in the original human practices of walking, building, and dwelling" (2015b, p. 265). These ideas lie in clear extension of the concern that Heidegger expressed towards the end of his life: the possibility of dwelling in a global and increasingly uniform world civilisation, made uniform by the spread of technologies.

In a 2006 paper, Borgmann lists large scale economic, environmental and political challenges and concerns at a level of generality that makes them familiar to most of us. Challenges, such as environmental degradation or economic injustice, are at times met with a technical solution. New devices are engineered, or existing ones redesigned – a type of response at times derided as a technological fix or "solutionism."[2] Another technologically informed response calls for the development of a kind of ethics that is appropriate to such large-scale prob-

---

[1] See Zimmerman (1990) and Wright (1993) for an exploration of Heidegger's interpretation of *Antigone*.
[2] The expressions are those of technological optimist and long-time director of Oak Ridge National Laboratory, Alvin M. Weinberg's and pessimist Morozov's (2014), respectively. See Johnston (2018) for an overview of the development of the idea of a technological fix.

lems. In this vein, Shannon Vallor has pointed to similar global issues and suggests that they also present a challenge for "human flourishing in our present moral condition" (2016, p. 117). According to her, crucial to meeting these challenges is "our ability to encourage the wider, even global, cultivation of the *technomoral virtues*" (2016, p. 117, her emphasis). Vallor joins a tradition of relying on virtue theory in reflection on the global challenges and opportunities related to technology. Borgmann was an early proponent of drawing on virtue ethics in analysing and responding to the phenomenon of technology.[3] In contrast with Vallor, Borgmann's overarching concern is that of the home and the local environment. He notices how issues such as environmental degradation and global injustice are relatively well understood, and that often, solutions for the problems exist. Still, he suggests that a sustainable environment will not give us a sense of belonging; a prosperous economy will fail to make us happy and pursuing social and global justice does not repair moral abandonment. "My suggestion is that for a proper understanding of our cultural malaise we have to get a grip on technology as a cultural force" (2006b, p. 352). Borgmann has, for decades, remained in agreement with Heidegger that there *is* a malaise, and suggests: "To act on this suspicion [of an ailing culture] is the beginning of philosophy" (2003, p. 119).

In offering his own, more empirically informed diagnosis as well as suggestions for care and cure, he is casting philosophy in a therapeutic role.[4] Borgmann's analysis of the malaise is two-pronged. The first is Heideggerian, as Borgmann explores what it means to dwell, to know one's way in one's environment, and how technologies can both strengthen and obscure the understanding of one's place in the world. Accordingly, in more of his writings, Borgmann offers detailed descriptions of homes, such as those of Thomas Jefferson and Frank Lloyd Wright, and he frequently relies on accounts of the history, culture and infrastructure in which his home in Missoula, Montana, is set.[5] The second adds

---

[3] Another book-length study that relies on virtue theory in philosophy of technology is Schultze (2002).
[4] Hadot (1995) is an influential exposition of this understanding of the role of philosophy.
[5] Borgmann rarely speaks of Being as it was explored in the previous chapter. Yet, to the extent that dwelling is central, I suggest Borgmann is a more faithful Heidegger interpreter than Malpas, to whom the recognition of nearness of Being "...is not a matter of coming into the vicinity of some single place, but rather of coming to recognize the placed character of being as such. Such a recognition is always articulated in and through the particular places in which we already find ourselves and no one such place can have any priority here" (Malpas, 2008, p. 309). It is not clear from the surrounding passages what kind of priority Malpas has in mind, but being at home does seem to have priority not only in the *order cogniscendi* in Heidegger's thought: how we get to learn about the virtues and get our bearing in our environment.

virtue theory to Heidegger's focus on the homely. It explores how technologies in our immediate environment can strengthen or frustrate the fostering of virtues. While disorientation is Borgmann's preferred way of speaking of the malaise along Heideggerian lines, a conception of the good life plays a central role in Aristotelian inspired diagnosis: "[T]he just society remains incomplete and easily dispirited without a fairly explicit and definite version of the good life" (1984, p. 91). A good life, in turn, is to Borgmann explicated in terms of excellence and happiness. Borgmann characterises existence under the device paradigm as unhappy (1984, p. 145), and the pleasures derived from consumption as "flawed... when we measure it against standards of excellence and undertake it to attain happiness" (1984, p. 139).

In 1984, Borgmann marshalled empirical, sociological evidence to the effect that both excellence and happiness were in decline in American society, and he suggested that our uptake with technology was an important aspect of this decline.[6] Any way of operationalising the concepts of excellence and happiness will be contentious, and we shall discuss Borgmann's own attempts below. Put differently, making good the claim about decline requires saying something substantial about the good life. Here, Borgmann's source is located among those involved in deictic discourse: "[T]he reflective care of the good life has not withered away. It has left the profession of philosophy and sprung up among practical people. In fact, there is a tradition in this country of persons who are engaged by life in its concreteness and simplicity and who are so filled with this engagement that they have reached for the pen to become witnesses and teachers, speakers of deictic discourse" (Borgmann 1984, p. 201).[7] As we explore, his emphasis on simplicity is moderated, if not contradicted, by his appeal to what John Rawls (1971) called the Aristotelian principle and by his emphasis on the rich and complex ways that focal practices engage us. When giving an account of the happy – *i.e.* well-functioning – human life, Borgmann emphasises parti-

---

[6] Borgmann suggests that sociological evidence must be guided by "intuition and firsthand experience" (1984, p. 101). See (1984 pp. 99ff & 127ff) for his discussion of the decline of excellence, which he understands as literacy and education, physical vigour and skill, acquaintance with arts and proficiency in artistic practices and levels of compassion towards those suffering from hardships. It is repeated in his 2006 work, *Real American Ethics*, but here with scant reference to empirical investigations.

[7] In such works as Norman Maclean's *A river runs through it*; Colin Fletcher's *The complete Walker*; Roger B. Swain's *Earthly Pleasures*; Robert Farrar Capon's *The Supper of the Lamb* and George Sheehan's *Running and Being*. Fandozzi (2000) convincingly adds films, such as *Babette's Feast* and *Local Hero*, to modes of deictic language that can bear testimony to the importance of practices and places.

ally that humans dwell and partially that they are sophisticated social and material beings that flourish when their dormant capacities are developed.

To understand the cultural force, Borgmann replaces the concept of *Gestell* with the concepts of pattern and paradigm. In this way of continuing Heidegger's thought, "Gestell" is transformed into a pattern of tool use and interaction with the world that Borgmann suggests can increasingly be seen across different spheres of private and communal life. The pattern is identified in obvious and largely tangible settings, like those associated with transportation (cars, first-class flights), education and entertainment; in intangible, social ones, such as insurance and unsuspected ones, such as cool whip (Kraft Heinz' non-dairy whipped topping) and suburban lawns.[8] While we have seen how technologies associated with production played an overarching role in Marxist thought on technology, a viewpoint Borgmann also locates in Arendt, Borgmann stresses: "Much is learned from Arendt's analysis of the vulgar and disorienting aspects of technology as a system, devoted primarily to production and consumption. But I am not sure that Arendt's notion of Labour reveals them unambiguously. Technology shows its force most disturbingly as it dissolves the tradition of cooking and the celebration of family meals, both ferial and festal" (1984, p. 59).[9] Positioning himself against modes of philosophical inquiry exemplified by trolley problems, as well as more recent developments in social epistemology, Borgmann finds in much philosophy a lack of interest in what he calls content, as opposed to procedural, epistemology. Content epistemology concerns "...questions [of] *what* people typically know in our society, what they are capable of knowing, and what they should be expected to know" (Bendick & Borgmann, 2017, p. 173). Borgmann can be seen to subscribe to the Heideggerian view of the role of philosophy and poetry as pointing to the often homely objects and practices of importance. Borgmann's book-length 1999 study on the nature of information accordingly concludes with lengthy analyses of the particular areas of Montana where Borgmann has lived and worked for decades, its history, peoples and wilderness.

---

8 Others have taken up Borgmann concepts and analysed farming (Thompson, 2000) as well as extended Borgmann's analysis of energy consumption (Geerts, 2017).
9 As explored by Barney (2004), in spite of their differences, Arendt and Borgmann are clearly united in emphasising the importance that the permanence of things can constitute for the human subject: "For a society of labourers... the most important task of the human artifice... is to offer mortals a dwelling place more permanent and more stable than themselves" (Arendt, 1958, p. 151).

In addition to relying on the concept of a paradigm, Borgmann uses the concept of character to describe technological culture.[10] The concept itself is technological in origin, deriving from the Greek word for the tool used for engraving. Like "identity", the concept has a complex history that draws on Greek philosophy, medieval theology and, in the 20th century, sociology and psychology. Only in recent decades has it forcefully re-entered philosophy as a central term in virtue ethics. The importance of this word for Borgmann's philosophy of technology is double. First, it is one way of conceiving of technology as autonomous and exhibiting a systematic influence on people apart from what people and communities themselves wish to do with technology, when asked in a reflective moment. Second, characters are shaped by the natural, material and social environment, which can help foster such traits as being resilient, kind or carefree. Borgmann's pessimistic outlook, formulated in terms of the device paradigm, has one of its sources in the way he thinks the device pattern shapes the characters around him.

As Kuhn suggested in his discussion of the concept of a paradigm, convincing others to see things a certain way, according to a given pattern, is a complex matter. To establish his vocabulary and its concomitant claims about technological culture, Borgmann does not, in the first instance, rely on general principles. Rather, his deictic discourse involves talking about things in ways that serve to bear testimony to their complex and engaging character when compared with what he calls devices. Deictic discourse appeals to kinds of experience already residing with the reader, with a view to her being convinced of the relevance of the pattern for understanding everyday, technological existence. Once a pattern is seen, Borgmann can offer "apodeictic" (1984, p. 77) abstractions, which he does by means of concepts like "commodity", "machine", "availability" and "engagement." Borgmann rejects seeing philosophy primarily as the exercise of proposing general principles and finding counterexamples: "The brain of every mainstream philosopher has been programmed to react to whatever general claim by racing through its instances in search of devastating counterexamples" (2003, p. 124). Rather, Borgmann has in his authorship stayed with explorations of the relatively simple pattern that he proposed in his 1984 book, and he has analysed such phenomena as literacy, community, forms of leisure, eating, navigating, exercising and the wilderness in the light of different technologies. To Borgmann, the purpose of exploring this pattern is more than mere under-

---

10 While forms of technological determinism and autonomy loom large in philosophy of technology (cf. chapter 4), the point of appealing to the notion of character seems to have escaped notice from the academic community. Borgmann himself does not focus on it either, but the related concept of a pattern. Mitcham (2000) is an insightful exception.

standing. It is ultimately to explore and elicit active assent to a form of life marked by engagement and dwelling.

In the sections below, I offer an account of some of the major themes in Borgmann's 1984 *Technology and the character of Contemporary Life*. In addition to Borgmann's work on religion, the themes and concepts found here resurface in several of his later works, such as *Holding on to Reality* (1999) which focuses on informational technologies. The themes concern the possibility of a good life, and the environment in which an ethos – a shared view of what a good life is – can survive and thrive among people who are highly intertwined with modern technologies in their everyday lives. Borgmann speaks of a time pretechnological and his overall narrative remains that of a modern malaise. His criticism of particular information technologies, perhaps coupled with his insistence on the importance of "traditional morality" (1984, p. 171) and the overarching narrative of a "twofold loss" of "great things and great practices" (2010, p. 16), seem to have led some philosophers to cast him as nostalgic, and in late writings, he partially agrees.[11]

There is a sense in which the charge is correct. The etymology of nostalgia has to do with being homesick. It is, exactly, practices traditionally associated with the home – cooking and eating meals, providing shelter and warmth – that Borgmann thinks have suffered at the hands of technologies and have left us disoriented. However, being nostalgic is often taken to mean longing for other times merely on account of being historical. Whether Borgmann in fact longs for earlier times or not, what we must do below is unearth the reasons that Borgmann might have for his longings – reasons that can be understood and recognised without reference to the mere fact that states of affairs are of the past. After discussing the device paradigm, I survey how this is achieved on a platform of virtue ethics with a distinct Heideggerian bent. I then conclude with Borgmann' suggestions for a reform of the device paradigm.

6.2 A pattern of disengagement

Borgmann located the device pattern in unassuming, and then everyday objects and practices like stereos, cool whip, life insurance, central heating systems and *Defender*, a 1980's video game. Below, we shall draw on some philosophical vocabulary in order to present Borgmann's thought at a sufficient level of generality. In the spirit of deictic discourse, I shall introduce key concepts of Borgmann's

---

[11] See *e.g.* Feenberg (1992) and, in particular, Cutrofello (1993).

by way of describing technological aspects of my environment: what keeps my house warm during the winter and where I go to exercise and explore what some – to my mind erroneously – call the last wilderness in Denmark, during my time of recreation.

Being located in Denmark and not built according to nearly zero-energy standards, my house requires heating for more than half the year. I require a *commodity*, and I am, to a great extent, lumbered with the decisions made by previous owners of my house. The house came with a natural gas-fuelled central heating system, having previously been equipped with an electricity-powered heating system. Though my ignorance gradually decreases over the years, I have little knowledge of the *concealed* workings of the *machinery*. It presents me with a dial, six buttons and a small display, offering me various messages that I fail to understand completely. Much more conspicuous is the sticker next to the display, informing me of a phone-number to call in case of "problems with the heating." Apart from the quarterly bill, I am, to a great degree, *disburdened* and *no engagement* on my behalf is really needed for my house to be kept sufficiently warm. The gas boiler undergoes yearly maintenance by a professional, who in turn far from fully grasps the workings of the *device* in its layers of complexity. During the occasional breakdown (I have taken out an *insurance* against incurred costs, and choose not to rely on more knowledgeable friends and neighbours), the repairman – *available* within 24 hours at the touch of a button on my phone – frequently opts for not repairing and rather chooses to replace some of the complex circuit boards and other elements of the boiler. Over the duration of my more than 10 years of ownership, there has been a distinct change in the attitude of the repairmen. From encouraging me to engage with and understand the nature of central heating and the gas boiler, to menacingly enquiring whether I have been tinkering with the device, before repairs and maintenance is undertaken. To my understanding, it is currently fed by gas delivered by Russian energy company Gazprom, but whatever geopolitical reservations I might have about my *consumption*, they are unlikely to influence the way gas is procured as part of the national strategy for securing energy *availability*.

The italicised words in the previous paragraphs characterise the main pattern, the device paradigm, that Borgmann identifies in Western culture. In short, a device is "composed of two parts: the machinery and the commodity" (2006b, p. 356). The machinery in large parts conceals the workings of the technology, while being perceived primarily, if not exclusively, in terms of the commodity it offers for consumption. Borgmann (2004, 2006a) distinguishes what he calls cultural, or moral, commodification from economic commodification. In Borgmann's writings, the concept of commodity should not primarily be considered a matter of something being subject to financial exchange, where the process is that of moving goods from other different spheres – public ones or intimate ones – into that of the market. Rather, the Latin etymology that suggests being suitable and convenient – a commodious way of making goods available – is central to Borgmann's use of the word. While economic commodification can serve to account for forms of injustice, Borgmann suggests that moral commodification is largely "blameless". Moral commodification serves to account for what Borgmann and Charles Taylor describe as "a loss of resonance, depth, or richness in our human surroundings" (Taylor, 1991, p. 6, cited in Borgmann, 2006, p. 150). Like Heidegger, Borgmann suggests that the device paradigm is a way of relating not just to inert things in our surroundings, but also to each other: "The most troubling extension of [the pattern] is yet to be recognised. The availability... and the absence of demands... we seek in persons as well" (2003, p. 17). A device makes for a contrast with a focal thing or practice, and moral commodification, to Borgmann, is a matter of divorcing goods and practices from the context of place and time. I go on to describe two cases of focal things: an inrigger and Borgmann's most cited example, a hearth. Here, the italicised words centre on the mode of engagement with my environment that the thing both offers and demands.

Like many people of my age with a work-life that involves negligible physical exertion, I regularly spend time doing physical exercise. Living where I do, I have *chosen* to have those activities of my life involve a *thing*, a rowing boat. At times, I will use an inrigger, a type of rowing boat predominantly used in Scandinavian countries, and once in the Olympic Games. Though still in small scale production, they are slowly fading out of existence, but are still in use in rowing clubs in Northern European countries. Using an inrigger for exercise and recreation places *demands* on one and requires that one gets one's *bearings*, socially and geographically. You need to know the *surrounding waters* – its shallow parts and their use by others, such as fishermen, the navy, swimmers, divers and those who prefer speedboats. You need to foster sound *judgment* whether or not you set out to sea at any given time. Someone needs to be the cox and agree with rowers on pace and destination. You need to hone the *skill* to actually row well, avoiding the unpleasant and possibly *dangerous* experience of catching a crab with your oar: having a rowing stroke go wrong in a way that results in the handle of the ore being pressed against you with great force. An inrigger requires *manning* by either three or five people, so the availability of recreation and exercise is at the mercy of social cooperation. Also, cooperation and sharing of *skill* are required for the *maintenance* of the delicate *wooden* boats – work that is often undertaken out of *season*, when the waters are *too cold* and *unsafe* for the majority of rowers. As you frequent the century-old rowing club, you inevitably learn about the *history* of the people and the city. This is learnt through *conversation* with senior rowers as you take brief breaks on a trip; when you share a meal; through the paintings, photographs, plaques and trophies one finds on the premises of the rowing club. Once a year, the club hosts a *ceremony* for new rowers, featuring a senior rower dressed up as *Neptune*, coming to baptise the junior rowers. The *history* of each boat – its acquisition, previous users, trips, major maintenance works, as well as events associated with it, furthers your knowledge of the boat's surroundings. As already suggested, there are dangers involved in rowing, for example in the event of a capsize in cold waters. Rowers prepare for it and exercises, or submits to, judgment and *authority* over others to avoid it. *Death* is encountered: when members of the club die and are commemorated, or more disturbingly when, on rare occasions, dead bodies are discovered in the water by rowers.

While the inrigger and the focal practice it supports and requires is of some age, being a rower does not entail being in any kind of principled opposition to the use of sophisticated, modern technologies. Both in and out of season, rowers often use fairly high-tech equipment of the kind used in the fitness-centre a few hundred meters away, when they improve their strength and stamina in rowing ergometers. The techniques involved in use of the ergometer are cruder than those involved during actual rowing. Nevertheless, there are other kinds of *sophistication*, of a technical kind: on the internet, you can compete with other rowers, each using their ergometers in real-time. Generally, rowers happily sport the latest heart rate monitors, textiles and other technologies as part of the rowing practice, to excel in it. That is to say, the internet connected ergometers and GPS technologies, pieces of modern technology in their own right, here have their rank and place in relation to the focal thing, the inrigger, and the practice of rowing.[12] Neither are focal practices opposed to investigations carried out by natural sciences: studies of fluid dynamics as well as the human physiology can enrich the practice.

The inrigger and the practice that supports its use to a great extent fit Borgmann's more general description of focal things and practices:

> They are concrete, tangible and deep, admitting of no functional equivalents; they have a tradition, structure, and rhythm of their own. They are unprocurable and finally beyond our control. They engage us in the fullness of our capacities... A focal practice, generally, is the

---

[12] This mirrors Borgmann's reflections on proper and improper use of various information technologies when being in the wilderness (cf. 2015b, p. 263f.). Also, detailed descriptions of the practice of care and its activities allows van Wynsberghe (2016) to reflect which (robotic) technologies you can introduce into health care without doing damage to the practice and the goods internal to the practice.

> resolute and regular dedication to a focal thing. It sponsors discipline and skill which are exercised in a unity of achievement and enjoyment, of mind, body and the world, of myself and others, and in a social union. (Borgmann, 1984, p. 219)

Time constraints leave maintaining another example of a focal thing, a hearth, out of the question. The latin "focus" means hearth and was only later used in mathematical and optical senses. The activity of maintaining a hearth is one of Borgmann's examples of a technological practice that contrasts with the device paradigm. The hearth would serve as the architectural, practical, social and religious centre of a household – "the hearth sustained, ordered and centered house and family" (1984, p. 196). Its user would need knowledge about how to choose, chop, split and store firewood, negotiate the risks associated with cutting it, as well as light and maintain the fire and clean the fireplace; the hearth would be placed centrally in the house; religious symbols were placed here (later, trophies from achievements and family pictures at a fire place would replace the symbols) and of course, cooking would take place here. In speaking of *the* user, I have glossed over how the hearth helps structure the different roles of a household, from roles in cooking meals to gathering, preparing and storing the firewood.

Actions are intentional under a certain description. I have described my activity of rowing, with its focal thing, the inrigger, as one that has the goal of maintaining my health. In contrast with activities associated with historic, overarching and more culturally dominant focal practices, such as the Christian religion, it is fully legitimate for me to describe my activity in different ways. Getting away from people, taking in the sights, getting new friends, learning about the local village are all acceptable ways of describing my activity. The activity was deliberately chosen, against competing alternatives such as the fitness centre across the waters – largely identical to many thousands spread across the world. As a way of staying healthy, choosing the fitness centre would undoubtedly disburden me in more ways, and would likely be a more efficient way of achieving my goal. Though having gas heating in my house was not my choice, were I to choose a more efficient gas heater, rather than, say, a focal thing like a Finnish mass oven, this would be a choice with two options, both with the goal of heating my house.

Consequently, when Verbeek suggests that "[f]ocal practices... never serve specific goals" (2002, p. 77), this does not accurately reflect Borgmann's distinction between focal things and devices. In the case of the hearth and the inrigger, both are readily seen to involve goal-directed activities – a warm house and physical health and strength. It is the demands that these focal practices place on us and the ways they structure and orient our dwelling that are of importance and distinguish them. Having a sufficiently rich and fine-grained description of our practices in terms of activities allows us to see the different ways that technologies shape, sustain or challenge our practices and shape our habits. It is the richness and moral qualities of the demands and possibilities that are integral to focal things that are neglected under the device paradigm. A subclass of focal things, such as the wilderness, is a goal in itself and does not exist "in-order-to." Having a central fireplace can hardly be considered an intrinsic good or activity, valued and undertaken purely for its own sake. It will mostly be for heating or comfort. At any rate, Borgmann's examples of focal things and surrounding practices that have goals such as warmth, health and entertainment are initially of more service in analysing technology than the "ultimate" focal things. Yet, he will likely maintain that a detrimental relation exists between the use of devices and the appreciation and knowledge of things of ultimate importance.

While Borgmann is content to speak of things and practices being "tightly interwoven" (1984, p. 219), Haworth (2000) proposes two models of the relation between focal practices and focal things: the guardian model, exemplified by horse riding, has a devotional character, according to which "the purpose of a focal practice [is] to guard in its undiminished depth and identity the thing that is central to the practice" (Borgmann, 1984, p. 209). The other model – the internal goods model – relies on MacIntyre's (1981) emphasis on the honing of skills and there being criteria of excellence in a practice, whose worth lies in the practice itself.[13] Haworth suggests that the two models are frequently and jointly reflected in Borgmann's examples, and that one can place examples of focal practices on a spectrum. There is a "realistic" end of the spectrum, where the practitioners do not consider their practice integral to the being of the focal thing. Divine worship and navigating the wilderness are clear examples here. At the other end of the spectrum, traditions, practices and their concomitant concepts of excellence have a more overarching influence on the way practitioners view the good of the practice: it would not exist if it was not for the practice. Japanese tea-making is a good example here.

Borgmann's characterisation of the cultural malaise can be summed up in the claim that devices to an increasing extent replace things and focal practices, by inserting machines – material and non-material – between humans and ends. This makes for a "characteristic and constraining pattern to the entire fabric of

---

[13] This seems to be the standpoint found in Borgmann's late discussion of the wilderness (Borgmann, 2015b) and is also the view suggested in Haworth's discussion of Borgmann's earlier work.

our lives. This pattern is visible first and most of all in the countless inconspicuous objects and procedures of daily life in a technological society" (1984, p. 3). In music streaming services replacing CD's which together with other historical forms of information storage, have been able to, on occasion, replace live performances; in forms of fast-food replacing a home-cooked, communal meal and insurance replacing the support of a community. In short, making commodities available "instantaneously, ubiquitously, safely, and easily" (1984, p. 77), resulting in a "pervasive transformation of things into devices that is changing our commerce with reality from engagement to the disengagement of consumption and labour" (1984, p. 61). Procuring warmth, leisure and nourishment were traditionally associated with demanding and skilled practices, and the device pattern has thoroughly challenged many of these practices, some to the point of near extinction.

The concept of a pattern would seem to allow for irregularities (as in the series "2,4,6,10,12,14"), for seeing two different patterns instantiated in the same set of objects, or indeed, to see no pattern where others do. "2, 4..." can be correctly continued in accordance with at least two different patterns, and we may find that the pattern "+2" is more clearly instantiated in other regions of the number series. Much of the criticism of the idea of a device pattern can be understood along one of two lines. First, whether Borgmann's assessment of the pervasiveness of the pattern in contemporary culture is correct, and second, whether a given instance in fact fits the pattern. Frequently, critics have followed Borgmann in offering the kind of detailed descriptions that he encourages and have argued by way of pointing to a different pattern in the same set of object. This has most often been a matter of seeing information and communication technologies a wholesome kind of technology use that diverges from the one associated with the device paradigm and the negative assessment which the paradigm entails.[14] It is noticeable that critical commentators have rarely, if at all, taken up his discussion of the case of the pattern that Borgmann finds most disturbing.[15] I sug-

---

[14] Verbeek (2002, 2005), Kellner (2000) and Feenberg (1999) have offered varieties of this criticism of Borgmann's idea of a device paradigm. For example, Feenberg (1999) points to counterexamples of edifying and engaging patient meetings taking place online, and Kellner points to examples of uses of the internet that "might help overcome the individual isolation, apathy, and sullenness that have alienated large sectors of the public from our polity and from other people" (2000, p. 244). As argued immediately below, *some* amount of such examples, even if successful, are compatible with the existence of a pervasive device pattern – of a technological culture having a certain character.

[15] Both Selinger (2013) and Vallor (2016) discuss the mores associated with the dinner table in the light of Facebook's 2013 TV spot "Family Dinner", to which we return below. None of them clearly rely on Borgmann in doing so. Vallor's Borgmann is mainly concerned about "gourmet

gest that commentators have at times overstated the persuasive strength of using deictic discourse to discern and demonstrate patterns. Social and historical phenomena are far more complex than number series, and the possibility of meaningful disagreement about patterns on this background is to a great extent possible. That is to say, presenting counterexamples to the pattern only gains strength as an argumentative strategy as they begin to match, in numbers and significance, the many places where the pattern *does* become visible in everyday life. More specifically, there are likely uses of communication technologies that do not fit the pattern that Borgmann sees in contemporary technological culture. Indeed, they can be understood and appreciated on the background of Borgmann's account of focal practices and things.

In addition to helping us understand the world, identifying a pattern or a certain character trait should equip one with a measure of success in predicting phenomena – something that Borgmann himself does not emphasise. A kind character can certainly act out of character but can generally be expected to exhibit kindness in her dealings with others. To the extent that information and communication technologies have become devices that make commodities available for consumption rather than engage and challenge our various faculties, I suggest the device pattern enjoys some measure of success in predicting developments since it was proposed in Borgmann's 1984 book. For example, at the turn of the millennium, early stages of optimism regarding the qualities of the internet were visible when critical commentators offering counterexamples to Borgmann's device pattern. In 2000, Kellner hailed the internet as "one of the few decommodified spaces in the ultracommodified world of technocapitalism" (2000, p. 246) and described it as a force for good in political life. With the proviso about social and historic phenomena mentioned above, subsequent developments suggest that Borgmann's device pattern – using technologies to make commodities readily available for consumption – is the pattern most clearly seen when one surveys the continued social shaping of the internet.[16]

---

cooking" in so far as it serves to "cultivate personal excellences and can be used to honor 'focal things'" (Vallor, 2016, p. 30). Frischmann & Selinger (2018) dedicate an appendix to a discussion of "Modern Meal Times" and Barney (2004) discusses the structuring aspects of the seminar table and contrasts it with forms of e-learning.

16 I cannot here make the case, but the internet in the Western world certainly *appears* increasingly commodified, with many highly valued companies creating their value from services (entertainment and advertisement) offered here. The challenges for democracy that arise from information distribution based on seeing users as consumers rather than citizens gained wide attention based on the writings of Sunstein (2007) and Pariser (2011). An earlier survey of competing visions of the internet was carried out by Feenberg and Bakardjieva (2004). A melioration of the challenges that commodification of information presents for political communities and

Borgmann suggests that the pattern of commodity procurement has emerged over approximately three centuries, and he considers it encapsulated in the promises of technology: disburdenment, liberation from misery and toil, and enrichment – notions "joined in that of availability" (1984, p. 41). The transformation from practices and things to availability through devices comes out clearly when one compares technologies slightly more than a century apart: from a time when "coaches and sleighs were not heated" (1984, p. 41) to using your *device* (which in 2020 often just means a smartphone) to activate another: for example, the heater in your electric car a few minutes before entering it. The device conceals its workings, does not engage us and crucially, tends not to foster any skill, knowledge or virtue. A thing, in contrast with a device, "is inseparable from its context, namely, its world, and from our commerce with the thing in the world", while commodities "are free of local and historical ties" (1984, p. 81).

6.3 Things: orientation and the good life

In what ways do focal things and practices assist us in achieving the good life? In answering this question, Borgmann draws on a range of themes in virtue theory and adds to that the Heideggerian theme of orientation. In what follows, we shall discuss these in turn.[17] First and foremost, like a virtue is a chosen, settled disposition, chosen for the right reasons, contemporary focal practices frequently involve an active choice that in turn can help settle a range of morally significant dispositions. The voluntary character makes for a contrast with some of the historical cases of focal practices that Borgmann points to. In past times, there has probably been little genuine choice when using a hearth for heating. The alternative would have been misery and discomfort. In present times, we mostly choose to engage in one and not another, and we have the choice whether or not to be engaged in a focal practice at all. For centuries, before being scattered by various forces, the churches and its practices had a uniform and a highly structuring effect on its cultural surroundings, but it was also a very dominant practice. You might not go to church or in other ways get your bearings there, and you were an outsider for that very reason. You might not want to grow vegetables to supplement your diet, but circumstances would force this on you, along with the discipline, skill and knowledge it demands. In contrast, contem-

---

democratic processes has been attempted through value sensitive design by Bozdag & van den Hoven (2015).

17 In my presentation of Borgmann's appeal to virtue theory, I am reliant on expositions of virtue theory such as Russell (2009), Annas (2011), Athanassoulis (2013) and Hursthouse (2011).

porary culture exhibits a diaspora of focal practices, many of which are found on the fringes – homely, inconspicuous and dispersed. All of these practices cannot co-exist in any single life: one cannot simultaneously centre, say, the musical instrument, the boat, the wilderness, the vegetable garden, the running track, the fishing rod and the salmon in a single life. On the background of the affluence and possibilities offered by a range of technologies and social change, each practice exists in a space of alternatives, mostly unfettered by social or economic necessity.

Contemporary practices are themselves demanding, but predominantly chosen. This nature of focal practices can help us understand a general challenge to the fostering of virtues that is amplified by the device paradigm. According to Aristotle, most virtuous persons will initially have habits fostered on them before the actions that flow from the habits are understood, appreciated and actively chosen. It is not just parents and virtuous persons – *phronemoi* – that can help initiate and sustain these habits from an early age. Focal practices play a role in necessitating certain habits and dispositions that are conducive to virtue. Unfortunate people strive to become virtuous despite their natural and developed tendencies, and some fail to become so. Aristotle characterised those characters as being continent (encratic) and incontinent, respectively. Unlike virtue, the traits of the continent and incontinent are unstable and only exist in a possible and frail moral progression towards being virtuous.

Borgmann emphasises the technologically shaped nature of the situations in which the continent and incontinent struggle to make the right decisions on their way to virtue, and finds a lack of attention to material detail in much philosophical ethics: "[T]here is this assumption in theoretical and practical ethics that life unfolds on an empty stage, or at least the belief that, when it comes to doing the right thing, the props on the stage of life don't matter much... Technological devices... channel the typical ways we behave" (2006a, p. 11). For example, in discussion of his key example of a focal practice, the culture of the table contrasted with technological eating, Borgmann appeals to continence and incontinence: "We all have had occasion to experience the profound pleasure of an invigorating walk or a festive meal. And on such occasions we may have regretted the scarcity of such events" (1984, p. 206). Why do these brief glimpses of the splendour of focal practices remain episodal? "The reason lies in the mistaken assumption that the shaping of our lives can be left to a series of individual decisions. Whatever goal in life we entrust to this kind of implementation, we in fact surrender to erosion... On the spur of the moment, we normally act out what has been nurtured in our daily practices as they have been shaped by the norms of our time... it would take superhuman strength to stand up to this order ever and again" (1984, p. 206f.).

Not only are we by nature equipped with different dispositions. We might know what is good and desirable, but struggle with a weak will – *akrasia*. Faced with the commodious nature of the device paradigm, this struggle is intensified. To the extent that habit is central to virtue, the idea of a struggle against an inclination to not do what leads to being virtuous acquires a distinct technological embodiment in Borgmann. Habits are different from virtue, in so far as the latter requires reflection; yet, habits are crucial for becoming a virtuous person. With the proviso that we are yet to say a little more about what the good life consists in according to Borgmann, he can be seen to suggest that our technological environment, absent of focal practices, makes us less likely to achieve virtue through persistent training of our dispositions. We are more likely to become incontinent and choose the easy option that places few demands on us. This is not a matter of the mere ability or possibility that technologies do or do not foster and offer. It is a matter of what technologies actually will do to our characters and the actions that flow from them. So when Verbeek (2005, p. 188 f.) levels a criticism of Borgmann by suggesting that CD-players *can* be a technology that foster engagement with Bach's works, Borgmann responds: "The problem lies in the slide from '*is* more engaging' to '*can* involve themselves intensely'. Yes, people can so involve themselves; it's important to point that out. But do they? What's the aggregate effect of all the devices at people's disposal?" (Borgmann, 2005, par. 18). This is clearly a call for a virtue theoretic assessment of technology emphasising the engagement and habits it fosters rather than the (mere) possibilities it offers and the abilities it might help raise.

Facebook's 2013 TV-spot "Family Dinner" appeared designed to drive home Borgmann's contrasting of "technological eating" with the "enactment of generosity and gratitude" found in the "focal event par excellence" which, among other things, "requires and sponsors memorable conversation" (Borgmann, 1984, p. 204 f.). The TV-spot features an adolescent girl being bored, like everyone else, while sat at a lavish family dinner. An elderly family member's long-winded rambling about the purchase of cat food is the immediate cause. By using a device (a new development in Facebook's communication platform), conveniently and instantaneously communicating with her far more exciting friends is a live option that is quickly seized upon. The TV spot illustrates this by transporting these more interesting events and persons into the scene of the family dinner. Cultural critics have discussed the conventions that this TV-spot both suggests and challenges, and how a generalisation of the Facebook-enabled behaviour would be utterly detrimental to the social fabric of an extended family. The recognisable challenge facing the young woman is almost a microcosm of Aristotelian themes in the light of the device paradigm, if we consider the dinner table to be the training ground for a range of virtues. Ideally, the young woman would be able to rely on an already practically wise person – a *phronimos* – to observe and learn how to stop the family member in her tracks in a respectful and caring manner. Alternatively, this is simply an exercise in patience, which might be what she is able to observe in the *phronemoi* around her. Lacking the required patience or judging it an inappropriate response in the context, she would need to muster both courage and practical, conversational skill to end the stream of tiresome and dull talk in a way that balances a number of considerations (the state and history of the talkative, elderly family member, among other things). In doing so, there is a slight chance that she might chip away at a possibly strong and unfortunate habit of a family member.

The TV-spot effects a stark contrast with the focal aspect of the meal, as it makes present a family history of recipes, of regional habits and immemorial skills of cultivating plants and butchering animals. It is the ready availability of information that allows the young woman to turn away from conversation, and it invites us to contrast the "fluidity of information technology with the stability of the things and practices that have served us well and we continue to depend on for our material and spiritual well-being" (Borgmann, 1999, p. 202). The particularities and history of a communal place structured by a thing is invaded by the availability of uniform space. Exploring Goethe's perception of the flawed conversational skills in his otherwise erudite and knowledgeable friends, Borgmann (2015a) joins Sherry Turkle (2011b) and many others in seeing this kind of availability as detrimental to the practice of conversation. Conversation at a dinner table (or elsewhere) is not only a training ground for habits, and eventually, virtue, when a *bonus pater* or *mater familias* enforce the practice in the right way for the right reasons. Borgmann suggests that our being in the world is attenuated by the lessening of demands for the kind of knowledge required to engage in a conversation.[18]

This technological microcosm leaves out many aspects of virtue theory, and it is a genuine possibility that other training grounds for virtue could be found online. The criticism of the use of technology it embodies is subject to a more general complaint, also levelled against virtue theory: it favours the traditions (a settled, non-negotiable way of eating) and persons of privilege (the ageing family member who is able to flout conventions of conversational turn-taking)

---

18 See his discussion of content knowledge and world appropriation that takes place during conversation (2015a). He frames his discussion as the opposite of the micro perspective of conversational analysis. Borgmann explores how Goethe complained about the nature of some conversation to friends of his: "They [the correspondents] struck me as billiard balls that blindly move around on the green surface without knowing each other and that, as soon as they touch each other, run all the farther away from each other" (cited in Borgmann, 2015a, p. 220).

while it serves to "repress the ardours and enthusiasms of the young" (Russell, 1945, p. 188). As suggested in the previous section, we might overlook patterns with focal qualities while criticising this particular social media platform on this occasion, or in more generalised criticisms of the erosion of focal practices by new technologies. Yet, we can point to some of the key qualities such a practice should have: sufficient permanence and requirements of discipline to foster habits that can eventually result in a virtuous character. In virtue theory, this, in brief, means succeeding in attaining a good life.

The young woman fails to engage with her immediate social surroundings and the topics they entertain in their conversation. Engagement is one of the defining features of focal practices, but in itself, a concept that includes many forms of relation to one's environment. For example, when Verbeek (2002) criticises Borgmann for using the concept ambiguously, Verbeek divorces "engagement" from its virtue theoretic setting in Borgmann's writings. When he sums up Borgmann's position as one that "centres around the concern for engagement with reality" (2002, p. 75), the road is open to making almost anything of Borgmann's position.[19] Specifically, Verbeek's allegation of an ambiguity rests on a reading where "pretechnological" focal practices are considered entirely in the light of their burdensome requirements, while contemporary ones are entirely on the realistic end of the spectrum, leaving out the practical, virtue theoretical aspects as well as the Heideggerian ideas about place and orientation, explored below. When Verbeek suggests that "[t]he engagement [contemporary] focal practices evoke is of an entirely different nature [than pretechnological ones]. Efforts and pains are not crucial here for Borgmann, but meaningfulness" (2002, p. 76), the difference is rather that orientation and formation of habits were imposed by necessity and mores onto the individual to a greater extent than what is the case today. Exertion and meaningfulness are not two completely different forms of engagement, but frequently, go together in Borgmann's examples of focal practices and things.[20]

Another criticism of Borgmann's approach is levelled by Vallor, who is sympathetic towards a virtue-theoretic approach when discussing technology. She rightly locates in Borgmann a concern for excellence "understood as the cultiva-

---

19 Verbeek (2002) in particular understands Borgmann's position to be at one with those of Heidegger's, Jaspers' and Ellul's in making alienation from reality a key theme, and to Verbeek's mind, wrongly presupposing a notion of authenticity. This analysis certainly appears at odds with the exposition offered in previous chapters.

20 To wit, also in my own example: those who excel in rowing as a highly competitive activity regularly throw up from exertion during ergometer training. Of course, their activities centred around a rowing boat are differently described than mine.

tion of social, physical and intellectual capacities or virtues" (2016, p. 30) but finds his approach wanting on a number of counts. In addition to rejecting an answer to Heidegger's fundamental query about dwelling with a version of Vallor's idea of "global human family" (2016, p. 30), Borgmann's account is considered "…ambiguous and incomplete. How are we to determine what counts as facilitating engagement and what counts as its subversion? What *specific* excellences are most worth developing in focal practices?" (2016, p. 30). In demanding a more complete and explicit account of specific virtues, Vallor is pointing to one of the challenges in virtue theory, the enumeration problem (cf. Russell, 2009, pp. 145ff). Virtue theorists give different accounts of the specific virtues. Russell suggests Aristotle offered an open "laundry list" while Plato remained with four. The stoics and Aquinas offered a more tidy, hierarchical version with cardinal virtues and more specific ones subsumed under these. The *Virtues Project*[21] at one point listed 71 virtues, including the 52 virtues for each week of the year. Vallor discusses technologies in the light of 12 virtues. How should we structure our account, and what level of granularity should an account exhibit? Further, any virtue-informed action, like that imagined to be carried out by the young woman at the dinner table, must balance several, if not a totality of, virtues in order to hit the mark (she must not just be courageous, but also kind), which means that active reflection on the action requires knowledge of several virtues. Vallor demands from Borgmann to know more about which.

Borgmann does offer answers that admittedly are very general in character. Firstly, he acknowledges the need for a "definite vision of the good life" (1984, p. 91), and chastises liberal democracies for in fact *not* leaving this for people to settle within general constraints. Instead, in a veiled manner, he suggests that liberal democracies do answer the question of the good life along technological lines: "Politics has become the metadevice of the technological society" (1984, p. 107), with regular competitions between political parties to make *more* goods readily available. The openness of the political forum for dealing with questions of ultimate significance – a definite vision of a good life – does not equate emptiness. It is a place where the device paradigm can rule and offer consumption and withdrawal from engagement. Of course, contemporary politics would be an unlikely place to look for notions of excellence and a good life; I mention political frameworks and prevailing philosophies to remind the reader that liberal democracies are meant to allow for a great degree of openness in answering the question.

---

21 The Virtues Project "is a global grassroots initiative to inspire the practice of virtues in everyday life, sparking a global revolution of kindness, justice and integrity" (2019).

For slightly more specific notions of excellence, Borgmann relies on a bareboned version of the Classical and Judeo-Christian framework, including intellectual aspects of excellence. The excellent person is a world citizen who understands scientific and historical aspects of the world; this person exhibits virtues of gallantry and charity and is accomplished in arts. Borgmann readily admits that these virtues continue to be altered and have been so in the past by movements such as chivalry, humanism and the Renaissance. Likely, this is a far cry from the specificity that Vallor requests. Is this lack damaging to Borgmann's analysis of technological culture?

Vallor offers relatively little motivation for requiring something more specific. She may think her own, more systematic work with 12 virtues constitutes just that, to a sufficient extent. In any case, there is no reason Borgmann's relatively coarse and unsystematic list of virtues could not be refined and systematised. Indeed, he does this himself in his 2006 work on ethics, relying on a distinction between personal and political ones and discussing them in turn. More importantly, Aristotle readily identified and distinguished new items, such as magnificence, on his "rambling list of virtues" and Russell thinks Aristotle's reasons for doing so will generalise: "Where we have distinctive, new contexts and demands for virtuous action, we must also find distinctive, new virtues" (2009, p. 149). The concept of context looms large in virtue theory, and in Borgmann's 2006 book on ethics, a range of virtues, personal and political, are discussed in the light of e.g. Bill Gates' smart home. We can with the notion of ever-changing contexts point to a different motivation for specificity that can be gleaned from Vallor's writings: an existing framework might be unsuitable to "an increasingly rapid, transformative, global, unpredictable... technological change" (Vallor, 2016, p. 119). We have already encountered reasons for thinking that the unpredictability of technological change is overstated, at least at the level of philosophically informed analyses. Borgmann's device paradigm would arguably have proved a better guide to the social shaping of the internet than the idea of an anarchistic cyberspace informed by radical, yet democratic ideals. Yet, even on the assumption that technological development is increasingly rapid and unpredictable, this would not speak uniformly in favour of higher levels of granularity in listing and reflecting on virtues. The work of generalising and adapting fewer virtues might well be more intellectually fruitful.

Another set of considerations that speaks in favour of remaining with relatively few virtues when offering the broad cultural diagnosis, is Borgmann's pluralism concerning focal practices. They range from the culturally marginal fly fishing to the once-dominant Christian religion. There is no reason why one could not do an Islamic version of Borgmann's analysis. He remains open to the emergence of new focal practices, and certainly, there is no pretence of completion in his mention of focal things and practices. What unites them is their resistance to the device paradigm and the way they allow for bodily, social and intellectual engagement as well as gaining orientation in one's environment. In addition to these general features, focal practices, with their histories and particular contexts, will have as part of their fabric specific values and virtues. For example, should a community centred around hacking succeed in measuring up against the qualities that Borgmann sees in more traditional focal practices, excelling in coding will likely demand and foster some virtues particular to those practices.

In further detailing the good life and to carry out a discussion of practices "measuring up", Borgmann relies on something even more general, the "Aristotelian Principle". It aids Borgmann in offering an account of another requirement for virtue. "Just as a piece of land has to be prepared beforehand if it is to nourish the seed, so the mind of the pupil has to be prepared in its habits if it is to enjoy and dislike the right things" (Aristotle, 1976, 1179b19f). Being continent and reasoned in one's habits is not sufficient for being virtuous. Finding pleasure in doing the right thing is a requirement for the virtuous person. The Aristotelian principle was given its name by John Rawls and implicates the relation between pleasure, motivation and excellence. In brief, the idea is that we take greater pleasure in activities where we to a greater extent excel, and this motivates us to act. A similar principle can be found in the writings of John Stuart Mill, who emphasised higher pleasure as a matter of intellectual complexity, aesthetic imagination and engagement of moral sentiments. Borgmann adopts Rawls' version of the principle, which is formulated as follows: "[O]ther things equal, human beings enjoy the exercise of their realized capacities (their innate or trained abilities), and this enjoyment increases the more the capacity is realized, or the greater its complexity (Rawls, 1971, p. 426, cited in Borgmann 1984, p. 213).[22]

In Borgmann's thought, the principle serves two purposes. First, it is called on to throw light on the reported sadness of the scarcity of the experience of a festive meal and an invigorating walk. Rawls suggests the principle is "relatively strong and not easily counterbalanced" (1971, p. 426). Meanwhile, Borgmann

---

[22] It is beyond the task undertaken here to ascertain the origin of the principle. Rawls offers textual evidence from the *Nicomachean Ethics*. Meanwhile, Annas' (2011) discussion of the requirement for pleasure completely bypasses Aristotle's writings, opting instead to draw on Csikszentmihalyi's (1991) concept of flow. Her account of flow, in turn, emphasises engagement in ways that closely resembles Borgmann's account of skilled participation in focal practices. Much contemporary, popular discussion of habit relies on neurophysiological accounts of pleasure. See *e.g.* Duhigg (2012).

suggests that the principle is readily counterbalanced by the device paradigm. He contrasts the availability of classic fiction with actual media use, and the availability of cookbooks with actual dining practices, and concludes that "something is evidently missing in Rawls' political ethics" (2006a, p. 83). The device paradigm is a, if not *the*, strong counterforce that persistently challenges the kind of enjoyment the Aristotelian principle points to. Subscription to the principle – what people "actually know" about excellence – coupled with the force of the device paradigm accounts for the sadness. This is readily construed as widespread *akrasia* – weakness of will in the face of *knowing* what is good – under the device paradigm. And again, one avenue of an antidote for *akrasia* consists in attaining to the right habits, fostered in practices and communities.

Second, making complexity a mark of excellence, Borgmann employs the principle to offer one among more normative criteria concerning the practices and their relative quality. Why not call playing "Defender" (Borgmann's 1984 example), or in early 2020s, playing CS:GO, a focal practice on an equal footing with fly fishing, and celebrate that, as it is increasingly done in eSporting events? Indeed, a case can be made that playing CS:GO does require skills of speed, endurance, discernment and cooperation that in certain respects match and exceed those involved in fly fishing or cooking a meal from the ground up. In wanting to motivate the "considered judgment" (1984, p. 214) of ranking fly fishing higher in terms of the required skills and knowledge, he has to qualify the concept of complexity being appealed to in the principle. Borgmann here seems to opt for the number of skills and forms of knowledge involved in a practice. The fly fisher relies on knowledge about seasons, of the hatching of insects, water movements as well as sophisticated hand movements, and Borgmann can count more forms of skill at work when one excels in fly fishing than what he could in the computer games and cultures of work surrounding computers which he discussed in 1984.[23]

---

23 One can discuss whether his counting is correct and no wholesale criticism of computer games is implied in Borgmann's philosophy of technology. Only, they will have to enter and shape the social and material fabric of individuals, families and communities in a way that engages individuals in more of their capacities. Siyahhan & Gee (2018) provide a fascinating insight into the lives of families playing computer games, and how these can shape and foster forms of engagement. Borgmann does discuss the practice of those who "devote their lives to the design and construction of computers" (1984, p. 216). He finds it flawed as a focal practice: it has unhappy social arrangements and is largely disembodied. To the counter that so is poetry, Borgmann suggests that poetry allows us "to comprehend the world more fully and so are empowered to inhabit it more appropriately" (1984, p. 217). Aspects of Borgmann's indictment of computer culture, based on Kidder (1981), are largely borne out by the more recent ethnographic study of coders, found in Thompson (2019).

So far, we have explored the more Aristotelian inspired aspects of the good life. Finally, the trout is able to orient one's environment in ways that a computer game rarely can. This is the more Heideggerian inspired answer to the good of focal practices and things, suggested by this analysis of fly fishing: "The trout is a focus of the health and fertility of a drainage or even of a continent" (1984, p. 216). In exploring this topic of orientation, Borgmann repeatedly returns to the architectural themes that also occupied Heidegger. One gains orientation and a sense of one's environment through focal practices, while the device paradigm characteristic of technologically advanced cultures makes us lose our sense of direction. In his exploration of the architectural themes, Borgmann offers a linguistic excavation of his own. Borgmann reminds us that the expression "to orient something" is a linguistic remnant from a historical, overarching focal thing: the church building. To orient something would mean to build a church "with the longer axis due east and west, and the chancel or chief alter at the eastern end" (1984, p. 79). While a thing centres one's life by making different elements fit together in a meaningful whole, the device has a disorientating effect. The medieval church or the Greek temple were structures that their users could rely on for orientation as they gathered and disclosed the land. Not so with the typical modern office tower. Though massive and imposing, it has none of these features. It "is not accessible either to one's understanding or to one's engagement" (1984, p. 67), and "stands as a metaphor for the whole society desire for independence from its natural setting" (Socolow 1976, cited in Borgmann, 1984, p. 67). In this way, the machine-like nature of the gas boiler is also found in architecture, and what they share Borgmann again puts under the heading of "machinery". To Borgmann, his criticism is clearly expressed in Le Corbusier's dictum that a house is a machine for living in, and Borgmann finds architectural examples of "functional indifference" or "radical invariability" (2003) also in shopping malls. One can easily imagine one way of getting luxury goods (at the mall) replaced with another (online shopping). Borgmann suggests that this functional indifference of the mall, frequently being coupled with designers' "attempts to give malls and shopping centres a striking spatial or historical appearance", (2003, p. 49) is the cause of what he calls mall nausea. The disorientation from a modern, technological structure fits the pattern of the device paradigm. Unlike a thing that orientates, most eminently exemplified by the Parthenon, "high rise towers... disclose themselves through their refusal to disclose a world" (2010, p. 14).

Borgmann holds little hope for a similar orienting power to emanate from modern examples of monumental technologies. In 1984, he discussed what some commentators have described as the cathedral-like structure of the Robert Rathbun Wilson Hall at Fermilab and the significance of the launch of the first space shuttle. He found that these marvels compare unfavourably with the cathedral. While the intricate principles of construction of all three are intransparent to laymen, the construction of a cathedral – lasting generations – would be more open to the surrounding community. More importantly, while it is possible to find significance in space travel and fundamental physics, Borgmann insists that they do not engage communities and individuals in the same way: "What do these objects tell us about the beginning and end of all things? About the order of society and the universe? How can they be comprehended in a profound if unsophisticated manner by ordinary people, and how can such people participate in them firsthand?" (1984, p. 160). With such rhetorical questions, coupled with his suggestion that the increasingly widespread device paradigm is erosive of historical examples of moral training grounds with no comparable substitutes being provided by that paradigm, he joins a number of philosophers in their overall pessimistic view of technology. We now turn to Borgmann's suggestions for a reform.

6.4 Reform and design as antidotes for akrasia

The challenge remains to overcome the rule of technology through the practice of skilled, focal activities. Some focal practices have been instated by a founding act, such as the eucharist and the communion, which were commanded to be practised regularly. Christianity, in a sense, was privileged by having clearly identifiable sources of opposition, allowing the young religion to steel itself. In contrast, the device paradigm is harder to identify as the pervasive and mighty opposing force it is. The device paradigm has no founding act or clear hierarchical, social structure, and devices do not present the same moral urgency as violent persecution or as the process of working out your salvation with fear and trembling. At a general level, the challenge becomes that of initiating practices and guarding the often humble and scattered existing ones.

A reform of technology must recognise and challenge the device pattern itself, rather than suggesting a reform within the paradigm. This latter kind of reform would mean procuring more of a good, such as energy combined with low levels of atmospheric CO_2, or equality in distributions of goods. A reform *of* technology does not address such problems in their own right. Borgmann's thinking seems to be that if one takes care of the small, local things, then the global ones will take care of themselves. Focal practices disclose the significance of things and humans, and as such "engenders a concern for the safety and wellbeing of things and persons...both locally and globally" (1984, p. 220). The reform would protect and sustain focal practices while restraining devices to their prop-

6.4 Reform and design as antidotes for akrasia — 147

er place of sustaining a functioning everyday life. The rowers can take their car to the rowing club and the boats, but they would likely buy cars that protect the environment that they enjoy in their focal practice. The challenge becomes "to distinguish what on moral and cultural grounds should be recovered and what should be left to technological devices" (Borgmann, 2010, p. 16).

These are the personal aspects of a reform. They focus on the personal sphere, that of the family and its material, technological environment – the home. As for politics, Borgmann's suggestions remain probing, and are offered at the level of cities and larger infrastructures. Though focal practices and things each have their particularity and rarely co-exist in any single life, a companion to the Aristotelian principle – apparently overlooked by Borgmann – would be a first step for a more general recognition: "As we witness the exercise of well-trained abilities by others, these displays are enjoyed by us and arouse a desire that we should be able to do the same things ourselves" (Rawls, 1971, p. 428). To the extent that this is true, it could undergird a general appreciation of, and discourse about, focal practices beyond one's own, if any. Borgmann distinguishes wealth (arising from focal practices) and affluence (as measured in GDP or equivalents) and suggests that social justice is a matter of redistributing monetary affluence to allow for wider access to the wealth that focal practices offer. Likely, a reform of the paradigm would go against its *raison d'être* of making goods available efficiently. Consequently, a reform of the paradigm would mean less affluence in areas of our lives, making the question of redistribution pertinent.

In contrast with Heidegger's thought, humans are not restricted to pointing to existing or forgotten practices and *Gelassenheit*. As suggested by the Churchill principle, design is an ethical endeavour. Corresponding to our judgment of excellence in professions that procure health, education and justice, Borgmann proposes that "we think of design as the excellence of material objects" (1995, p. 13). The task of design becomes twofold: it is partially a conservative trusteeship, concerning historical modes of dwelling and being engaged, partially a more creative artisanship that seeks to create an engaging material culture. Borgmann frequently reflects on the design of cities. The device paradigm is most clearly seen and felt in cities, and also here, Borgmann counsels engagement, contrasting culture as something one takes in, typically in pristine, historic cities, with something one engages in. Infrastructural edifices should have an intelligible design, allowing for modes of dwelling, such as walking, running, sitting, resting, shopping and beholding from different angles. Celebrations, small and large, should be encouraged and designed for, gaining a central place in cities.[24]

---

[24] There are many forms of celebrations and things to celebrate. In addition to religious cele-

Working as a philosopher, Borgmann does not fill out much of scientific, practical or empirical detail, but offers the contours of the task for designers: making ethics real by attending to the way things not just *can*, but generally *will* make us do certain things in a certain way. While the device paradigm rarely presents itself in the form of a moral crisis, *akrasia* is a moral failing that can present an opportunity for a designer to sustain the good life. *Akrasia* is often experienced on the background of deep matters of concern, and empirical studies revealing *akrasia* can be a starting point for designers to change tack from asking how users can be disburdened, to how they can be burdened in the right way. This should clearly not be a matter of making life burdensome for the users, for the sake of it. Nor should it be a matter of scripting behaviour, so that one ends up doing the right thing, largely as the result of the design of *e.g.* speed bumps or seat belt warnings. Rather, it should be a matter of designing environments and things in ways that respect human excellence. This would make easy the choice of taking on burdens of engaged and absorbed practices of caring for focal things.

Borgmann extends an invitation for designers to engage in conversation with users and communities, and to do so in language more specific than "comfortably vague terms such as 'green space', 'progress', 'family' and above all 'quality of life'" (2006a, p. 134 f). This is perhaps what most clearly sets Borgmann apart from other philosophers, such as Latour and Winner, who have emphasised the moral qualities of artefacts: ethics in its design garb will have to speak more clearly about the homely, focal things of importance to the way that people dwell.

---

brations, our culture frequently entertains celebrations of man's strength in sports. Here, Borgmann praises the central location of Camden Yards Ballpark in Baltimore (1995, p. 21), which contrast with the location of many football stadiums in Europe, placed in driving distance from city centres.

7 John Dewey: The making of tools

7.1 Introduction

What can we know about reality? Thinking about this question with full generality has, since the writings of Kant, been approached by taking into account a subject that in experience exhibits both receptivity and spontaneity, the latter being understood as the "faculty for bringing forth representations itself" (Kant, 1997, A51 / B 75). Among the impressive range of questions that Dewey engaged with, he kept returning to the same kind of questions about human knowledge and reality that Kant treated and have remained at the centre of philosophy ever since. With Dewey, the idea of spontaneity became one of active use of productive skills: human experience, and practical inquiry with its instruments, were pervasive themes in John Dewey's treatment of a range of philosophical questions, including questions related to realism and idealism. While Kant took himself to have affected a Copernican revolution in philosophy, Dewey sought to do for philosophy what Darwin had done for biology. Dewey gave pride of place to an active, constantly adapting organism in a natural environment and applied this outlook to a range of standing questions in philosophy.

In contrast with other founding figures in the philosophy of technology, such as Karl Marx and Martin Heidegger, a would-be reader with an interest in philosophical reflection on technology is not clearly directed to any particular selection of readings in Dewey's extensive writings, and the theme features far less clearly in the reception of Dewey's philosophy than that of Heidegger's and Marx's.[1] Books and articles dedicated to exploring Dewey's view of technology are relatively scant, and, while Dewey's ideas have had an overarching influence in educational science, he is largely absent in the many contemporary discussions of educational technologies, again, in contrast with Marx and Heidegger. One reason for this is likely that it has not been sufficiently considered how Dewey's thought is closer to what Mitcham called an engineering philosophy of technology. In contrast to a humanities philosophy of technology, the engineering

---

[1] *The Cambridge Companion to Dewey* (Cochran, 2010) contains no chapters dedicated to Dewey's conception of technology and does not attempt to identify him as a philosopher of technology of any kind. Hildebrandt's (2003) discussion of realism, antirealism and reception of Dewey has few discussions of technology and the use of tools. The very noticeable exception is the authorship of Larry Hickman, who in several writings has sought to bring into focus Dewey's philosophy of technology (1990) and develop it (2001). Dalsgaard (2014) suggests that key themes of Dewey's align closely with what Dalsgaard calls design thinking.

perspective "begins with the justification of technology or an analysis of the nature of technology itself...[I]t then proceed to find that nature manifested throughout human affairs and, indeed, even seeks to explain both the nonhuman and the human worlds in technological terms" (Mitcham, 1994, p. 62). This means that technology and use of tools rarely become the subject of critical scrutiny in the way it does in the humanities philosophy of technology, but rather acquires an omnipresent quality in Dewey's writings. This perceived lack of a critical approach made Dewey the subject of criticism from a range of thinkers in the humanities tradition, including Marcuse and Mumford.[2] To thinkers in the critical tradition, "instrumental reason" was the entry point for sweeping criticisms of contemporary society and subjectivity. To Dewey, intelligent use of instruments was paradigmatic for how an organism copes with an ever-changing environment.

As a consequence of his overall approach, Dewey never made the kind of dramatic and pessimistic claims about technology that one readily finds in other traditions, and that has long reverberated among academics and intellectuals. Dewey displayed a different mood of thinking, one that sought, also in philosophy, to contribute in its own way to the betterment of humans in the face of an ever-changing and, at times, uncertain environment. He considered technology fundamental in this task: "Technological industry is the creation of science. It is also the most widely and deeply influential factor in the practical determination of social conditions. The most immediate human problem of our age is to effect a transformation of the immense resources the new technology has put in our hands into positive instruments of human being" (LW15, p. 275). While several thinkers in other traditions have bemoaned the encroachment of technological or instrumental modes of thought into other spheres, such as politics or family life, Dewey's version of pragmatism was characteristic in its insistence that the modes of inquiry that have proved successful in science and engineering, should be applied to political and moral problems. He suggested that a role for philosophy could be to aid a "sense of a social calling and responsibility",

---

[2] Under Mumford's heading of "The pragmatic acquiescence" (1926), Dewey was criticised for a pragmatism that put "means at the expense of ends, technique at the expense of moral imagination..." (Westbrook, 1991, p. 382). See also Stemhagen & Waddington (2011) for a helpful discussion. Both Horkheimer (1947) and Marcuse (2011b), in different ways, accused Dewey of succumbing to a narrow focus on instrumental reason. Dewey was aware of this and countered that the emphasis on instruments and practical consequences that were an integral part of his emphasis on inquiry placed little restrictions on the kinds of consequences that could be explored. They could be "aesthetic, or moral, or political, or religious in quality – anything you please" (MW10, p. 366).

making it clear to engineers and scientists that "ideals are continuous with natural events" (MW10, p. 366), and that the use of tools presents us with our best possibilities for the attainment of such goals. The extraction of ore from a mountain was not a regrettable process of human domination and manipulation, but a picture Dewey repeatedly returned to, in order to model human use of language as well as historical changes for the better and the more refined. Contrary to Heidegger's view, manipulation and reduction of objects "from their status of complete objects" as Heidegger would express it, was considered by Dewey as genuine progress in knowledge, particularly when compared with what Dewey suggested was a flawed, Greek understanding of technology.

Influence of Dewey's philosophy has likely been further hindered by the fact that at a late stage mainly is the concept "technology" itself tentatively placed at the centre of Dewey's enormous corpus. Dewey presented the concept as an interpretive key to his thinking: "It is probable that I might have avoided a considerable amount of misunderstanding if I had systematically used 'technology' instead of 'instrumentalism' in connection with the view I put forth regarding the distinctive quality of science as knowledge" (LW15, p. 90, footnote 3). This remark would seem to place science at the centre of his thought, and Dewey did look to science as a model for his concept of an inquiry. Inquiries, however, be they everyday or of a sophisticated scientific kind, are technological through and through. Discussion of, and reference to, the use of tools is seamlessly integrated into Dewey's treatment of many philosophical themes, and his engineering approach to key philosophical questions was ill appreciated by many of his contemporaries. For example, Dewey's discussion of logical operation to be treated in the following section – a key theme in the philosophies of early Wittgenstein and in Russell's thought – is carried out under the title of "Essays in Experimental Logic" and soon involves illustrations and arguments that feature "a variety of wheels and cams and rods which have been invented with reference to doing a certain task" (MW10, p. 353). Later in the same discussion, the question of realism is replaced with one of practical consequences: "We do not measure the worth or reality of the tool by its closeness to its natural prototype, but by efficiency in doing its work... The Theory proposed for mathematical distinctions and relations is precisely analogous" (MW10, p. 356).

Such remarks are typical of Dewey's writings. His quotidian style often lacked the precision that many philosophers take pride in. He brought to entrenched philosophical debates a different perspective, drawing on biology, engineering and holistic forms of philosophy. Seeing unity or sameness across a range of phenomena where others see distinctions and differences was characteristic of Dewey's mode of thought. In particular, the notion of a tool was used to characterise the functioning and development of a simple biological entity as well as the operations of a logician at work. In an analytical fashion to take things out of their context runs counter to the overall tenor of Dewey's thought. Considering phenomena apart from their context – be it historical, biological or social – was one of the fundamental errors that Dewey identified in the thought of those with whom he debated. The failure to take seriously Dewey's use of technological language in his reflection has meant that ideas often associated with other philosophers found an earlier, if not first, expression with Dewey. Specifically, commentators have emphasised themes from engineering and tool use in both Wittgenstein's early and later philosophy of language.[3] As we explore further below, this had long been a central feature in Dewey's philosophical reflections on language. Like Wittgenstein, Dewey sees uniformity of action as a key aspect of an account of language: both in what lies at its organic foundation and the social coordination we hope to achieve by using it.

One can trace two strong currents in the reception of John Dewey's thought. One presents Dewey as a thinker concerned with the nature and importance of education and democracy; the other presents him as a proponent for a pragmatist standpoint in a discussion that, in different guises, continues to vex areas of philosophy: realism and antirealism. In this latter context, Richard Rorty and Hillary Putnam have been influential in developing a stance on realism that claims inspiration from pragmatist philosophers such as Dewey. In the field of education and the learning sciences, Deweyan notions of situation and context have been extremely influential, perhaps most so through the work of Jean Lave's 1988 *Cognition in Practice*. This landmark piece in the science of learning suggested that cognition is distributed across a body and its setting, rather than merely being embedded within them. In Lave's work, the unit of analysis for cognitive science was to be "the whole person in action, acting with the settings of that activity" (1988, p. 17). As we explore below, this reverberates very strongly with Dewey's emphasis on the notion of a situation, and the two thinkers offer the concept of a problem centre stage when understanding cognition.[4]

---

[3] For some early examples, see Nordmann (2002) and Hyder (2002). An issue of *Techné: Research in Philosophy and technology* is dedicated to facets of Wittgenstein's reflections on technology. See Coeckelbergh et al. (2018).

[4] In 1988, the year of the publication of Lave's ethnographically informed book on learning, Ellen Lagemann suggested that "one cannot understand the history of education in the United States during the 20th century unless one realizes that Edward L. Thorndike won and Dewey lost" (1989, p. 185). Two fundamental ideas of Dewey's resurfaced in Lave's extremely influential work. Firstly, the need for studies of learning in contexts other than that of the lab. In "Context and Thought" Dewey would express this more generally in terms of "the fallacy of neglecting context" (LW6, p. 21). Associated with this is the "the analytic fallacy", where one divides a phenomenon up for the purposes of interpretation and control, but frequently overlooks the purpos-

The two currents in Dewey's legacy are reflected in his intellectual background and career. He was trained in Hegelian philosophy as well as an empirical psychologist under G.S. Hall and founded psychology laboratories at Michigan, Minnesota, and Chicago. At the University of Chicago, he developed the Laboratory School and did foundational work in empirical education research. He left Chicago in 1904 and moved to Columbia University. There he joined the philosophy department, which helped shift the focus to problems more squarely located within philosophy, exemplified by his discussion with Bertrand Russell. Naturally, this latter focus, his self-description as well as reliance on ideas from in particular Peirce's statements on pragmatism, locates Dewey's as a pragmatist. The meaning of this, however, is notoriously hard to pin down. In 1908, Arthur Lovejoy could publish "The Thirteen Pragmatisms", and the interpretation of selected themes in Dewey's thought at the hands of pragmatists such as Richard Rorty, Hilary Putnam and Robert Brandom display considerable variety. Menand's study of the Metaphysical Club at Harvard in the 1870's – arguably the birthplace of pragmatism – offers a flavour of the mode of thinking that located technologies at the centre of pragmatism:

> They [Holmes, James, Peirce and Dewey] all believed that ideas are not "out there" waiting to be discovered, but are tools – like forks and knives and microchips – that people devise to cope with the world in which they find themselves. They believed that ideas are produced not by individuals, but by groups of individuals – that ideas are social. They believed that ideas do not develop according to some inner logic of their own, but are entirely dependent, like germs, on their human carriers and the environment. And they believed that since ideas are provisional responses to particular and unreproducible circumstances, their survival depends not on their immutability but on their adaptability. (2001, p. xi f.)

In this characterisation, we see several key aspects of Dewey's thought, that we explore in the sections below. First and foremost, the discussion of reality and the relevance of technologies in addressing the question of realism is what ties the two pragmatist thinkers in this volume – Dewey and Latour – together, and serves as our entry point in section three below. Further, we see in Dewey a continuous reliance on biology in his philosophical outlook. This was integral to his naturalism, according to which all aspects of humans are understood as

---

es of the learners' actions and the history relevant to the context. In both cases, the use of "fallacy" was more a linguistic ploy to attribute fundamental errors to the opponent rather than careful identification of a fallacy. Secondly, the concepts of "situation" and "transformation" were central to Dewey's philosophy: "A higher organism acts with reference to a spread-out environment as a single situation (LW1, p. 214). Dewey used "situation" to speak about all that is involved in a transaction between a human and their environment.

something within nature. Take Rosenberg's dictum, "the universe grows knowers", and add to that the centrality of action, crystallised in Peirce's recommendation of Alexander Bain's definition of belief as "that upon which a man is prepared to act," as central to pragmatism, we then have the main tenor of the naturalistic and action-oriented approach that Dewey brought to philosophy.

From Hegel, Dewey also inherited a holistic approach to thinking, which would lead him to see individual entities as part a whole and their being as a matter of constant becoming. Beginning your analysis of say, experience, with individual entities (such as sense-data), Dewey considered a fundamental mistake. If we place Dewey in a more traditional metaphysical landscape, where entities, structures or events are considered to be what is fundamentally real, Dewey joined the ranks of process-metaphysicists. The philosophical task of matching the idea of a static world – "reality" or "creation" – with the processes of a living organism in a changing, developing world was approached by critically addressing the metaphysical idea of reality. While generally critical of the metaphysical tradition, Dewey did offer his own stance, along the lines of a study of being *qua* being or to Dewey "the most general traits manifested by existences of all kinds" (LW1, p. 412). To Dewey, concepts of events, becoming and change are the most fundamental categories with which to understand nature and reality: constant relationship, contingency and movement are shared features of what exists: "Every existence is an event" (LW1, p. 63). Yet, his interest is not in presenting an argument about what reality at the most fundamental level consists of. When describing metaphysics, he relies on a very consequential, human tool: map making.[5] Metaphysics is "a ground-map of the province of criticism, establishing base lines to be employed in more intricate triangulation" (LW1, p. 310). Ordinary maps are clearly maps *of* something, and Dewey consistently rejected the charge of subscribing to a form of idealism. Dewey emphasised the practical and perspectival qualities of maps. There are no maps of the world that are "a view from nowhere". There are different projections according to human interest, such as navigation over sea (the Mercator projection) or area of land mass (Gall-Peter's projection) or being transported on the underground grid in London (railways with land and places overlaid). It is in its usefulness that the value of a map lies, and in mapmaking, representations of reality and values and interests intertwine very tightly. An important part of their utility consists in making representations that are accurate in respect that they aid the organism in certain challenges or endeavours. Dewey thought that emphasising

---

[5] A Deweyan account of metaphysics as maps of the prototypically real is offered by Boisvert (1998).

malleability and events as lying at the bottom of reality was a more helpful metaphysics to human beings as they construct societies, design education and think up theories.

Below, we turn first to Dewey's engineering approach to logic and then, in the final section, to his discussion of metaphysics. Here, we explore how Dewey's suggestion that the development of the idea of reality – central to discussions of realism and metaphysics – was given an unrealistic expression by Greek philosophers' ideas of construction and tool use.

7.2 The inquiring organism and its tool of tools

While contemporary analytical introductions to realism and antirealism tend to neglect a position clearly identified as the stance of pragmatism or that of John Dewey specifically, one still finds discussion of pragmatism in treatments of theories of truth. In different ways, notoriously treacherous to survey, the topics of truth and what there is are connected, for example by way of truthmaker theory.[6] If utterances, propositions or other truth bearers are true, there is *something* that makes a given sentence true: facts, states of affairs that obtain, objects or some other philosophical term of art that describes reality at a high level of abstraction. At least some of these truths are true independently of the fact that minds are involved in making these statements. They are true *anyway*. In the context of discussion of theories of truth and realism, pragmatism tends to be assigned one of two roles: analytical philosophers with an interest in theories of truth will tend to present a pragmatic theory of truth as one among several non-realist theories of truth, one that is distilled from writings of William James, John Dewey and Charles S. Peirce. Alternatively, pragmatism has been relied upon to reject the whole discussion between realists and antirealists as somehow deeply flawed.[7]

Dewey himself was embroiled in discussions of realism. The more specific question of the reality of logical constants brings out key aspects of Dewey's technology informed approach to the philosophy of language and logic. Mainly in response to themes in Frege's philosophy, Russell and Wittgenstein were developing their views on the nature of logic, which would include the question of

---

[6] See also the treatment of these questions in chapter 5.
[7] Rorty's idea of a "World Well Lost" (1972) and Putnam's internal realism (1981), I take to be examples of this strategy. I have previously argued that Putnam's version of realism, along with many others, remain unclear in its attempt to distinguish internal and external realism (Hansen, 2010, p. 34 ff) and therefore does not achieve what it sets out to do.

the nature and reality of logical constants. For years, Russell held what is called a substantive account of logic: logic is a topic neutral, maximally universal science, dealing with inference. Being a science and offering truths, it requires an ontology. Russell does not offer an exhaustive list of logical constants, but at one point suggests "formal implication, material implication, the relation of a term to a class of which it is a member, the relation of *such that*, the notion of a relation, and truth" (Russell, 1903, p. 11). Opposed to this realist view of logic, his student, Wittgenstein, would claim about his own work: "My fundamental thought is that the 'logical constants' do not represent. That the *logic* of the facts cannot be represented" (1922, 4.0312, his emphasis). Russell's position might seem unusual when we take paradigmatic objects to be physical objects,[8] but furnishing the world with atemporal, abstract objects is a regular feature of the kind of philosophy that Frege, Wittgenstein and Russell helped found.[9]

This sketch of a sophisticated and intricate discussion of the possible logical furnishings of the world suffices to bring into focus, on a number of counts, Dewey's technology-informed approach to philosophy and its problems. In "Logical Objects", Dewey addressed the question of realism that Russell and Wittgenstein had discussed. His approach to philosophical analysis that emphasised the importance of context, would at first sight look like a point of agreement. Frege had originally underscored the importance of considering the meaning of words only in the context of a proposition, making the context principle one of his three fundamental principles (cf. 1884, p. x). Frege believed that at the root of philosophical misunderstandings – such as those he took to be on display in psychologism – lies the failure to take account of this context. The context-principle was, in different ways, adopted by Russell and can be found throughout Wittgenstein's writings. In *Experience and Nature*, and subsequently in "Context and Thought", Dewey also confronted what he saw as an impulse to abstract and consider phenomena apart from, and as independent of, a wider context. With Dewey though, "context" took on a wider significance, in that he took aim mainly at the resistance to seeing things from a developmental or genetic perspective. One of the symptoms of failing to do so was exactly the mode of thought that had informed Russell's thinking and arguably reached a pinnacle in the atomism

---

[8] We can make the same observation as Latour did regarding context: when people speak of objects, they frequently think of a middle-sized object, the size of pumpkin, drawn in the air (recounted in Lave, 1996, p. 22). At a late stage, Quine suggested: "Bodies are assumed, yes; they are the things, first and foremost. Beyond them there is a succession of swindling analogies" (Quine, 1981, §2)." Such remarks suggest an unclarity concerning the concept of an object, and *inter alia*, realism, that Dewey addresses.

[9] For sustained and classic defences, see Hale (1987) and Wright & Hale (2001).

of Wittgenstein's early work: what Dewey called the analytical fallacy. According to this, a phenomenon – such as a valid inference – is decomposed into its parts, while purpose, history and the process of genesis are ignored. This is perhaps the most fundamental difference between Dewey and those with whom he debated about the nature of logic and language. While Russell and Wittgenstein sought to offer an account of ordinary language in terms of logical atoms – elementary propositions that picture the world – and their subsequent composition by means of being subject to logical operators (such as Wittgenstein's N-operator), Dewey would begin his analysis with an inclusive whole, and from there, consider differentiations *within* that whole.

This approach has a range of implications. It matters to the nature of the questions that philosophers set out to answer and how they frame them. Dewey emphasised *The Problems of Men* rather than Russell's *The Problems of Philosophy* (1912). This is not so much a matter of not wanting to do philosophy, but one of pointing to widespread neglect of the genesis and context of the questions in philosophy. Early Wittgenstein seemed to have given representation pride of place in his account of language, though logical operators were not in the business of picturing anything. In contrast, Dewey the naturalist would see language as the tool of a biological being adjusting its practices to cope with its natural and social environment. At the root of thinking was not picturing, nor, as Grice would later give priority, intentions, but problems. Finding out how things are anyway – the view of reality from nowhere – is not the end-station of human knowledge. Rather, a constant process of refining tools as a part of dealing with problems is what humans are engaged in, and modes of abstract philosophical thought finds its worth in so far as they contribute to this process. We turn now to a sketch of Dewey's approach to questions traditionally treated in the philosophy of language, but approached through his notions of problems and inquiries.

Problems arise on the background of an organism being in a contented state of equilibrium. For most of their lives, chickens and humans alike have experiences of being fed and warm, at ease in their environment. They carry out routine activities and have immediate experiences in which they delight rather than reflect. Indeed, much of our experience is unproblematic and not, as such, the subject of reflection or knowledge. We enjoy an evening with friends, we enjoy a painting and we quench our thirst – some of Dewey's paradigmatic cases of experience. Yet, at times, when a problem arises, patterns of action have to be adjusted. Dewey's description of this alters more of the received philosophical vocabulary and we shall briefly explore his definition of an inquiry. What is stable and where an individual "is at home, consistently at one with its own preferences" can become precarious, and the individual somehow becomes "at odds with its surroundings" (LW1, p. 188). For example, I get off the bus in a foreign town, and my GPS devices malfunction. In this way, without a map or a clear idea of my location and how to get to my destination, I do not know my way about, and my environment attains a different and unnerving quality. My habitual modes of action have to be adjusted – "*we* are doubtful because the situation is inherently doubtful" (LW12, p. 110). The problem pertains not to a subject, but to the organism in this particular environment.

While the notions of self-evidence in different ways were central in Frege and early Wittgenstein[10], problems and the uncertainty that go with them are pivotal in Dewey's philosophy and other philosophical concepts – a mind-independent world, certainty, reality, inference, proposition – are relativised to that. In *Essays in Experimental Logic*, Dewey insists that "thinking would not exist, and hence knowledge would not be found, in a world which presented no troubles" (MW10, p. 332)[11]. For example, the concept of an object becomes a matter, not of carving an existing world at its joints, but of making something sufficiently stable to be treated as a means to an end. Objects "present stability, recurrence at its maximum" (LW1, p. 116) and allow for control.

A precarious situation is an opportunity for the organism to refashion the whole of which it is a part. This can be done in more or less fruitful and constructive ways. In *The Quest for Certainty*, Dewey suggests two fundamental modes of response to uncertainty. One is forms of appeasement, where one adjusts to the powers that decide our fate. Among them are forms of magic, self-discipline and general acquiescence in the face of problems. The other way of responding seeks to change the world through the invention of arts (cf. LW4, p. 4f.). This was the ideal response according to pragmatists, and to Dewey, an integral part of this response meant carrying out an inquiry. Dewey developed this concept over more than four decades, and in his 1938 *Logic: The Theory of Inquiry*, he offered this definition: "Inquiry is the controlled or directed transformation of an indeterminate situation into one that is so determinate in its constituent distinctions

---

[10] To wit, one of Wittgenstein's reasons for penning the Tractatus Logico-Philosophicus: "…it is remarkable that so exact a thinker as Frege should have appealed to the degree of self-evidence as the criterion of a logical proposition" (Wittgenstein, 1922, 6.1271). Their concerns, of course, were different than the attempts at foundationalism in epistemology where the idea of self-evidence has played an important role.

[11] As much philosophy has discussed, in pragmatism, the concept of truth becomes relativized to those of a successful inquiry or of warrant. Yet, we can always ask of a successful inquiry if its result is true, which would seem to suggest that the concept of truth extends beyond inquiry. This, Dewey would either condemn as an idle question, or rephrase as a question about future inquiries and the warrant they will offer a given statement.

and relations as to convert the elements of the original situation into a unified whole" (LW12, p. 121).

Inquiry is on more counts a technological activity, as it aims at and actively undertakes change and control of the environment. It does not begin with a doubting subject faced with a world, but a whole situation experienced as being *somehow* wrong. Having gotten off the bus and not knowing my way about, I am yet to consider what exactly the problem is. A second stage of inquiry moves from a situation being indeterminate to "The institution of a problem" (LW 12, p. 112). How a problem is conceived and thought about will shape the next phase of the inquiry. Is it, for example, a problem with the devices in my possession or the satellites they rely on? Is it a problem of navigation, mental wellbeing or of eyesight? To define a problem is "to be well along in inquiry" (LW12, p. 113), as it, in my imagined cases, suggests quite different ways of proceeding. The third stage is a search for possible solutions, where "the first step then is to search out the *constituents* of a given situation which, as constituents, are settled" (LW12, p. 113). Perhaps the correct functioning of the satellites is settled as a fact, which makes the situation slightly more determinate and amenable to formulation of solutions. The fourth stage, reasoning, involves getting clear on key concepts in the hypothesis and finally, active experimentation and observation takes place – getting to a stable situation again through practice and action is the ultimate arbiter regarding the possible product of inquiry: knowledge and subsequent new avenues of contentment and harmonious, consummatory experiences. I might develop a new habit (bringing a paper map) when entering unknown areas by expanding my palette of different tools for navigating through unknown cities. Both in using language to think up new procedures and in testing out plans and hypotheses, tools have a key role. Stability is typically not the order of the day in our environment for long stretches of time, and certainly not in the fundamental processual nature of reality, but something we can aim at creating through invention – a stabilisation created for our purposes.

To Dewey, naturalised logic became a matter of a systematic account of the conditions of the inquiries that the organisms undertake, so that it offers an "important aid in proper guidance of further attempts at knowing" (MW10, p. 23). Tools – among them logic – is simply what the organism uses as a means to resolve the problematic situation and subsequently create knowledge. What is typically conceived as the a priori character of logic is a matter of being a very stable tool. The logical connectives serve us consistently in countless situations: "*If* I do not get my device to work, *then* I must rely on a different tool for navigation". Tools can be organic or extra-organic, physical or mental. Hands, hammers, conceptual maps, modes of inference and metaphysics, can all be tools that aid the organism in a problematic situation. In essence, a stick used as a tool to get one's bearing is not different from an organism developing sensation in order to achieve the same. The human skin is not an important marker when understanding the nature of tools, and neither is the mind, if conceived as an inner state. Further, what a tool is on a given occasion is relative to its use on that occasion to solve this or that specific problem, Finally, what a tool is, is not necessarily defined in isolation from what the goal is. As Dewey formulates it, ends are not absolute, but always ends-in-view. As we saw, as means are developed and situations re-evaluated, the nature of the problem might be refashioned, and means and ends are in that way reciprocal. In many contexts, new means of navigating presents new possibilities and sometimes, new ends.

In Dewey's discussion of Russell's understanding of logical objects, Dewey makes the question one of technical action: "…I assume that inference is an occurrence belonging to action, or behavior, which takes place in the world, not just within the mind or within consciousness…. It belongs in the category where plowing, assembling the parts of a machine, digging and smelting ore belong – namely, behavior, which lays hold of and handles and rearranges physical things" (MW10, p. 92). Dewey's account of logical objects is that just as behaviour like "walking, plowing, eating, blacksmithing, etc. need and evolve distinct instrumentalities, organs, structures for [their successful prosecution], the presumption is strongly in favour of the statement that the operation of inference has its own peculiar characteristic tools and results" (MW10, p. 93). Though there are many differences, Dewey invites us to see a "therefore" as we see a hammer. Losing sight of the useful, pragmatic contexts of making inferences is to Dewey at the root of the question of logical objects, or what he calls the lost souls of philosophical theory.

By turning away from seeing not just logical operators, but also language more generally, as primarily in the business of representing the world or expressing intentions to communicate, and instead seeing logic as "tools of… secure and fertile inquiry" (MW10, p. 96), Dewey relegated the questions of truth and reality, and gave primacy to a different understanding of logic. His naturalistic approach will have him see language quite generally as a matter of a biological entity using tools, while he criticises early analytical philosophy for "…the abstracting of some one element from the organism which gives it meaning, and setting it up as absolute" (EW1, p. 163).

That is not to say that language, with its possibilities of reasoning, representation and expression of intentions was unimportant to Dewey. He considered language the "tool of tools" (LW1, p. 146) for the organism, and Dewey offered an outline of how some signs come to get meaning-bearing qualities. The meaning-bearing qualities of certain physical things, inscription, drives much study of language in the analytical tradition. This is frequently attested by the framing of the question found in introductory chapters in text-books in the philosophy of language: "How do certain sequences of noises or marks, then, have a feature that is both scarce in nature and urgently in need of explanation: that of *meaning something*" (Lycan, 2018, p. 2). To understand Dewey's position on tools, we should consider how tools used by an animal can have the relevant quality of being meaningful.

To Dewey, the process-metaphysicist, both mind and language are emergent properties from lower plateaus of sentient being. Over time, habitual responses arise, and as we have seen, on occasion, modes of response to a situation will have to be reorganised. Habitual actions can become problematic which means that various dispositions in the organism must be rearranged: a disposition to curiously interact with and explore the world – by combining seeing and reaching – becomes at odds with a strong disposition to avoid pain, and the child who holds a finger to the burning candle acts and adjusts its dispositions. This was James' example that Dewey discussed in his famous article, *The Reflex arc*.

Habits of curiosity and pain avoidance will furnish an infant with conflicting responses to a bright object. Experienced pain from the flame will result in one habit of response, curiosity, being fused with a habit of pain avoidance. What characterised the emergence of mind is the ability to separate anticipation and consummation through what Dewey calls "distance receptors". The step from anticipation to consummation is hardly present in lower animals. In contrast with prelinguistic babies and lower animals, fully evolved human beings and higher mammals are characterised by the fact that they can respond also to what is far away in time, so that they act with "reference to a spread-out environment as a single situation" (LW1, p. 214). Dewey contrasts the use of distance receptors of a higher organism with the behaviour of a hen. It is stimulated by the feed-spreading hand to avoid the perceived threat and then by the stimulus to eat. In contrast with higher primates, its behaviour suggests that anticipation and consummation are not kept separate, and no negotiation of habits seem to take place. They shy away as soon as the hand moves, and immediately return for the feed. Dewey discussed the sign that a bird that takes to air offers the rest of the flock. The flock responds to a sign of danger, but we ascribe no intention to the bird that so expresses something to the rest of the flock. The coordinated adjustments of behaviour have adaptive value, but in the bird case, they are based on reactions to stimuli to danger (the first bird) and each other (the flock).

When we add to this mode of simple behaviour a separation in time of event and consequence as well as reliability in patterns of behaviour of others –reflexes and habits – we have the first beginning of language: a tool used to influence the behaviour of others predictably by means of signs for things not immediately present. With increased complexity of the organism comes the ability to see stimuli as something distant that can be represented and considered in the light of problems and alternate causes of action. That is to say, rather than immediately coordinating impulses, organisms can use a tool. "A tool is a particular thing, but it is more than a particular thing, since it is a thing in which a connection, a sequential bond of nature is embodied" (LW1, p. 102). Using tools allows for grasping the temporal step, which opens the possibility of signs being representations of aspects of the environment and representing a situation in order to effect a reconstruction of its objects, is key to several stages of an inquiry.

What characterises a mind is a level of complexity where different habits find their place in ever more complex patterns, and the subordinated habits function as organic instruments. A stimulus to engage in one mode of action – reaching out for the bright object, say – becomes a sign for something else – pain. At the level of mere sentience, phenomena such as the red bull being in a state of anger from seeing red or the infant feeling pain, is a pervasive and vague feature. With the emergence of mind, the organism begins to receive different signs, each in a logical space of possibilities. Brightness goes from being a stimulus that pervades the organism to be a distinct sign for something else. This Dewey exemplifies with the train driver, where seeing red makes up part of a distinct pattern of response (braking the train when seeing red). This pattern – if seeing red, then brake train – will have to be negotiated with other patterns relevant to the situation (keeping the train driving when in motion until station is reached) and possibly, different possibilities of fitting "seeing red" into the situation (the brake lights of a car or a sunset). That is to say, stimuli should not be considered "outside" objects that set in drift a dormant, inactive organism. Responses to events are dependent on the whole milieu where events are found, and part of a situation is an organism with existing, habitual reactions. The act of sensing is developing under the patterns of habitual response into 'seeing-for reaching-purposes' (EW5, p. 99). In reality, seeing and acting (reaching) are closely intertwined rather than substitutes.

Again, representing a situation with the help of distance receptors with a view to rearranging it, is an integral part of the sophisticated inquiries that humans undertake. This is Dewey's entry point for thinking about language with full generality. In contrast with semantic theories of language, pragmatics – what we use language to do – comes before semantics. The temporal structure of the experience of higher primates allows for a range of activities to be seen as instruments, and language, in virtue of its central role in representing the rearranging of a situation, becomes the tool of tools. Many of the problems that animals encounter are problems with other organisms. Much language use arises and is modified in response to questions of social coordination – it has adaptive value for a group of organisms: "Language is always a form of action and in its instrumental use is always a means of concerted action for an end" (LW1, p. 145). Using language to cooperate can help resolve a range of precarious situations.

Reliance on observed patterns in behaviour (such as those associated with gaze and certain noises) might enable some higher primates (e.g. vervet monkeys) to deceive their peers with use of false alarm calls. Yet, it all takes place on the background of seeing patterns in events and in actions among peers. Some tool use is happenstance: in any given situation, we will use a range of hard objects – a stone or a lamp – to put a nail in a wall. Yet, the hammer is the institutionalised tool for carrying this out, and effective language-use likewise requires that its tools become institutionalised: "A stick even though once used as a lever would revert to the status of being just a stick, unless the *relationship* between it and its consequence were distinguished and retained" (LW1, p. 148, Dewey's emphasis). Perhaps the most strongly and consistently institutionalised tools are the logical operators, but language in general is a store of relatively fixed tools for making things happen.

Dewey's understanding of language is more inclusive than typically suggested by both philosophers of language and philosophers of technology: "To be a tool, or to be used as means for consequences, is to have and to endow with meaning" (LW1, p. 146). This conception of a tool runs counter to "text-book instrumentalism"[12]. Text-book instrumentalism typically relies on a conception of a human being with fully formed intentions and desires that are then carried out through reliance on a tool that is in itself devoid of intentionality, meaning and value. To Dewey, being a tool is already to be something that has meaning, and one particular useful kind of tool is linguistic meaning. When something is a tool, it shares with meaningful linguistic signs the temporal distance that allows for an organism to use signs: the split between anticipation and consumption. What exactly the means and the ends are, is something that is analysed after a successful inquiry has been carried out.

So far, this is only a rough sketch of what is being developed into a richer theory of meaning in bio-semiotics and bio-semantics. It will need to address a range of issues associated with a successful theory of language: an account of compositionality and an account of the relation between a singular consciousness and social conventions in language use. To Dewey, such a theory will neither begin with the ascription of mental states, *a la* Grice's theory of meaning

---

[12] This understanding of "instrumentalism" is replicated without being endorsed in Tiles & Oberdiek (1995), Verbeek (2005) and Dusek (2006).

that takes its beginning with communication intentions. Neither would it operate with a ready-made world, fit for being represented, as the starting point for a truth-conditional semantics. Rather, it would look at the needs of an evolving, social entity, and the formation of habits of tool use and consider what adaptive value this tool – language – has for a group of animals. During Dewey's lifetime, perhaps the questions of truth and realism were the most pressing for the philosophical community that interacted with Dewey. A frequent response would be that his account left no room for the intuition that we presented at the beginning of this section: That his understanding of language and mind takes too little account of the ready-made world in which the human mind finds itself. It is to Dewey's concern with the worldly side of the question of realism that we now turn.

7.3 The world well built: a history of philosophers' view of technology and creation

The previous section placed a narrow concern about the reality of logical constants and then language use more generally in a far more encompassing philosophical outlook that emphasised tool use – be it hands, feet or apparatuses – of an organism faced with a problematic situation. To many philosophers, this was an unacceptable relativisation and neglect of the questions that had long been at the centre of philosophy, and much of Dewey's writing consists of efforts to answer and accommodate more traditional philosophical concerns. For example, Dewey's philosophical outlook had him entertain discussions of the reality of the past.[13] Dewey, however, would emphasise that philosophical questions themselves have a history and genesis, and he would bring these aspects to bear in the discussions in ways foreign to much philosophy of his time.

Questions of the past matter as long as they leave traces in present inquiries. Historical understandings of technology are still with us and unearthing them assists Dewey in reconstructing philosophy in a way that makes it more fit for what he took to be its purpose. Regardless of whether one shares the view of philosophy that Dewey subscribes to, his contributions to discussions of realism are interesting in their own right as contributions to the tradition of philosophy concerned with realism. Further, it is a clear source of continuity with Bruno Latour,

---

13 Since then, Michael Dummett has raised the question, from his "The Reality of the Past" (1968) to his 2002 Dewey Lectures (2004). Dewey's discussion of the truth of statements about the past and the reality of the past are found in "A short Catechism of Truth" (MW6) as well as in responses to Arthur Lovejoy's criticisms.

explored in the following chapter. In addition to offering his own, tool-based account of logical operators, Dewey offered a historically informed account of how the question of realism attained such a central role among philosophers as well as scientists.

To Dewey, the source of the question concerning realism is found in incongruent views of reality on one side, and experience and inquiry on the other side. In brief, reality is thought to be fixed, while experience as considered by the tradition is fleeting and the process of inquiry is a constantly ongoing process of reconstructing problematic situations. To Dewey, this discrepancy motivates a history of views of technologies and their role in creating objects. "Creation" is a more religious laden word for one side of the question of realism and truth as correspondence. Dewey was critical of standing conceptions of realism, and he named the pattern of reasoning that led to its positing *the* philosophical fallacy. The fallacy consisted in "the conversion of eventual functions into antecedent existence" (LW1, p. 35). What serves as tools in once problematic situations, perhaps consistently, are converted into something pre-existing that our linguistic practices must measure up against.

Dewey attempts a description of central features of the history of philosophy by detailing how these antecedent existences came to shape our philosophical thinking. This is undertaken by shifting away from looking at "creation" as a noun signifying a complex thing, and rather looking at the tool-informed process of creating. Dewey does not offer what is so frequently seen, namely, a history of technology in terms of phases defined relative to dominant technologies (such as informational or energy technologies), nor the ownership of technologies, as is found in Marx's idea of both pre- and post-capitalist communisms, or indeed, as an epoch of the way Being presences. He considers the ways philosophers have considered the process of making and tool use.

This becomes a history of philosophical views of toolbased making, presented as a matter of stages and moods. Dewey begins his account on a note that offers a nod to the kind of experience that Heidegger emphasised, and which contrasts with technological making: "Human experience in the large, in its coarse and conspicuous features, has for one of its most striking features preoccupation with direct enjoyment: feasting and festivities, ornamentation, dance, song, dramatic pantomime, telling yarns and enacting stories. In comparison with intellectual and moral endeavor, this trait of experience has hardly received the attention from philosophers that it demands" (LW1, p. 70). These activities, and objects, however, reflect what Dewey calls final objects, subject to aesthetic enjoyment with a certain immediacy. "One might think that philosophers in their search for some datum that possesses properties that put it beyond doubt, might have directed their attention to this direct phase of experience, in which objects... are something had and enjoyed" (LW1, p. 73). While the notion of self-evidence had been a major driver in Frege's logical axioms and Wittgenstein's attempt to answer the question of the nature of logic, Dewey underscores that "human interest in the things of sport and celebration is the most conspicuously obvious of all. In comparison, the 'self-evident' things of philosophers are recondite and technical" (LW1, p. 74). Along with this, "useful labor and its coercive necessity" is equally self-evident. In matters of labour, humans turn away from "absorption in direct having" and turn to seeing things in the light of "what it will do to other things – the only way in which a tool or an obstacle can be defined" (LW1, p. 74).

Dewey's account of the philosophical understanding of tools and creation is one of genuine progress from a flawed Greek mode of thinking. Greek thinking is one of the stages of history, and within this stage, Dewey traces significant movement. In short, the problem with Greek thought as handed down to us and in still in operation was that it was carried out by people who were liberated from the *necessities* of providing for comfort and recreation. They held a low opinion of artisans in so far as the philosophers were concerned with truth and knowledge. Borrowing an expression of Latour's, these people where Janus-like thinkers: they relied heavily on the images of production in their thinking, but considered the mode of knowledge involved in production lower than practical and theoretical knowledge. Being engaged with difficult material in a complex and changing world was *demeaned*. I have already mentioned Plato's reference to carving when thinking about conceptual work and its relation to reality. The chapter on Borgmann made brief mention of the technological origin of the concept of character; Aristotle relied on artisans for his analysis of the four causes; the concept of "episteme" is derived from a verb meaning "to be able". This concept, rather than "eidenai" (awareness) or "gignoskein" (acquaintance) was at the centre stage for Greek theories of knowledge.

In spite of this use of concepts gathered from intelligent use of tools in the Greek fashioning of philosophy, the background and context of tool use was ignored. In brief, what was left was a consumptive uptake with the products of the craftsmen. The process of the creation of products was ignored by a class of people free from involvement with the means of production, and the relation became one of beholding, and as it is often emphasised: a spectator metaphysics emerged (cf. LW1, p. 78). More specifically, both Plato and Aristotle offered an account of the world in terms of fixed forms apprehended by the mind. To Plato, these forms were wrought by a demiurge – an original artisan – but this craftsman, along with his skills and activities, was then left out of the picture. The result of his work was forever fixed, for dialectically trained *minds* to grasp. Dewey suggested that the word "form" (eidos) had undergone a change from Homeric times, from "shape" or "what one sees" over Herodotus' "type or property" to Plato's form. Plato's model for reality was still that of an artisan – giving "technical structure of the resulting metaphysics" (LW1, p. 79) – but intellectually uprooted from its original setting: forms exist apart from the material and changing world. Theoretical knowledge was not the birth of science, but of philosophy. It offered an account of reality more congenial to minds and logical canons than hands, tools, malleability and precariousness. The model of reality, in being decontextualised from the technical context, was unrealistic.

Due to the organisation of Greek community that separated men and women with different functions, Plato and Aristotle were purely spectators of artisans and their works. As a result, experience afforded no model for a conception of experimental inquiry or of reflection efficacious in action. "In consequence, the sole notability, intelligibility, of nature was conceived to reside in objects that were ends, since they set limits to change" (LW1, p. 81). After having relied on artisans to inform their thinking, "they spurned the things from which they derived their models and criteria" (LW1, p. 91). This mattered in metaphysics: "The social division into a laboring class and a leisure class, between industry and aesthetic contemplation, became a metaphysical division into things which are mere means and things which are ends" (LW1, p. 103). The latter are self-sufficient items that can be known in themselves through reason, while the former can only be known in their subordination to something else. Malleability, manipulation, trial and error all became excluded from knowledge par excellence by a host of extremely influential thinkers. As Hickman puts it: "The Greeks took the task of objectification so seriously that they overshot their mark" (1990, p. 91).

Yet, while failing to engage in practical science such as physics – "born of the... crafts and technologies of healing, navigation, war and the working of wood, metals..." (LW1, p. 106) – the Greek philosophers did take things forward from the times of Homer: "If Greek thinkers did not achieve science, they achieved the idea of science" (LW1, p. 104). "Local" beliefs about natural events were lifted out of their context of occasions of origin and use. Logical relationships became an ideal of inquiry and "thinking was uncovered as an enterprise having its own objects and procedures" (LW1, p. 103). Dewey points to another upside to Greek thinking and experience: Greek experience had moved from a gloomy temper of life, emphasising how the often ill-fated humans were at the mercy of ill-tempered gods – a fate "to be neither bribed with offerings nor yet compelled by knowledge and art" (LW1, p. 105). The sophists and Plato display a different mood. There is misery, but different forms of human knowledge and control can remedy this. As "inventions, tools, techniques of action and works multiply" (LW1, p. 105), the gods recede and worship of them becomes more of a moral matter. Yet, relying on the thought of Gilbert Murray, Dewey suggests that the Greeks would soon lose their nerve, and philosophy would shy away from even their few avenues of making – such as that displayed in designing a Republic – to intellectual work being purely a matter of gaining access to the non-natural realm, exemplified by the reported excesses of scholastic philosophy.

The stage of the modern era made for a return to the following idea: science can be a "resource in world of mixed uncertainty, peril, and of uniformity, stability" (LW1, p. 105). It can control and multiply objects that are fulfilling and good, and at the centre of science lies tools. However, an unfortunate inheritance from the Greeks reared its head in modernity, when the practice of science took shape. Dewey saw many manifestations of it but considered it most fundamentally to be responsible for the attempted pairing of the presumed *objects* of science – the reality that science is about – with human ends and appreciation. How understand the dualism of "nature as a mathematical-mechanical object" (LW1, p. 107) and a sensory world of both ends and freedom? Dewey makes a sweeping suggestion: "If the proper object of knowledge has the character appropriate to the subject-matter of the useful arts, the problem in question evaporates. The objects of science, like the direct objects of the arts, are an order of relations which serve as tools to effect immediate havings and beings" (LW1, p. 111). In this passage, Dewey seeks to establish the antecedent by a comparison with extraction from crude ores. Science and technology here both operate through a "similar operative technique of manipulation and reduction" and "physical science would be impossible without the appliances and procedures of separation and combinations of the industrial arts" (LW1, p. 108). So, should we accept Dewey's focus on the tools in the activity of science, why would the problem from different kinds of dualisms, between nature and human knowledge and consciousness, persist?

Dewey's own favoured explanation lies in the intellectual shadows cast, by Greek theory of knowledge, on modern science: "The notion of knowledge as immediate possession of Being was retained when knowing as an actual affair radically altered" (LW1, p. 110). In short, reinventors of science such as Galileo and Kepler, had been excellent tool makers, creating lenses and smooth inclined planes as tools of inquiry. Also, they had revived the Greek idea of science as one of control but had been poor thinkers when it came to the full implications of their methods of inquiry. In spite of a lively curiosity, ancient science had been about demonstration of "final affairs", while the "life blood of modern science is discovery" and consisted in "knowledge dealing with instrumental objects" (LW1, p. 123) rather than final affairs. What Dewey calls differences in logic accompanied the two understandings of knowledge. Classification and definition were central to the former, and discovery was a matter of subsuming a particular under a universal. To Dewey, the church would find this spectator view of reality congenial and was able to expand the given truths and discuss the acquisition of them – reason and revelation. What was eminently *practiced*, but only dimly understood by the likes of Galileo and Kepler, was that science is an affair of *"making* sure, not of grasping antecedently given sureties" (LW1, p. 124). Of course, sureties – objects – are one of the results of a successful inquiry and may be enjoyed as such. But other inquiries will make these objects themselves become unsure, and ultimately, "[w]hen things are defined as instruments, their value and validity reside in what proceeds from them" (LW1, p. 124). To Dewey, the account that these scientists gave of their work, separating what is known from their skilled use of tools, were deeply at odds with what they practised.

So, given a corrected view of inquiry as a process of transformation of an entire situation, what are we to make of the idea of a ready-made world for science to investigate and track? The constant comeback is that facts, after all, are discovered, and the world is one of objects, and if not, then at least its structures are what our best sciences continue to *latch on to*. Dewey will not deny that existence of *something* prior to any inquiry, but would not equal this *something* with the objects of an inquiry. What does he offer instead to not be entirely open to a charge of idealism? Can we make do merely with different objects resulting from different inquiries that humans make, or does the conception of ourselves in the world not lend itself to something like a view from nowhere of the world *as it is* – "the question at issue is what the real is" (LW1, p. 128).

In *Experience and Nature*, Dewey is willing to concede something to idealism, in so far as it has emphasised "the part played by intelligence" in finding the objects of knowledge. Only, idealism had taken the "work of thought absolutely and wholesale", rather than seeing constant and practical reconstructions based on previous reconstructions. That is to say, Dewey finds that idealism is guilty of "neglect that thought and knowledge are histories" (LW1 p. 127). For example, when speaking about sense-data, constructions from which at the hands of some philosophers have ended in a form of idealism, such thinkers have failed to see both the organic and intellectual developments behind talking about experience in that way.

As indicated at the outset of this chapter, much reception of Dewey has sought to develop an answer to the question of realism. In the following chapter, we go on to suggest that Bruno Latour is an important heir to Dewey's thought. Placing inquiry at the centre of his philosophy, Dewey saw himself as offering a more "empirical empiricism" (MW10, p. 19). Latour has given technologies and their interconnection a key role in his own "more realistic realism". Perhaps more important to Dewey was the spread of the technological approach to human activities embodied in science to other spheres of human activity. Most clearly, in the organisation of democracy and education, but in principle, in any arena of human life – from romance and partnership to climate change – that from time to time presents itself in a way that suggests something is wrong.

8 Bruno Latour: Networks and fabrications

> If gunshots entail, as they say, a "recoil effect," then humanity is above all the recoil of the technological detour.
> (Latour, 2013, p. 230)

8.1 Introduction: from situations to networks

Latour was trained in philosophy and theology in France. He continues to be extremely prolific, and his writings straddle topics typically treated in branches of philosophy, political science, sociology, history and psychology. Integral to his thinking is a fundamental questioning of the way we understand scientific knowledge creation, with its divisions between political, technical, psychological and natural reality, as well as a distinction between facts and values. He has been instrumental in shaping the field of science and technology studies and is considered a co-founder, with Michel Callon, of actor-network theory. While philosophy was infused with themes from biology at the hands of Dewey, Latour can be seen to have introduced to philosophy some of the lessons he learned from a stint as an anthropologist in Abidjan. Working for the Office de la Recherche Scientifique et Technique Outre-Mer (ORSTOM), a development aid agency, from 1973 to 1975, he explored the local understandings of competence and how these views were related to a strong tendency to fill managerial positions with French nationals rather than local Ivoirians. While undertaking empirical studies of technical projects and scientists at work, he has worked at Centre de Sociologie de l'Innovation de École des Mines and, since 2006, the Institut d'Études Politiques de Paris, or Sciences Po. His work attracts interest from a range of disciplines within academia, and it has different strands such as theories of modernity, sociology, and history and philosophy of science.

Latour toys with a range of genres, from that found in Wittgenstein's *Tractatus* to a murder mystery. From his 1979 *Laboratory Life – The Social Construction of facts* to his 2013 *An Inquiry into modes of existence – An Anthropology of the Moderns*, Latour has relied on the imagined figure of the anthropologist studying the convictions, materials and techniques of a foreign people that has its particular convictions, outlook and traditions. In spite of having addressed an unusual range of topics in his career and tried to rethink their mutual relation, Latour reasserts his focus on metaphysics in his 2013 work. In more of his later writings, a question similar to that which Dewey discussed in his interactions with professional philosophy features prominently:

> Everything hinges on the question of CORRESPONDENCE between the world and statements about the world. Some will say that if there is any subject that ethnology ought to avoid like the plague, it is this famous *adequatio rei et intellectus*, at best good enough to serve as a crutch for an elementary philosophy exam. Unfortunately, we cannot sidestep this question; it has to be faced at the start. Everything else depends on it. (Latour, 2013, p. 71. His emphasis)

When addressing this standard question in philosophy, he draws on his extensive studies of the nature and workings of laboratories, considering them a model for understanding both the linguistic and worldly side of the question of correspondence. This is perhaps the clearest way that Latour draws on themes concerning the nature of technology in order to contribute to philosophy. He mirrors Dewey in stressing the importance of a genetic account of philosophical questions, and in discussing both the worldly and linguistic sides of the question of correspondence in that way. While Dewey studied conceptions of reality among philosophers, Latour explores images of reality found among scientists. The situations within which organisms achieve reference to things, in Latour's thinking becomes motley networks of texts and inscriptions that form the background allowing for successful reference

Having studied labs with methods and ideas from history and semiotics, combined with the approach of an anthropologist, Latour's thinking and analysis rely on an enormous range of texts and ideas.[1] To the extent that they come from philosophy, they are mainly from what one still calls "continental" philosophy, and he frequently transforms their ideas to get his own points across. In addition to themes from theology, semiotics and historiography of science also loom large in Latour's thinking. This chapter presents Latour's writings in a rather different constellation from the one he normally finds himself in, when approached as a philosopher. He is presented as a philosopher of technology who has mirrored and developed the approach Dewey brought to questions traditionally treated in philosophy. Like Dewey, Latour discusses both sides of the question of realism. He brought an empirical approach to the question of how reference to things is achieved, particularly in a scientific context. Furthermore, drawing on themes from theology and religion, he has explored the ideas we

---

[1] The excellent biography of Latour offered by Schmidgen (2015) makes clear just how diverse the thinkers and scientists are. They resist categorisation and range from theologians such as Bultmann, studied in his doctorate, to ethnographer Augé, the manager of ORSTOM, during his time of working there, poet Péguy and linguist Greimas. At the University of California, he attends Lyotard's lectures on Nietzsche. Finally, Latour frequently mentions the philosopher of technology, Simondon, with approval. Ideas from such figures, and many others, frequently surface in his writings, and sometimes the ideas are altered or reversed for Latour's purposes.

have of truth production and how these ideas influence the image we carry of what is referred to: reality. This division of topics also shapes this chapter. The second section treats Latour's account of reference to things in a scientific context. His analysis of widespread ideas of the reality, that science is taken to track and discover, concludes the chapter.

Hennion, one of Latour's collaborators at the Center for the Sociology of Innovation where Actor Network Theory was developed, has suggested that themes from pragmatism are helpful when approaching Latour's work (Hennion, 2016). Latour makes use of a Deweyian term of art, inquiry, in the title of and throughout his 2013 work – a work that in many ways summarises the intellectual work that began to take form in the laboratory almost 40 years earlier. In this work, which otherwise mentions very few other thinkers in its printed version[2], Latour frequently relies on the ideas of James. However, when Latour is appropriated by those with a philosophical interest, it is predominantly in light of themes from Heidegger.[3] Associating those two can certainly make for a meaningful approach, and it would seem that Latour has both embraced the comparison and resisted it. While the Heidegger that Latour presents is too out of tune with the one presented in chapter 5, we can use a central idea of Heidegger's both to see the resemblance and to understand Latour's resistance to being associated too closely with Heidegger.[4] Latour begins his inquiry by suggesting that the moderns suffer from homelessness. "The Moderns" is Latour's expression for what he takes to be a widely shared *Weltanschauung* concerning the relations between fact and value, politics, law and science. To Heidegger and Borgmann, homelessness is central to the modern malaise. With his inquiry into modes of existence, Latour wants to draw up a sketch for a new home for the moderns, one that helps them understand the relations between truth production and modes of existence found in technology, politics, poetry, science, morality, or-

---

[2] In an attempt to make the humanities more digital and participatory, the book leads an online life, where those who sign up can comment on the work, and more background material can be assessed.
[3] Harman (2009) is an influential commentator who has approached Latour's work in this way. Riis (2008, 2016) also associates the two thinkers.
[4] At times, Latour seems to ascribe to Heidegger the viewpoint that technology is entirely autonomous: "Man – there is no Woman in Heidegger – is possessed by technology, and it is a complete illusion to believe that we can master it. We are, on the contrary, framed by this *Gestell*, which is one way in which Being is unveiled... Technology is unique, insuperable, omnipresent, superior, a monster born in our midst which has already devoured its unwitting midwives" (1999b, p. 176). No such position emerges from a sympathetic reading of Heidegger, and we can speculate, as Kochan (2010) does, that Latour presents Heidegger in a rather unnuanced way, in order for Latour's own conception of modernity and technology to look more appealing.

ganizations and other kinds of beings that intermingle. He takes the moderns to suffer a "generalized housing crisis" (2013, p. 23) in that they never manage to establish a proper home – a household – in modes of existence such as "the economy" or "the ecology". With Latour, dwelling becomes a matter of reorganising our thinking about these different modes of being, and Latour sounds distinctly Heideggerian when he asks about the moderns: "Why would they wander in the permanent utopia that has for so long made them beings without hearth or home..." (2013, p. 22). Latour's sketch of an intellectual map relating different modes of existence ends up resembling a house with three levels.

These ideas supplement another key concept of Latour's, that of the parliament. As we saw, Heidegger also refers us to the meaning of "thing" – originally the word for a political assembly in Nordic languages. To Heidegger, what the thing assembles is the fourfold, and his concept of dwelling is closely tied to the fourfold. Latour naturally draws on the meaning of the French verb "parler" – to speak – as the background for the word "parliament". He emphasises the many varied voices that are heard in the parliament of the moderns. Below we explore how theoretical entities are given a voice by complex technical and social means. Latour would consider it too reductive that a gathering should be a matter of the fourfold only: "[Heidegger] had only four folds" (2004, p. 235). Latour's account of modes of being – he counts 15 – that intertwine and translate in different ways through networks is more complex. It will presumably allow the moderns to "speak better" – with greater felicity – about the metaphysical outlook they more or less explicitly draw on to understand themselves and their world.

Before modelling Latour's thinking on that of Dewey's in more detail, we note how Latour's writings reiterate and contribute to several of the themes that we have encountered in previous chapters. Langdon Winner explored the notion of giving technology a voice in the form of Frankenstein's monster, pleading with its creator for due care. Winner considered this to be a relevant way of understanding autonomous aspects of complex technological systems and the kind of relation we should have to it. While working at the Center for the Sociology of Innovation, Latour and his assistant Nathanial Herzberg undertook a detailed study of a failed transport system, Aramis. Design and construction of the transport system with platooning carriages was initiated in 1969 and finally abandoned almost 20 years later. Latour's genre-hybrid *Aramis, or the love of Technology* (1996) offers a detailed example of Winner's take on Shelley's work, as Latour documents how managers, engineers and politicians tried to bring a complex system to life. On more than one occasion, the system itself, in the arduous process of coming into existence as a fully-fledged member of Parisian society, is offered a struggling voice of its own. Norbert H., one of the leading investigators of the death of Aramis, reiterates Winner's reading of Frankenstein: "Victor abandons his own creature...The monster is none other than Victor himself" (1996, p. 83). Unlike some of Latour's studies of scientific objects, Aramis concerned a complex network of rails, carriages, computer code and doors, and the role of creator was distributed among a collection of different actors. Latour's mix of murder mystery and sociology concludes that no one person killed off Aramis. It failed to find its place and affection in the collective of things, people and institutions. Or, as Latour would simply call them, actants.

As we explore in the following section, "actant" becomes a basic metaphysical category for Latour. In addition, the concept assists him in reflecting on the question of technological determinism that was explored in chapter 4 – the relation between human agency and mastery, and the imperatives, laws and attempted persuasions that technologies present us with. In contrasting his own thought with that of Heidegger's, Latour changes some of the fundamental premises of the discussion of technological determinism and autonomy. Neither humans nor technological devices should be seen to have a volition of their own when they in fact are joined together. Like Dewey, Latour draws on studies of animals to emphasise that the division of humans as ends in themselves that use means as intermediaries quickly becomes strained, and it is strained in the history of humans as well. "In the wake of pioneering work on chimpanzeean 'industry', we now begin to discover long periods in pre-history when technical ability preceded the emergence of human language by several hundred thousand years. It increasingly seems to be the case that human self-development appeared within a nest or a niche already inhabited by abilities, by know-how and technological objects" (2002, p. 248). Like Dewey, who did not consider the skin as an unfailing point of demarcation between organism and tool, Latour sees in humans and tools actants that combine in different ways, creating new hybrids. This view applies not just on a grand scale. It also applies to the sociological analyses where technological determinism is typically discussed. The principle of symmetry that bids historians and sociologists to apply the same kind of reasoning to both successes and failures in studies of science and technology also applies in discussion of determinism. Rather than seeing human mastery over a tool or the opposite, Latour sees how different actors can combine. Discussing the NRA slogan "Guns don't kill people – people kill people", Latour finds the Heideggerian conceptual tools too crude and wanting. With the gun and the citizen combined, we have a third actant: "The citizen-weapon" or "the weapon-citizen" (cf Latour, 1999, p. 179). Latour calls this kind of technical mediation interference, where two actants create a new actant out of both: "Technologies never truly appear in the form of means" (2002, p. 251).

One would object that the relation still seems asymmetrical between the two original actants. Human actants remain the source of action and ultimately, they build guns, while guns don't build anything. To counter the objection, Latour introduces a second kind of technical mediation between actants: composition. While not implying originality to any of the two, Latour's line of thought is, to a great extent, a reiteration of Winner's argument. With the complex nature of practically any technology, the floor is taken, and no single person rarely designs and builds things. Relying on his concept of competence which he studied in Abidjan, he suggests: "Provisional 'actorial' roles may be attributed to actants only because actants are in the process of exchanging competences, offering one another new possibilities, new goals, new functions" (Latour, 1999, p. 182). As Dewey expressed it, ends are always ends-in-view, and new means will adjust our ends: "If you want to keep your intentions straight, your plans inflexible, your programmes of action rigid, then do not pass through any form of technological life" (2002, p. 252). In addition to black boxes, Latour speaks of a fourth mode of technical mediation: delegation. Speed bumps (in French, "a sleeping policeman", cf. 1999, p. 186) do the work of police officers through the combined, but absent, agency of town officials, people living by the road, engineers and constructions workers, giving their agency presence through a technical delegation. Engineers and designers in particular have the ability to mediate signs and warnings (slow down!) into concrete and pavement. What goes for the absent actors on the road goes for society in general and holds it together: "I live in the midst of technical *delegates*" (1999, p. 189). While Winner discussed avenues of challenging the apparent mastery of complex technological systems, Latour finds that we had better do away with the concept of mastery all together. Rather than being an instrumentalist who ascribes mastery to humans, or a determinist who ascribes mastery to technological systems, modern man in the parliament, always in search of forms of dominance, must learn: "[T]here are no masters anymore – not even crazed technologies" (2002, p. 255).

For our purposes of discussing reference and reality, the immediate context of Latour's thinking is seen to be that of Kuhn's notion of a disciplinary matrix. Kuhn was an early and very influential exponent of a movement that described the nature and development of science *not* in terms of its ability to track the truth about the make-up of the world – the facts. To Kuhn, a disciplinary matrix – or paradigm – is the background on which normal science proceeds. Kuhn famously suggested that scientists working in different matrices "practiced in different worlds" (1962, p. 150). This remark attracted much criticism, which centered on the idea that this amounted to a form of constructivism. While Kuhn denied such implications of his work, Latour has developed Kuhn's thinking in two directions. First, he has thoroughly explored one aspect of Kuhn's concept of a paradigm: the instrumentation it entails. Second, he has not shied away from taking the idea of constructivism seriously. As a consequence, he has faced the same kind of criticism that made Kuhn retract and rephrase his position. Latour is even cited twice in Sokal's (1996) infamous mockery of parts of academia and he ended up being one of the "French targets" in the science wars. On the question of constructivism, however, Latour has doubled down and explored the idea of making and building implicit in the charge of constructivism.

Kuhn made use of the phenomenon of a Gestalt switch, such as that made possible by the duck-rabbit image, to convey the idea of revolutionary leaps in the history of natural science. Latour resists the idea of any big, qualitative changes in the sciences, and rather wants us to have "a stereophonic rendering of fact-making" (1987, p. 100). The two channels allow us to simultaneously hear the kinds of reasons that are offered when science is in the making, as well as the reasoning offered when the facts are made and take on a life of their own – away from laboratories and in the thinking of philosophers and scientists alike. Both products (facts) and technical social processes feature in science, but Latour suggests that the stereophonic sound-image is out of sync when solidified in scientists' understanding of their practice and its resulting descriptions of reality.

In this chapter, we also emphasize a less immediate context as Latour's work is placed in extension of Dewey's. What speaks in favour of this juxtaposition of thinkers who, in many respects, appear unrelated in the history of ideas? Perhaps the strongest thread running through the works of Latour and Dewey is the question of realism and the reliance on the theme of technologies in approaching it. While Dewey offered what he took to be a more empirical empiricism, inspired by developments in biology and psychology, Latour has sought to offer what he calls a "more realistic realism" (1999, p. 15), relying on anthropological methods to explore the tools that are used in science and our views of reality. Both thinkers have taken empirically and scientifically informed approaches to questions in philosophy and placed tools at the centre of their answers to philosophical questions. Dewey explored the philosophical background of ideas of realism among Greek thinkers and its historical development. Latour has been more directly engaged with scientists and their instruments in his exploration of realism. Emphasising the importance of a genetic account, Latour suggests: "If one ever comes face to face with a technical object, this is never the beginning but the end of a long process of proliferating mediators…" (1999, p. 192). While Dewey spoke of and warned against "the conversion of eventual functions into antecedent" (LW1, p. 34) to diagnose a misguided ascription of autonomy to factual discourse as it emerges from a complex process, Latour has drawn on pictures from the study of religions to diagnose a similar movement: scientists create the conditions for actants to emerge and be spoken of, and then treat them like they never had a hand or a tool in this. There is a fetishistic cult of the fact.

Understanding how questions become questions as part of a more inclusive inquiry, for Latour, becomes a matter of undertaking studies of what goes on in the lab, before the point is reached where the facts about reality can be more or less settled, and objects emerge. Finally, at a general level, both Dewey and Latour can be seen to be engaged in modes of holistic thinking in addressing philosophical questions of agency and reality. Dewey saw misguided approaches in philosophy that separate aspects of a situation and ascribe antecedent existence to them, and generally thought that neglect of environmental context was detrimental to understanding both the human subject and their world. Latour also espouses a form of holism. At times, Latour puts it strongly and with full generality: "There is no sense in which humans may be said to exist as humans without entering into commerce with what authorises and enables them to exist" (1999, p. 192). In addressing questions of reality and subjectivity, Latour has given pride of place to networks. As with Dewey, the division between human subjects and their tools is broken down and made relative to that of a situation (Dewey) or a network and forms of technical mediation (Latour). To both Dewey and Latour, being an object is about offering resistance, and to Latour, an object is no stronger – no more real – than the network on which it can draw.

Though Latour in no way seems to have entered the fray of the question of language and reality through engagement with Dewey or other pragmatists, on multiple occasions he ends up debating varieties of the same question; furthermore, he is reported to have been met with the same incomprehension among those who read him. Dewey was met with stark criticism from his colleague in philosophy, Woodbridge, on account of his take on the question of idealism and realism and "antecedent surities".[5] A widely quoted review of one of Latour's key works – *Science in Action – How to Follow Engineers and Scientists through society* – was similarly met with something bordering on ridicule: "Surely, you are joking, Monsieur Latour!" (Amsterdamska, 1990). According to Amsterdamska, the biggest blow to Latour's work would come by establishing that it was a case of social constructivism. Whether or not this criticism ultimately sticks to his work, it is certainly one that Latour wanted to disassociate himself from: the word "social" was omitted from the second edition of his work co-auth-

---

[5] See the account of the exchange on realism between Dewey and Woodbridge in Hildebrandt (2003).

ored with Woolgar, making it *Laboratory Life – The Construction of facts*. If one were to put a label on his thought, technological constructivism regarding scientific objects would be slightly better, though Latour will always emphasise the motley of law, persons, text and materials in the network. It is the instruments and their setting in a lab that plays a pivotal role in Latour's contribution to the question of reference and reality.

Dewey and Latour both wish to place themselves in-between different camps arguing over realism, and considerations of technologically mediated construction play a central role in carving out this position. While meeting similar opposition, Latour and Dewey were far apart when one considers the philosophical tradition within which they worked and were trained. However, there is at least one common ancestry in the work of Gabriel Tarde. Dewey credited him with being instrumental in creating social psychology and with raising awareness of "the necessity for reducing the gross phenomena of social life into minutes events which may then be analysed one by one" (MW10, p. 55). Latour also speaks favourably of Tarde, and Dewey's construal of his significance captures well the spirit and approach of Latour's work.

8.2 The network behind reference to things

To understand the artefacts of different peoples, anthropologist Malinowski would counsel his fellow scientists to get off the veranda and move among the peoples they wished to study. On the veranda, you see decontextualized objects that are frequently misunderstood when seen only on the veranda. Rather, one should see the objects – spears, masks – in their original setting to gain an understanding of the nature of their existence – what they are and what they do. Latour's invitation to follow the work of the neuroendocrinologists at the Salk Institute at La Jolla in the years 1975 and 1976 allowed him to do an ethnography of the making of a scientific fact. After Latour left the research facility where he had carried out his empirical work, the director of the research institute, Roger Guillemin, received the Nobel Prize in Physiology or Medicine together with Andrew Schally, for their discoveries concerning the production of peptide hormones in the brain. Thus, it was, by received standards, a very successful case of science that Latour had studied, though by studying biology, chemistry and neurology, he deviated from the tendency among philosophers to analyse branches of physics, mathematics and astronomy. An aspect of the methodology that was brought to bear on studying the laboratory was that the researcher would systematically inquire about the subjects' own understanding of what they were doing, rather than immediately interpreting the activities of people as a matter of "representing facts" or "engaging in power struggles".

It is this empirical work, along with other studies in science, technology and society, that he draws on in his 1987 *Science in Action – How to Follow Scientists and Engineers through Society* – a work that is key to understanding Latour's later pronouncements on ontology and reference. In the discussion of reference and ontology in his *An Inquiry into the Modes of Existence*, the lab is the "Archimedean point" (2013, p. 147). In terms of metaphysics, the "laboratories are to metaphysics what fruit flies are to genetics" (2013, p. 153). Laboratories make for a particularly clear and useful sample of something more general – both reference to and shaping of what we call reality. When thinking about the linguistic side of the relation between words and things, laboratories are an exemplary way of making clear what is generally the case with reference: "If we have to grant such importance to laboratory studies, it is because they let us see even more clearly how rare and complicated it is to establish a correspondence between the two modes [of words and existence], something that the idea of an *adequatio rei et intellectus* completely concealed" (2013, p. 89).

In his 1987 book, Latour's approach to discussion of reference is two-pronged: he presents what at first sight appears to be a brand of instrumentalism in philosophy of science, while attacking what he takes to be its strongest alternative: appeals to nature or reality. Rather than speak of explanatory strengths of positing the existence of facts, Latour emphasises alliances and the multifarious networks that objects can enter into as they help account for instrument read-outs. The genre appears to be that of a textbook for science and technology studies, and he counsels the would-be student: "We study science *in action* and not ready-made science or technology; to do so, we either arrive before the facts and machines are blackboxed or we follow the controversies that reopen them" (1987, p. 258).

By mentioning instrument read-outs, we have begun close to the *terminus* of Latour's account of scientific facts. Echoing Dewey, Latour insists that the practice of science evolves around making something more or less sure – to change what Latour calls the modality of statements into given facts. While problems were foundational to Dewey, crisis and controversy seem foundational to Latour. It is under such conditions that actants will come into, or fade from, prominence. To stress such adversarial aspects, Latour's account of science in action begins with the figure of a dissenter being offered an unrealistic amount of time and attention from a laboratory director. This doubting character begins by taking issue with the scientific articles where, to many, facts are first encountered simply in virtue of scientific entities being referred to in them. In one of Latour's examples, the presence of an object – a hormone – is being questioned. This quickly leads the dissenter from the scientific text itself into the kind of citation network familiar to any scientist. Scientific articles typically set the stage by citing previous works that function as black boxes: their findings are considered as given facts. The modality of a statement is frequently omitted or simplified when a given paper is cited by one published later, and some facts become so black-boxed that they exist free of a given text: "Who refers to Lavoisier's paper when writing the formula H_2O for water?" (1987, p. 43). The network of texts is one place where the scientific process of *making* sure can be readily observed. Articles can be met with either giving up, going along or re-enacting. Re-enacting with a view to changing the modality of a fact is a costly affair, and it is extremely rare that texts are opened up, taken apart and critically assessed. As Latour suggests, most texts are simply ignored with no uptake from the scientific community, while a small minority are used in other texts as part of their attempts at securing facts. The dissenter can pursue a strategy of cutting off support from previous text to the one being considered and criticised, which, in Latourian terminology, is a matter of making an alliance weaker.

Scientists insist that central claims made in texts – reference to things and facts – originate in the lab, so the dissenter follows the lab director here. Leaving the world of texts, the dissenter is led to one of instruments, guts of guinea pigs and different scientists and engineers at work. The assay, in particular, is what is taken to measure the presence of an object. "The instrument, whatever its nature, is what leads you from the paper to what supports the paper" (1987, p. 69). Disagreement and persuasion – the domain of rhetoric – is now a matter of lab technologies, parts of animals, readouts and texts intermingling in constellations that the dissenter sets out to trace. In this setting, persistent dissent results in the presentation of a physiograph that displays readouts – a curve – from the reaction of slices of guinea pig gut to endorphin, morphine and naloxone. Of course, it doesn't display this to the dissenter, but the scientist assumes the role of a spokesman for the endorphin, pointing to a readout while claiming the presence of the entity in question.

In addition to reference, this is where Latour will speak of representation. In doing so, he echoes Wittgenstein's account of the naming of objects in the Tractatus. Here, Wittgenstein will speak of a name standing in for (*Vertreten*) objects when talking about reference. The German word is frequently used for that of an ambassador speaking on behalf of a nation. Neither hormones nor assemblies of people can speak clearly, if at all, of their own accord, and a relation is established through a complicated set of rules and arrangements that allows for this. When people represent people, these rules are mostly of a social character: only as part of a complex structure like a state can we have an ambassador that speaks on its behalf, and in times of trials of strengths within and between nations, the tie can be broken. When people speak for scientific, theoretical objects, the arrangements allowing for the representing are mainly technical. To Latour, reference to things is a matter of "technical resources that are under [the scientist's] command" (1987, p. 36).

A focal point for all these resources is what Latour calls inscription devices, which he defines as "any set-up, no matter what its size, nature and cost, that provides a visual display of any sort in a scientific text" (1987, p. 68). In addition to the guinea pig ileum assay, examples of instruments are particle accelerators, a tank built in an abandoned gold mine that detects solar neutrinos and entire research institutions providing, through surveys and register data, graphs that say something about, for example, people's voting tendencies or the rate of inflation. This definition makes instruments relative to a given research setup. Some setups will depend on thermometers and Geiger counters – once instruments – that are now typically blackboxed in a research setup, as their measurements are completely uncontroversial. They are intermediate, used in the service of a final read-out that ends up in the text. A primatologist, equipped with pen, paper and binoculars and making notes from observations of baboons, is an instrument.

Watching readouts from a physiograph measuring contractions of a gut being subjected to various substances makes dissent increasingly costly, deadly, messy and technical. Latour's at times humouristic exposition allows for an unrealistic amount of dissent being met with patience from the laboratory director, as various black boxes are questioned and re-opened. Resisting adoption in the disciplinary matrix, the dissenter can in principle turn any black box into fields of contention: machinery for measuring contractions of the gut can be taken apart. The machinery and physics involved in using the high-pressure liquid chromatograph that makes the hormone available for the gut set-up, can be questioned. Again, doing science – being critical of the claims of the scientists, yet engaging constructively – means being involved with an entanglement of, in the first instance, labs, instruments, texts and persons, making Latour at one point use Lyotard's concept "techno-science" for the endeavour of making, questioning and further securing scientific facts.

The dissenter wanted to question claims about the makeup of the world – what there is. Specifically, she questioned whether a certain hormone should feature on the list of what exists. What the systematic doubt has partially reconstructed is the kind of trial of strength that entities undergo, in order to be considered part of the fabric of the world, of reality. Latour uses the same concept that was the focal point of his studies of managers in Abidjan, competence: "[E]ach performance [presupposes] a competence which retrospectively explains why the hero withstood all the ordeals" (1987, p. 89). In his African study, he had deconstructed the concept of competence as an explanation for the performance of European and African workers, respectively. In so far as the competence becomes the seed for ascribing a pre-existing essence to the theoretical actants in the laboratory, Latour would likely be critical. Yet, Latour uses the concept to capture the action-based foundation of reality: "Tell me what you go through, and I will tell you what you are" (1987, p. 91). A thing – an *actant* – is what it does: it reacts to a range of trials and *is* this list, prior to being given a name: "Endorphin..., *is* this list readable on the instruments in the professor's laboratory. So is a microbe long before being called such" (1987, p. 90).

Facing a well-established opponent, Latour's dissenter has expectedly lost her battle. The spokesperson reading the instrument and the thing has withstood the trial. Should the dissenter wish to continue along her path, she might decide to set up her own lab. Here, she would draw out a different actant, and do as her guide at the first lab did: subject it to a range of trials "imposed on it either by the scientific objector and tradition... or tailed by the authors" (1987, p. 89) and speak on behalf of it to any would-be dissenter and seek alliances in texts and the scientific tradition. This is how establishing reference to things – and *inter alia*, reality – is described by Latour, ranging from mental diseases to transfinite numbers. For example, Cantor gave form to his new objects by "having them undergo the simplest and most radical trial" (1987, p. 90) of one-to-one correspondence. You go from a scientist making himself a spokesman for an actant that is the force behind the inscription on an instrument, and eventually end up meeting no or little dissent and resistance from the scientific community, but uptake in a network of scientific papers.

Latour worked out his 1987 account of science in action while working closely with the director of the Center for the Sociology of Innovation, Callon, to whom *Science in Action* is dedicated. In addition to inscription, the concept of a network increasingly entered Latour's work as Callon and Latour made the concept of actors in networks central to their sociological analyses. To Latour, reference to things cannot be separated from the networked context in which the naming takes place. This is expressed succinctly in Latour's study of Pasteur's discovery of another scientific entity, the microbe: "The word reference designates the quality of the chain in its entirety, and no longer adequation rei et intellectus" (1999, p. 69, emphasis omitted). To understand what secures reference to things, we have to follow an entire network of texts, inscription devices, inscriptions, laboratories, more or less competent engineers, technicians and spokespersons. Together, they make up the historical trials of strength that are entertained between nodes in the network that attract the most attention: the actants subjected to trials and their spokespersons.

With the development of the internet, we have become used to thinking that the information that travels across a network does so untransformed. "Facts and machines are like trains, electricity, packages of computer bytes or frozen vegetables: they can go everywhere as long as the track along which they travel is not interrupted in the slightest" (1987, p. 250). This makes for a contrast with the subject of Latour's early theological work. Here, the inscriptions of Jesus' sayings and their subsequent travel in the Christian tradition regularly require translation. Indeed, one of the motivations for Latour largely abandoning the reliance on networks in his sociology was the development of the world wide web, obscuring some of the points associated with other kinds of networks, where travel requires forms of translation. On the world wide web, technical solutions, such as the transport layer security protocol, are put in place to ensure that the data package sent from one node is identical to the one received at another. However, for scientific-cum-technical networks to safely convey an inscription, it must translate material into a certain fixed form. Achieving this means procuring what Latour calls "immutable and combinable mobiles", and it is the task of what he calls centres of calculation to help offer this. Expressed in graph theory, these centres have a high degree of centralization, and their task is to make the inscriptions "circulate better by increasing their mobility, their speed, their reliability, their ability to combine with one another" (1987, p. 232). Scientists do their convincing through networks, are convinced as part of such and making their work fit for travel is the work of centres of calculation. Not to be confused with contemporary data centres, Latour's expression suggests their task to be the production of something "with the flat surface of a paper that can be archived, pinned on a wall, and combined with others" (1987, p. 227). Latour has in mind institutions like astronomical observatories and official census bureaus. They collect traces and inscriptions and make them readily available for subsequent use, ensuring stability and long-term use. This is an important role in various shows of force in scientific work.

Anthropological studies of tools, machines, the intricate circulation and citations of scientific texts, calculations centres and spokespersons might seem interesting to some, and their findings unsurprising to those who are already embedded in such networks. What has attracted critical attention from both philosophers and sociologists is the claim that such inquiries have any bearing on the question of reality, and in its more general study, metaphysics. While Kuhn recoiled when it was suggested that he was a constructivist of sorts, Latour did for a long time stick with the claim that, again, "Endorphin..., *is* this list readable on the instruments in the professor's laboratory. So is a microbe long before being called such" (1987, p. 90). To some, this flies in the face of the idea of a ready-made world that the scientist discovers and which offers the most plausible account of the progress of science. Before we delve further into the question of construction and reality in the concluding section, I briefly indicate how Latour's response can be placed in discussions of science and metaphysics.

By calling a scientific entity an actant, Latour has not denied its reality. The sortals by means of which we speak of scientific objects, such as microbes or gravitational rays, are themselves constructed by scientists. As Latour puts it, "[l]aboratories are now powerful enough to define reality" (1987, p. 93). In empirical matters, defining something is not the same as making it exist. Once described and being assisted in making an inscription in a sophisticated technical setting, the actant is able to enter into the kind of technical, political and societal constellations that makes it interesting to speak of. It resists trials, it makes alliances with other texts and public stakeholders; it has scientists and engineers speak on behalf of it. Only, what gives it sufficient strength is not the kind of disinterested theorising about facts that Latour's Moderns might suggest characterises science. It is a complex network of inscriptions, organizations, politics and people.

This is likely to leave the "realist" objector unsatisfied. Of course, science is a technical endeavour, but the scientific objects are in some sense there, prior to any scientist concocting the list of trials and subjecting the actant to it. Pushing this objection would seem like a demand that we speak of objects prior to them having descriptions associated with them – being defined by laboratories. That is, we are asked to speak of reality without helping ourselves to speaking of *these* kind of waves, microbes, hormones or numbers – to speak of them, before any scientist gives them their name and sortals in a form which in turn translates into a list of trials. To demand this is an invitation to engage in metaphysics – to speak of reality with full generality, apart from any particular region of what exists. Latour could abstain from this task, claiming that his work is fully in line with anti-metaphysical, naturalist strands of thought in analytical metaphysics and philosophy of science.[6] According to naturalism in metaphysics, what philosophy must do when thinking about what there is, is consult the best sciences and remain content with the answers found here. This is what gives us the furniture of the world – our list of what exists.[7] Putting things crudely, the only dif-

---

[6] I have in mind ideas that are critical of metaphysics as a philosophical discipline. The ideas can be traced to Carnap and Quine and have been defended in works by Ladyman & Ross (2007) and Maddy (2007).
[7] The comparison with naturalism in understanding Latour's "empirical metaphysics" (Hämäläinen & Lehtonen, 2016) can throw light on the disagreement that these authors have with Harman (2009) over Latour's metaphysics. Bearing in mind the distinctions between meta-

ference between Latour and naturalists in metaphysics is the character of the science journalism they undertake.

However, Latour has, on some occasions, gone further and attempted to establish a metaphysics – categories describing reality at higher level of generality. One example is his "Irreductions", a terse piece of metaphysics which he refers to as his "Tractatus Scientifico-Politicus" (1988, p. 234), with its form mimicking the style of early Wittgenstein and Spinoza. The exposition of his metaphysics is appended to his analysis of the different alliances between actors in Pasteur's discovery of the microbe. Like Dewey, Latour consistently remains with a kind of event-based metaphysics, with a Nietzsche-inspired concept of force at its centre. They both entertain discussions of the existence of mountains. Latour opens his 2013 work with describing the mode of existence of a mountain, and he would agree with Dewey that "The stablest thing we can speak of is not free from conditions set to it by other things" (LW1, p. 64). If we were to imagine complete stability, it would be "out of the range of the principle of action and reaction, of resistance and leverage as well as of friction (LW 1, p. 64).

At one point, his metaphysics (Latour will later draw on Whitehead's "proposition") has the world consist of actants. It has been called a flat ontology on account of its resistance to received forms of classifications and ontological levels, such as those relying on concepts of the human, scientific, minds, sentience, natural and artificial kinds (Harman, 2009). It is further flat in that to be an actor is not to be an instantiation of some kind of underlying substance. An actor is as an actor does, and force and strength are key aspects of this doing. Force is more a general metaphysical principle than it is a property of human agents. Doing is doing with others, and the strength of a microbe or a research facility is found in the network it is able to rely on, and what it has to compete against. As long as no-one reads your articles or books about other actors, both actors (you and your text) suffer a lack of strength. Again, being cut off from support does not mean not existing, and some theoretical entities proved powerful allies (microbes), while others did not (N-rays). Will the latter, supposedly non-existing entities, re-

---

physics and sciences introduced in chapter 5, I suggest Hämäläinen & Lehtonen conflate the tasks and conceptual tools of science and metaphysics. Science – what Latour studies in action – gives us a list of what exists, the "furniture of the world" by means of the sortals found in science and in this case, defined by laboratories. Saying that they are actants does not add further contents to the world, just as describing chairs as objects doesn't either. Metaphysics is the attempt to say something general about what the sciences describe, which naturally makes the categories different. Metaphysics can serve different purposes, such as explaining continuity between different theories in spite of surface difference in the things they historically have spoken of.

surface to fight another day? They might, as part of a very different network where they can display different kinds of strengths in different trials. Maybe hysteria is making a re-entry in contemporary psychology with different alliances in the form of inscriptions from brain scanners and troubled human beings, and answerable to lists in some ways similar to those it answered in the early 20th century.[8] Theoretical science, from physics to psychology, is the graveyard of theoretical entities. With his metaphysics, Latour has offered an account that can help us understand the development of science – questions that also consume more standard positions in philosophy of science, such as structuralism.[9] If there is a stability in what we speak about, it is a matter of force. "There is *no natural* end to controversies. They may always be reopened [...] In the end, interpretations are always stabilized by an array of *forces*" (1988, p. 197, Latour's emphasis). With the proviso that force is not the exclusive domain of human interaction, we can see how Latour position is far from a predominantly social constructivism.

8.3 Dummett and Latour on primitives and their images of reality

"For [Pasteur], constructivism and realism are synonymous terms" (Latour, 2010, p. 18).

Having followed Latour's dissenter through the lab, he has given us a picture of the actions and technically intricate constructions scientists undertake in order to arrive at successful descriptions of reality. Understanding this in the light of naturalised metaphysics, Latour has fundamentally done what this programme would have us do: take our cue from our best sciences when thinking about what there is. In at least two respects, Latour has likely swerved from this programme. He has gone on to offer a genuine metaphysics that generalised the

---

[8] To come full circle with the theological origin of Latour's interest in texts, on can point to the example of how Martinez-Badía & Martinez-Raga (2015) trace a new textual network for ADHD among a range of scientific texts from the 18th and 19th century and find evidence of it in the bible. Unfortunately, the paper loses much strength from its relation to a different force, one of predation. It is published by a journal that was once found on the list of predatory publishers compiled by Beall. Beall offered a contentious kind of calculation centre in the form of a filter – one that matters greatly for maintaining the flow in academic networks of texts.

[9] What partially motivates structuralism in philosophy of science is the attempt to account for the change of theoretical entities within the same sciences, primarily branches of physics, combined with the insistence that reality is progressively tracked by theories that speak of different theoretical entities (French, 2014; Frigg & Votsis, 2011).

methods and insights from his study of objects undertaken in the laboratory. Secondly, in line with his stereophonic view of science, he has inquired in far greater detail about the context of discovery when compared with at least some proponents of a naturalised metaphysics.

Writing and speaking of most kinds, involve the ability to orient your language to the listener – imagined or real. The same goes for philosophy, where a select kind of listener is frequently imagined, and based on common ground between listener and speaker, arguments are brought forward to dissuade the listener (or opponent) of his or her stance. Latour has relied on his idea of "A modern", and an oft-cited exchange between a working scientist and Latour has helped Latour frame his understanding of his work and design to his audience. Based on his anthropological study of science, and, not least, the apparent constructivist conclusions, Latour is asked by psychologist: "Do you believe in reality?" In response and upon reflection, Latour takes his task to be that of offering "a more realistic realism" (Latour 1999, pp. 1, 15).

One side of the question of realism, linguistic reference to things, was accounted for in terms of a network of actants – instruments, words, entities and people. A clear example of this network of relations between actants was found with the laboratory as the centre of the network. Thinking about the referents, reality, that science explores, Latour does not want us to see the actions and devices of scientists at work as concerning a different question than that of reality. He asks: "Do we really have to spend another century alternating violently between constructivism and realism, between artificiality and authenticity? Science deserves better than naïve worship and naïve contempt...Ask a physicist to turn her eyes away from the inscriptions produced by her detectors and she won't detect a thing... Only inside the closed walls of her ivory tower does she gain some access to the world 'out there'" (2010, p. 94). By following science in action, the channels in our stereophonic experience ought to align.

But the kind of image that scientists have of reality might have a variety of sources other than their practice. Ultimately, Latour suggests a picture where scientists end up conceiving of facts in what he calls "the acheiropoietic way" (2010, p. 78). This is the idea of Christian icons that miraculously appear with no hands being involved in their creation. A recurrent theme in Latour's works is the forgetfulness of the uncertainty and arduous process that leads to the fabrication of facts in the form of winning trials of strength. Being forgetful, Latour suggest that the scientist, after the process, will display certainty about his work almost purely based on the conviction that reality has spoken. In contrast with appeals to reality, Latour remarks concerning Pasteur's discovery: "The confidence in 'a way laid down' by Pasteur must therefore derive from something other than the facts, hard facts. The confidence was not one that came only

8.3 Dummett and Latour on primitives and their images of reality — 189

from Pasteur, but one that flowed back *on* Pasteur" (1988, p. 28). Central actors in this network were other stakeholders in French public health, and of course, the microbes themselves, as they were being shaped into something that could be seen and controlled. Retrospectively, it is this latter actor that steals the picture. The scientists put on the old side of the Janus face and tend to speak highly and forcefully of facts and reality in accounting for cases of successful practice of science – "nature with us" (1987, p. 94) – rather than the kind of collective that Pasteur was able to draw on.

Different modes of reasoning and persuasion can be required to convince the scientific listener about how to view the two sides of the language-reality relation. To think about reference, Latour introduced the sceptical dissenter. To think about reality, or the world, Latour ultimately draws on themes in studies of religion and something much stronger: the breaking of icons. The theme of religion was suggested by the formulation of the psychologist inquiring about Latour's belief (do you believe in reality?), and Latour recasts the nature of their dispute as one of images of science and reality. The science wars become refashioned as the image wars, and drawing on a comparison with religion, Latour addresses many of the same questions that Dewey did. What is our understanding of things made by hand and the tools in use and how does it measure up with images we have of reality? Dewey struggled to find a position that was both realist and recognised the activities and constructions of an organism in an ever-changing environment. Latour asks: "Is this made or is this real? You have to choose! What has rendered constructivism impossible in the Western tradition?" (2010, p. 81). In asking this, Latour was summing up and generalising a discussion not of scientific realism, but of the significance of Abraham's smashing of the idol shop of his father, as told in the Midrash Rabbah. Rather unusually for large parts of the philosophical tradition's discussion of realism, Latour aligns themes in empirical studies of religion, understandings of criticism and discussion of realism.

To draw Latour's reasoning closer to standing discussions of realism, I now explore how Michael Dummett and Latour have imagined and experienced themselves being met with incomprehension following their pronouncement on reality, and imagined orienting their speech to the character and outlook of the listener they are trying to convince. In doing so, they both rely on the notion of a primitive and concepts related to it, but put these notions to quite different use. Dummett is found in his role as expositor of Gottlob Frege. Frege readily allowed abstract objects on the list of what he thought there is – he was a realist about abstract objects such as the natural numbers. Number are referred to by numerals, who in turn feature in propositions that are uniformly taken to be true and syntactically appear to refer to objects. According to Dummett, that settles the question – numerals refer to objects.[10] Nominalists have objected to the existence of such objects on account of their lack of causal powers, and *inter alia*, the impossibility of causing our sensory apparatus to be affected by them, supposedly rendering knowledge about such postulated objects hard, if not impossible, to come by. In short, abstracts objects tend to become struck off the list of what exists by the nominalist, either because we would have no plausible account of reference, or because abstract objects are thought to be somehow odd or queer when compared with physical or ordinary objects. Replicating Latour's ideas of having too simplistic a view of reference, Dummett suggests: "…the nominalist challenge is a paradigmatic example of what Wittgenstein meant by comparing philosophical perplexity to the bewilderment of a primitive confronted with a sophisticated machine" (1991, p. 182).

Dummett does not combat the misconceptions of moderns, but of nominalists, who are, for different reasons, highly restricted in their view of reality and only allow concrete objects on the list of what there is. Also being met with dissent, Dummett reasons about another abstract object, the Equator:

> What should we say to correct the objector's misunderstanding? He is trying to conceive of the equator as actual object that has been stripped of its causal powers; naturally then, he cannot see what grounds we can have for believing in such an object. We have to teach him that it is an altogether different *kind* of object. We can do that only by patiently explaining to him the use, or the truth-conditions, of sentences containing the term 'the Equator'… When we have given these explanations, he will grasp that there is nothing problematic about the existence of the Equator; that its existence is not a hypothesis, but stands or falls with the proposition that the Earth rotates about an axis. Or, if he does not, we may abandon him to self-congratulation on his resistance to Platonistic superstition. (Dummett, 1991, p. 182)

The Platonistic superstition that Dummett suggests is misleading the nominalist dissenter, is that which concerns the existence of abstract objects. When insisting on reality being fully concrete, the often highly fixed view of reality held by the objector is inspired by an understanding of natural science as being concerned

---

[10] I explore this mode of reasoning in Hansen (2010), and an excellent exposition of this approach to questions of what there is, is offered by MacBride (2003). A traditional exposition of the question of reference to numbers and abstract objects generally relies on Benacerraf's dilemma between having a "consistent semantic" and a "reasonable epistemology" (Benacerraf, 1983, p. 403). On an understanding of epistemology that narrowly takes concepts of a human being with its senses being subject to causation by objects, epistemology speaks against the existence of abstract objects. Latour, at the outset of his study of the lab, would counsel that we "abandon knowledge about knowledge" (Latour, 1987, p. 7).

about non-abstract objects that can impinge, sometimes through instruments, on the sensory apparatus of humans.

An equally relevant Platonistic superstition, or myth, would be that of the public builder, the demiurge, discussed by both Dewey and Latour. I suggest that in both Latour's introductory tale of a meeting with a scientist, as well as the lines written by Dummett, we see how difficult it can be to persuade or reason with an objector about these kinds of beliefs. Both Dummett and Latour's anthropologist explore how to speak correctly about the different modes of existence. But Latour, rather than ultimately abandoning the objector – be it a scientist, nominalist or both – makes more elaborate attempts to further understand and diagnose the impasse that such general discussions of reality can result in. This he does by appeal to the notion of the imagery of primitives and moderns alike. While Dummett's objector is in some respects a simple case, as he insists on the centrality of parsimony or causality in his understanding of reality, Latour expects "a *plurality* of sources of mistakes" (2013, p. 53). Dummett is not engaged in offering the grand reordering of reality that Latour offers in his 2013 work. Yet, they share an interest in clearing up what they take to be misunderstandings about reality by exploring how it is spoken of. In what follows, we shall explore how to speak well about only two modes of existence out of the 15 that Latour identifies, those beings associated with technology and those beings associated with natural science.

First, while Latour draws on pragmatism more than semantics, he and Dummett are largely in agreement on some of the means for helping the objector. Latour finds that the moderns must patiently be explained the modes of truth production in the different modes of existence. Drawing on Austin, Latour speaks of felicity conditions for talking about different kinds of reality, or modes of existence. For Dummett, you have made a kind of category mistake about reality if you think it must always be spoken about – have truth conditions – that suggests we are talking about physical reality. That way, you will misunderstand the reality of the Equator. Latour's modes of being are more detailed and he asks: "why have the Moderns restricted themselves to such a small number of *ontological templates*, whereas in other areas they have caused so many innovations, transformations, revolutions to proliferate? Where does this sort of ontological anaemia come from?" (2013, p. 163). Latour would suggest that the anaemia partially comes from views of natural science as being somehow compartmentalized from considerations of social, legal and technical questions in their pursuit of the task of describing the world as it is. The most general expression of this is Latour's metaphysics. While earlier speaking of reality as a matter of relations of force between actants, in 2013 Latour says that being is relational, or "being-as-other". He contrasts this with "being-as-being", that describes the kind of substance metaphysics that both Frege and Aristotle would, in different ways, espouse (cf. 2013, p. 163). When we approach existence as "being-as-other" we are able to see the different alterations that take place in the network that allows us to speak of things.

Dummett was able to offer guidance for the objector who seemingly misunderstands the nature of language about the Equator because of his simplistic ontological template. What can Latour offer to the Moderns when they speak about the mode of existence he calls [TEC]nology? In 2013, Latour offered advice based on a summary of his positions as we have already encountered them in this chapter. The anthropologist studying the moderns cannot "do justice to technologies with the two patterns of 'Objects' and 'Subjects' as her only resources" (2013, p. 211). Speaking of "the social" and the "technical" will not suffice either: "As if a nuclear power plant, a drone, an eel trap, or a metal saw could be content to maintain itself in existence with the help of elements from two domains, the "social" and the "technological" – and these two alone" (2013, p. 212). Latour provides an answer to the question of definition that was raised in the introductory chapter of this book. There is no domain of technology, and it is, in this way, hard to make out as a mode of existence at all. "The more one studies technological arrangements, the more one considers their ins and outs, the less chance one has of unifying them in a coherent whole" (2013, p. 213). Technology is ubiquitous. Again, doing the slightest things – shifting position on the chair I am sitting on – involves mediation and negotiation of delegates. Talk about technology means talking about experts, economies and much else in the network. As it was learnt from the study of Aramis, this becomes particularly visible in the case of breakdowns and failed technologies. Latour reounts the breakdown of his car, which quickly has him take a detour through a complicated network of actors in order to get his car fixed. In such cases, technology can be clearly seen to be something political, economic, material, human and much more. Delegation and black boxes are everywhere. Only, we forget or we become lazy thinkers (Latour calls it "double click", to suggest the ease with which we expect to acquire knowledge) that only draw on notions of instrumentality, effectiveness or "the social" to understand the domain of technology. As his discussion of actants, means and ends demonstrated, this is much too simplified: "if there is an unworthy way to treat technologies, it lies in believing that they are means toward ends" (2013, p. 219). To speak well of technologies, one has to follow their many detours – one has always "to look beside it" (2013, p. 221) and follow its labyrinthine ways and the cunning of engineers and other actants as you do so. In a play on Heidegger's philosophy, Latour says that technologies are even better hidden than what remains hidden in *Aletheia*, and he also underscores the concept of event in understanding technology. We should not speak of things but use adjectives and adverbs – as in something being a technical issue. To speak of technology, we must speak of the movement of materials, people and ideas – not of a range of technical objects already functioning well. When doing this, what can be said of the mode of existence of technology? The concepts proper to following movements of things, ideas and tinkerers begins with concepts of "'[j]udgment','adjustment,'rectification' [and] 'fresh start'" (2013, p. 227) as applied to those involved in the process of innovation and design.

This is how we should understand the mode of existence of technology. What then of the kind of reality claims made by "realist" scientists? What sources of mistake can be found here? Latour takes issue with "...a violent separation between the theoretical form of life, which takes [the distinction] between objects and subjects seriously, and a quite different practical form of life in which we carry on in peace and quiet, without ever being able to make a definitive distinction between what we make with our own hands and what exists outside our hands" (2010, p. 29). Though often sceptical of the views that scientists have of their own practice, Latour draws out how close considerations of construction and discovery of reality are intertwined in Pasteur's own pronouncements on the nature of his science. Pasteur will speak about establishing facts as a matter of "a stand I am taking in this framework of ideas"; of facts "that cannot be irrefutably demonstrated" but instinctively interpreting "important developments" in a manner "consistent with the general results" and appealing to "the way I see it". Along such, to Latour, constructivist sounding pronouncements, Pasteur will also speak in ways that have a far more realist ring: Anyone "who judges impartially" will recognize that "...fermentation appears to be correlative to life" while competing views are "contradicted by the experiment" (Pasteur, 1922 *Oeuvres réunies par Pasteur Vallery-Radot*, cited in Latour 2010, p. 17 f). To the extent that naturalism is right in looking to natural science rather than philosophy when approaching questions traditionally answered by philosophers, Latour would have them take note of the proximity of pronouncement with a realistic and constructivist ring that come from some scientists as they reflect on their practice.

The final avenue of response to the objector relies specifically on themes from religion and turns Dummett's appeal to the primitive on its head. To Latour, the moderns are the ones who need to relearn the significance of building and constructing and making images. The primitive, used in a pejorative sense, is in fact the modern who has much too crude an understanding of what it means to construct something, and consequently, of the ways reality might be constructed. Though they live in big cities and are surrounded by sophisticated artefacts, "...their idea of creation, construction, production, is so strangely bifurcated that they end up claiming they have to *choose* between the real and the artificial. Anyone who thinks at all like an anthropologist can only remain dumbstruck before this lack of selfknowledge" (2013, p. 160).

Getting a clear view of how scientists, law makers and many others "carry on in peace and quiet", Latour searches for "a plausible passage between fetishism and iconoclasm" (2010, p. ix) and engages in a neologism that combines the concepts of fetish and fact: factish. In a grand historical overview, ranging from the Old Testament iconoclasm, over enlightenment rejection of old regimes, exemplified by Feuerbach's argument explored in chapter two, to Nietzsche's heralding of modernity with his philosophising with the hammer, Latour sees criticism as the smashing of images. When the amulet carrying, catholic Portuguese conquerors met with primitives, the Portuguese called their handmade objects of worship "feitiço" stemming from the Portuguese "to do, to make". In 1760, Charles de Brosses invented the word "fetishism", and associates the word with "fairy-objects" in his description of African religions. Latour underscores how neither primitives, Portuguese, nor moderns are image free. However, the primitives do not hide away the construction process in their religion and, as a consequence, refuse to see the dichotomy that moderns foist on them: real or constructed?

Rather than engaging in anti-fetishistic ridicule of the way the primitive is projecting his own powers onto the religious artefacts, what can the Moderns learn from the primitives' frankness about the constructed nature of their divinities, made of stone and wood? First, while created, the fetish does exert power: "how could anyone deny the efficaciousness of an object that is capable of so many prodigious feats" (2010, p. 9). Of course, the fetishist is accused of being mistaken by the origin of power. According to the anti-fetishist, the power lies with the human subject, and power should be restored to its rightful owner. However, with Latour's studies of the networks behind reference, he rejects the image of anti-fetishism as a simple matter of restoring power to the subject that has been somehow duped and mastered by its own creation. The power will have to be returned to a dispersed cloud of actors, to a collective, not one master.

What then of the distinction between facts and fetishes? This is the crux of the conviction of the moderns: the will and ability to detect the former sets them apart. Again, relying on the stage setting that Pasteur professes to engage in, Latour sees the original ambiguity of "fact", also at work in the French "le fait", as both "what somebody has fabricated" and "what no one has fabricated". The same will apply to the German "Tatsache". Linguistic evidence combined with evidence from his empirical studies of science leads Latour to conclude: "Facts are fabricated!... Whereas we fabricate them in our laboratories with our colleagues, our instruments, and our hands, facts are supposed to become, by some magical effect of reversal, something that holds up against any change..." (2010, p. 18). To remedy the double talk, Latour suggests we use the word "factish" to designate "a means of passage to establish continuity between human work and the ferment's independence" (2010, p. 19). Again, Latour will insist that his neologism is not driven by a wish to take sides in the science wars or prematurely seeing reality a certain way, for example as a matter of power struggles being settled. Latour insists that it is a matter of being able to give an account of successful science. Here, Latour finds little use of a distinction between facts and fetishes. The talk of belief that the scientist engages in when inquiring about Latour's belief in reality stems from an utter divorce of practical tool use and theoretical life, which forces a hard choice between facts and fetishes. Like Dewey's Greek philosophers disregarded practical life, Latour's Moderns suffer a form of belief in acheiropoieta – images made without hands. He suggests that the charge of fetishism, understood as being ruled by objects of your own making, completely fails to capture the practice of "primitive religions" or the work of artists and authors. Similarly, the idea of facts with no human hand in their making fails to capture the practice of scientists and their results. Once one "begins to size up practice" (2010, p. 20), primitives and moderns sound alike in their relation to their factishes. Their images are made, they are at times repaired and on occasion, smashed. This contrast with the kind of image that Latour calls "freeze-frame" characteristic of the acheiropoietic, realist scientist. Freezeframe amounts to extracting "an image out of flow, becoming fascinated by it... as if all movement had stopped" (2010, p. 84). Latour insists that he is not trying to drag down science by comparing their creation with those people believing in fairy-objects and constructed, religious icons. He is pulling everyone up: "Who knows most about paying equal respect to facts and fetishes? Why, obviously, those who have always gotten their factishes to say that they are used as passages for what goes beyond them when they are being constructed" (2010, p. 33).

Latour is unlikely to have offered an account of science that will persuade philosophers of science. Though religious, literary and scientific discourse may all create things that go beyond the creator, an insistence on the cumulative aspects of science, combined with the idea that they exhibit still greater explanatory powers, will likely leave the philosophers of science dissatisfied with the notion of factishes and actants. Yet, Latour has offered an intriguing account of the belief in reality among scientists and philosophers alike. Like the primitives, scientists create images. Latour counsels that their image of reality should be informed by actual studies of their own practice, as it reaches through complex networks to a focal point in laboratories in order to say something about reality.

Bibliography

Achterhuis, H. (2001). Introduction. In R. P. Crease (Trans.), *American Philosophy of Technology: The Empirical Turn*. Bloomington, Indiana: Indiana University Press.
Aitken, M. (2010). Why we still don't understand the social aspects of wind power: A critique of key assumption within the literature. *Energy Policy, 38*, 1834–1841.
Akrich, M., & Latour, B. (1992). A summary of a convenient vocabulary for the semiotics of human and nonhuman assemblies. In J. Law & W. E. Bijker (Eds.), *Shaping Technology/Building Society. Studies in Sociotechnical Change* (pp. 259–264). Cambridge, MA: MIT Press.
Albrechtslund, A. (2007). Ethics and technology design. *Ethics and Information Technology, 9*(1), 63–72.
Anderson, M., Anderson, S. L., & Armen, C. (2005). Towards Machine Ethics: Implementing Two Action-Based Ethical Theories. In M. Anderson, S. L. Anderson, & C. Armen (Eds.), *Machine Ethics* (pp. 1–7). AAAI Press.
Amsterdamska, O. (1990). Review: Surely You Are Joking, Monsieur Latour! *Science, Technology, & Human Values, 15*(4), 495–504.
Annas, J. (2011). *Intelligent Virtue*. Oxford: Oxford University Press.
Arendt, H. (1958). *The Human Condition*. Chicago: University of Chicago Press.
Aristotle. (1976). *Nicomachean Ethics* (J. A. K. Thompson, Trans.). London: Penguin Books.
Arthur, B. W. (2009). *The Nature of Technology: What It Is and How It Evolves*. New York: Free Press.
Athanassoulis, N. (2013). *Virtue Ethics*. London: Bloomsbury Publishing.
Babbage, C. (1835). *On the Economy of Machinery and Manufactures*. Londong: Charles Knight.
Barney, D. (2004). The Vanishing Table, Or community in a World That is no World. In A. Feenberg & D. Barney (Eds.), *Community in the Digital Age* (pp. 31–52). Oxford: Rowman & Littlefield Publishers.
Beard, C. A. (1927). Time, technology, and the creative spirit in political science. *The American Political Science Review, 21*(1), 1–11.
Benacerraf, P. (1983). Mathematical Truth. In P. Benacerraf & H. Putnam (Eds.), *Philosophy of Mathematics* (Second edition). New York: Cambridge University Press.
Bendick, R., & Borgmann, A. (2017). Explanation in philosophy and the limits of precision. *AI & Society, 32*, 164–174.
Beniger, J., R. (1986). *The Control Revolution: Technological and Economic Origins of the Information Society*. Harvard University Press.
Besmer, K. (2014). Dis-Placed Travel On the Use of GPS in Automobiles. *Techné: Research in Philosophy and Technology, 18*(1/2), 133–146.
Biesta, G. J. J. (2010). *Good Education in an Age of Measurement: Ethics, Politics, Democracy*. London and New York: Routledge.
Bimber, B. (1990). Karl Marx and the three faces of technological determinism. *Social Studies of Science, 20*(2), 333–351.
Blackburn, S. (2000). Enquivering. *The New Republic, 30*, 43–48.
Blok, V. (2017) *Ernst Jünger's Philosophy of Technology: Heidegger and the Poetics of the Antropocene*. New York, NY. Abdingdon, Oxon: Routledge.

Boisvert, R. D. (1998). Dewey's Metaphysics: Ground-Map of the Prototypically Real. In L. A. Hickman (Ed.), Reading Dewey: *Interpretations for a Postmodern Generation*. Bloomington: Indiana University Press.

Borgmann, A. (1973). Functionalism in Science and Technology. In *Proceedings of the XVth World Congress of Philosophy* (Vol. 6, pp. 31–36). Sofia, Bulgaria: Sofia Press Production Center.

Borgmann, A. (1984). *Technology and the Character of Contemporary Life: A Philosophical Inquiry*. Chicago: University of Chicago Press.

Borgmann, A. (1995). The Depth of Design. In R. Buchanan & V. Margolin (Eds.), *Discovering design* (pp. 13–22). Chicago, Il.: The University of Chicago Press.

Borgmann, A. (1999). *Holding On to Reality. The Nature of Information at the Turn of the Millennium*. Chicago and London: University of Chicago Press.

Borgmann, A. (2003). *Power Failure: Christianity in the Culture of Technology*. Grand Rapids: Brazos Press.

Borgmann, A. (2004). Is the Internet the Solution to the Problem of Community? In A. Feenberg & D. Barney (Eds.), *Community in the digital age* (pp. 53–67). Oxford: Rowman & Littlefield Publishers.

Borgmann, A. (2005, August 1). *What Things Do: Philosophical Reflections on Technology, Agency, and Design*. Retrieved from https://ndpr.nd.edu/news/what-things-do-philosophical-reflections-on-technology-agency-and-design/ Accessed on 17.01.2020

Borgmann, A. (2006a). *Real American Ethics*. Chicago and London: Chicago University Press.

Borgmann, A. (2006b). Technology as a Cultural Force: For Alena and Griffin. *The Canadian Journal of Sociology*, 31(3), 351–360.

Borgmann, A. (2010). Enclosure and disclosure on content and form in architecture. *AI & Society*, 25, 11–18.

Borgmann, A. (2015a). Knowledge and Conversation. *The Information Society*, 31(2), 212–222.

Borgmann, A. (2015b). The force of the wilderness within the ubiquity of cyberspace. *AI & Society*, 32, 261–265.

Bozdag, E., & van den Hoven, J. (2015). Breaking the filter bubble: democracy and design. *Ethics and Information Technology*, 17, 249–265.

Brey, P. (2010). Philosophy of Technology after the Empirical Turn. *Techné*, 14(1), 36–48.

Campanella, T. J. (2017). *How low did he go?* Retrieved from Citylab website: https://www.citylab.com/transportation/2017/07/how-low-did-he-go/533019/ Accessed on 17.01.2020

Carnap, R. (1932). Überwindung der Metaphysik durch logische Analyse der Sprache. *Erkenntnis*, 2, 219–241.

Castells, M. (2010). *The Rise of the Network Society* (Second edition). Wiley-Blackwell.

Cochran, Molly, ed. 2010. *The Cambridge Companion to Dewey*. Cambridge: Cambridge University Press.

Coeckelbergh, M., Funk, M., & Koller, S. (2018). Wittgenstein and Philosophy of Technology: Introduction. *Techné: Research in Philosophy and Technology*, 22(3), 287–295.

Cohen, S. A., & Hopkins, D. (2019). Autonomous vehicles and the future of urban tourism. *Annals of Tourism Research*, 74, 33–42.

Collingridge, D. (1980). *The Social Control of Technology*. London: Frances Pinter.

Crawford, M. B. (2009). *Shop Class as Soulcraft: An Inquiry into the value of Work*. New York: Penguin Press.

Csikszentmihalyi, M. (1991). *Flow: The Psychology of Optimal Experience*. New York: Harper.

Cutrofello, A. (1993). Must we say what "we" means? The Politics of Post-modernism. *Social Theory and Practice, 19*, 93–109.

Dalsgaard, P. (2014). Pragmatism and design thinking. *International Journal of Design, 8*(1), 143–155.

Davidson, D. (1986). A nice derangement of epithats. In E. Lepore (Ed.), *Truth and Interpretation: Perspectives on the Philosophy of Donald Davidson*. Oxford: Basil Blackwell.

Dennett, D. C. (1971). Intentional systems. *Journal of Philosophy, 68*, 87–106.

Descartes, R. (2006). *A Discourse on the Method* (I. Maclean, Trans.). Oxford: Oxford University Press.

Desmet, K., & Parente, S. L. (2014). Resistance to technology adoption: The rise and decline of guilds. *Review of Economic Dynamics, 17*(3), 437–458.

Dohn, N. B., & Hansen, J. J. (2018). Design in educational research – clarifying conceptions and presuppositions. In N. B. Dohn (Ed.), *Designing for Learning in a Networked World* (pp. 37–59). Oxon, Abingdon; New York: Routledge.

Dubos, R. (1968). *So Human an Animal: How We are Shaped by Surroundings and Events*. New York: Scribner.

Duhigg, C. (2012). *The Power of Habit*. New York: Random House.

Dummett, M. A. E. (1968). The Reality of the Past. *Proceedings of the Aristotelian Society, New Series 69*, 239–258.

Dummett, M. A. E. (1991). *Frege: Philosophy of Mathematics*. Cambridge, MA.: Harvard University Press.

Dummett, M. A. E. (2004). *Truth and the Past*. New York: Columbia University Press.

Duplessis, R. S. (1997). *Transitions to Capitalism in Early Modern Europe*. Cambridge: Cambridge University Press.

Dusek, V. (2006). *Philosophy of Technology: An Introduction*. Wiley.

Edwards, P. (2004). *Heidegger's Confusions*. Amherst: Prometheus Books.

Eldred, M. (2009). *The Digital Cast of Being: Metaphysics, Mathematics, Cartesianism, Cybernetics, Capitalism, Communication*. Frankfurt: Ontos Verlag.

Fandozzi, P. R. (2000). The Moving Image: Between Devices and Things. In E. Higgs, A. Light, & D. Strong (Eds.), *Technology and the Good Life?* (pp. 153–165). Chicago and London: Chicago University Press.

Feenberg, A. (1988). The Bias of Technology. In R. Pippin, A. Feenberg, & C. Webel (Eds.), *Marcuse: Critical Theory and the Promise of Utopia*. Bergin and Garvey Press.

Feenberg, A. (1992). *Critical Theory of Technology*. Oxford: Oxford University Press.

Feenberg, A. (1995). *Alternative Modernity*. Berkeley: University of California Press.

Feenberg, A. (1999). *Questioning Technology*. London: Routledge.

Feenberg, A. (2001). Whither educational technology? *International Journal of Technology and Design Education, 11*, 83–91.

Feenberg, A. (2005). *Heidegger and Marcuse: The Catastrophe and Redemption of History*. New York and London: Routledge.

Feenberg, A. (2010). Remembering Marcuse. In D. Kellner & C. Pierce (Eds.), *Philosophy, Psychoanalysis and Emancipation: Collected Papers of Herbert Marcuse*. (Vol. 5). London; New York: Routledge.

Feenberg, A. (2017a). *Technosystem: The social life of reason*. Cambridge, MA: Harvard University Press.

Feenberg, A. (2017b). The online education controversy and the future of the university. *Foundations of Science, 22*(2), 363–371.

Feenberg, A., & Bakardjieva, M. (2004). Consumers or citizens? The Online Community Debate. In A. Feenberg & D. Barney (Eds.), *Community in the digital age. Philosophy and Practice* (pp. 1–28). Oxford: Rowman and Littlefield.

Feuerbach, L. (2008/1841). *The Essence of Christianity* (G. Eliot, Trans.). New York: Dover Publications.

Fichte, Johann. G. (2009/1806). *Characteristics of the Present Age*. Gloucester: Dodo Press.

Fitzpatrick, K. (2011). The digital future of authorship : Rethinking originality. *Culture Machine, 12*, 1–26.

Flanagan, M., Howe, D. C., & Nissenbaum, H. (2008). Embodying values in technology: Theory and practice. In J. Van den Hoven & J. Weckert (Eds.), *Information Technology and Moral Philosophy* (pp. 322–353). Cambridge: Cambridge University Press.

Floridi, L., & Sanders, J. W. (2004). On the morality of artificial agents. *Minds and Machine, 14*, 349–379.

Floridi, L. (2013). What is a philosophical question. *Metaphilosophy?, 44*(3), 195–221.

Fogg, B. J. (2003). *Persuasive Technology: Using Computers to Change What We Think and Do*. San Francisco, CA: Morgan Kaufmann.

Forty, A. (2005). *Objects of Desire: Design and Society since 1750*. London: Thames and Hudson.

French, S. (2014). *The Structure of the World: Metaphysics and Representation*. Oxford: Oxford University Press.

Frege, G. (1884). *The Foundations of Arithmetic. A logico-mathematical enquiry into the concept of number* (Second rev). Oxford: Basil Blackwell.

Friedman, B., & Hendry, D. G. (2019). *Shaping Technology with Moral Imagination*. Cambridge, MA. London, England: MIT Press.

Friedman, B., Hendry, D. G., & Boring, A. (2017). A survey of value sensitive design methods. *Foundations and Trends (R) in Human-Computer Interaction, 11*(23), 63–125.

Friedman, B., Kahn, P. H., & Borning, A. (2006). Value sensitive design and information systems. In P. Zhang & D. Galletta (Eds.), *Human–computer interaction and management information systems: Foundations* (pp. 348–372). New York: M. E. Sharpe, Inc.

Friesen, N. (2011). The Lecture as a Transmedial Pedagogical Form: A Historical Analysis. *Educational Researcher, 40*(3), 95–102.

Frigg, R., & Votsis, I. (2011). Everything you always wanted to know about structural realism but were afraid to ask. *European Journal for Philosophy of Science, 1*(2), 227–276.

Frischmann, B., & Selinger, E. (2018). *Re-engineering humanity*. Cambridge University Press.

Gallie, W. B. (1956). Essentially Contested Concepts. *Proceedings of the Aristotelian Society, 56*, 167–198.

Gandesha, S. (2004). Marcuse, Habermas, and the critique of technology. In W. M. Cobb & J. Abromeit (Eds.), *Herbert Marcuse: A Critical Reader* (pp. 188–208). New York: Routledge.

Geerts, R.-J. (2017). Towards a Qualitative Assessment of Energy Practices: Illich and Borgmann on Energy in Society. *Philosophy & Technology, 30*(4), 521–540.

Gibson, J. J. (1979). *The Ecological Approach to Perception*. London: Houghton Mifflin.

Grossman, H. (1929). *The Law of Accumulation and Breakdown of the Capitalist System. Being also a Theory of Crises*. London: Pluto Press.

Gunkel, D. J. (2018). The other question: Can and should robots have rights. *Ethics and Information Technology, 20*(2), 87–99.

Habermas, J. (1970). Technology and science as ideology. In *Toward a Rational Society*. Boston: Beacon Press.

Hadot, P. (1995). *Philosophy as a Way of Life* (M. Chase, Trans.). Oxford: Blackwell.

Hale, B. (1987). *Abstract Objects*. Oxford: Basil Blackwell.

Hämäläinen, N., & Lehtonen, T.-K. (2016). Latour's empirical metaphysics. *Distinktion: Journal of Social Theory, 17*(1), 20–37.

Hamilton, E., & Feenberg, A. (2005). The technical codes of online education. *Techné, 9*(1), 97–123.

Hansen, S. B. (2010). *The Existence of God. An Exposition and Application of Fregean Meta-Ontology*. Berlin & New York: De Gruyter.

Hansen, S. B. (2012). Metaphysical nihilism and cosmological arguments: Some tractarian comments. *European Journal of Philosophy, 20*(2), 223–242.

Harman, G. (2009). *Prince of Networks: Bruno Latour and Metaphysics*. Melbourne: re.press.

Harvey, D. (2006). *The Limits to Capital*. London and New New York: Verso.

Haworth, L. (2000). Focal Things and Focal Practices. In E. Higgs, A. Light, & D. Strong (Eds.), *Technology and the Good Life?* (pp. 55–69). Chicago and London: University of Chicago Press.

Hegel, G. W. F. (1977). *Phenomenology of Spirit* (A. V. Miller, Trans.). Oxford: Clarendon Press.

Heidegger, M. (1966). *Discourse on Thinking* (J. M. Anderson & E. H. Freund, Trans.). Harper & Row.

Heidegger, M. (1968). *What is called thinking?* (J. G. Gray & F. D. Wieck, Trans.). New York, Evanston and London: Harper & Row.

Heidegger, M. (1971a). Building, dwelling, thinking. In A. Hofstadter (Trans.), *Poetry, Language, Thought*. Harper & Row.

Heidegger, M. (1971b). Origin of the work of art. In A. Hofstadter (Trans.), *Poetry, Language, Thought*. New York: Harper & Row.

Heidegger, M. (1971c). The thing. In A. Hofstadter (Trans.), *Poetry, Language, Thought*. New York: Harper & Row.

Heidegger, M. (1971d). What are poets for? In A. Hofstadter (Trans.), *Poetry, Language, Thought*. New York: Harper & Row.

Heidegger, M. (1974). *An Introduction to Metaphysics* (R. Manheim, Trans.). New Haven: Yale University Press.

Heidegger, M. (1977a). The age of the world picture. In W. Lovitt (Trans.), *The question concerning Technology. And other Essays*. New York and London: Garland Publishing.

Heidegger, M. (1977b). The turning. In *The Question Concerning Technology, and other essays*. New York: Harper & Row.

Heidegger, M. (1982). *The Basic Problems of Phenomenology* (A. Hofstadter, Trans.). Bloomington & Indianapolis: Indiana University Press.

Heidegger, M. (1996). *Being and Time:* (J. Macquarrie & E. Robinson, Trans.). Oxford UK & Cambridge (USA): Blackwell.

Heidegger, M. (1998a). Introduction to what is metaphysics. In W. McNeill (Ed.), *Pathmarks*. Cambridge: Cambridge University Press.

Heidegger, M. (1998b). Letter on humanism. In W. McNeill (Ed.), & F. A. Capuzzi (Trans.), *Pathmarks*. Cambridge: Cambridge University Press.

Heidegger, M. (1999). *Contributions to Philosophy (from Enowning)* (P. Emad & K. Maly, Trans.). Bloomington & Indianapolis: Indiana University Press.

Hennion, A. (2016). From ANT to Pragmatism: A Journey with Bruno Latour at the CSI. *New Literary History, 47*(2), 289–308

Hickman, L. A. (1990). *John Dewey's Pragmatic technology.* Bloomington: Indiana University Press.

Hickman, L. A. (2001). *Philosophical Tools for Technological Culture: Putting Pragmatism to Work.* Bloomington, Indiana: Indiana University Press.

Hildebrand, D. L. (2003). *Beyond Realism and Antirealism: John Dewey and the Neopragmatists.* Nashville, TN.: Vanderbilt University Press.

Hjort, P. S. (2012). *Besat af Vind [Occupied by wind].* Copenhagen: Saxo.

Horkheimer, M. (1947). *The Eclipse of Reason.* New York: Continuum.

Hursthouse, R. (2011). What does the Aristotelian phronimos know? In L. Jost & J. Wuerth (Eds.), *Perfecting Virtue: New Essays on Kantian Ethics and Virtue Ethics* (pp. 38–57). Cambridge: Cambridge University Press.

Hyder, D. (2002). *The Mechanics of Meaning: Propositional Content and the Logical Space of Wittgenstein's Tractatus.* Berlin & New York: Walter de Gruyter.

Isaacson, W. (2014). *The Innovators: How a Group of Hackers, Geniuses and Geeks Created the Digital Revolution.* New York: Simon and Schuster.

Ihde, D. (2008). The designer fallacy and technological imagination. In P. E. Vermaas, P. Kroes, A. Light, & S. A. Moore (Eds.), *Philosophy and Design: From Engineering to Architecture* (pp. 51–59). Amsterdam: Springer.

Jeansonne, G. (2006). *A Time of Paradox: America Since 1890.* Oxford: Rowman and Littlefield.

Joerges, B. (1999). Do politics have artefacts? *Social Studies of Science, 29*(3), 411–431.

Johnston, S. F. (2018). Alvin Weinberg and the Promotion of the Technological Fix. *Technology and Culture, 59*(3), 620–651.

Kant, I. (1997). *Critique of Pure Reason* (P. Guyer & A. W. Wood, Trans.). Cambridge: Cambridge University Press.

Kellner, D. (1984). *Herbert Marcuse and the Crisis of Marxism.* Berkely; Los Angeles: University of California Press.

Kellner, D. (2000). Crossing the Postmodern Divide with Borgmann. In E. Higgs, A. Light, & D. Strong (Eds.), *Technology and the good life?* (pp. 234–255). Chicago and London: Chicago University Press.

Kellow, A. (1996). *Transforming Power: The Politics of Electricity Planning.* Cambridge: Cambridge University Press.

Kidder, T. (1981). *The Soul of a new Machine.* Boston: Little, Brown and Company.

Kitchen, M. (2015). *Speer: Hitler's Architect.* New Haven: Yale University Press.

Kochan, J. (2010). Latour's Heidegger. *Social Studies of Science, 40*(4), 579–598

Konishi, K., & Bohbot, V. D. (2014). Spatial navigational strategies correlate with grey matter in the hippocampus of healthy older adults tested in a virtual maze. *Frontiers in Aging Neuroscience, 20*(5).

Kuhn, T. S. (1962). *The Structure of Scientific Revolutions.* Chicago: University of Chicago Press.

Kurzweil, R. (2005). *The Singularity is Near: When Humans Transcend Biology.* London: Viking Penguin.

Lachney, M., & Dotson, T. (2018). Epistemological Luddism: Reinvigorating a concept for action in 21st century sociotechnical struggles. *Social Epistemology*, *32*(4), 228–240.

Lagemann, E. C. (1989). The Plural Worlds of Educational Research. History of Education Quarterly, 29(2), 185–214.

Lanier, J., & Sequin, C. (2007). Hyperseeing the regular Hendecachoron. *Proc ISAMA 2007*, 159–166. Texas A&M.

Latour, B. (1987). *Science in Action – How to Follow Scientists and Engineers through Society*. Harvard University Press.

Latour, B. (1988). *The Pasteurization of France*. Cambridge, MA: Harvard University Press.

Latour, B. (1996). *Aramis, or the love of technology* (C. Porter, Trans.). Cambridge, MA. London, England: Harvard University Press.

Latour, B. (1999). *Pandora's Hope: Essays on the Reality of Science Studies*. Cambridge, MA. London, England: Harvard University Press.

Latour, B. (2002). Morality and Technology. The End of the Means (C. Venn, Trans.). *Theory, Culture & Society*, *19*(5/6), 247–260.

Latour, B. (2004). Why Has Critique Run Out of Steam? From Matters of Fact to Matters of Concern. *Critical Inquiry*, *30*, 225–248.

Latour, B. (2010). *On the Modern Cult of the Factish God*. Durham and London: Duke University Press.

Latour, B. (2013). *An Inquiry into Modes of Existence. An Anhropology of the Moderns* (C. Porter, Trans.). Cambridge, MA. London, England: Harvard University Press.

Lave, J. (1988). *Cognition in Practice: Mind, Mathematics, and Culture in Everyday Life*. New York: Cambridge University Press.

Lessig, L. (1999). *Code: And other laws of cyberspace*. New York: Basic Books.

Levine, N. (2012). *Marx's Discourse with Hegel*. Basingstole: Palgrave Macmillan.

Lovejoy, A. O. (1908). The Thirteen Pragmatisms. *The Journal of Philosophy, Psychology and Scientific Methods*, *5*(1 and 2), 5–12, 29–39.

Lukács, G. (1923). *History and Class Consciousness: Studies in Marxist Dialectics*. Merlin Press.

Lycan, W. G. (2018). *Philosophy of Language: A contemporary Introduction* (Third). London and New York: Routledge.

MacBride, F. (2003). Speaking with Shadows: A Study of Neo-Logicism. *British Journal for the Philosophy of Science*, *54*(1), 103–163.

MacIntyre, A. (1970). *Marcuse*. London: Fontana/Collins.

MacIntyre, A. (1981). *After Virtue*. Indiana: University of Notre Dame Press.

MacKenzie, D. A. (1984). Marx and the machine. *Technology and Culture*, *25*(3), 473–502. https://doi.org/10.2307/3104202

Mackenzie, D., & Wajcman, J. (eds.). (1985). *The social shaping of technology*. Milton Keynes: Open University Press.

Maley, T. (Ed.). (2017). *One-Dimensional Man 50 Years On: The struggle continues*. Halifax and Winipeg: Fernwood Pub.

Malpas, J. (2008). *Heidegger's Topology: Being, Place, World*. Cambridge, MA: MIT Press.

Marcuse, H. (1941). Some social implications of modern Technology. In Douglas Kellner (Ed.), *Technology, War, and Fascism: The Collected Papers of Herbert Marcuse* (pp. 39–66). Routledge.

Marcuse, Herbert. (1941). *Reason and Revolution*. Oxford: Oxford University Press.

Marcuse, Herbert. (1964). *One-dimensional man: Studies in the ideology of advanced industrial society*. Boston: Beacon Press

Marcuse, Herbert. (1967a). Liberation from the affluent society. In *Collected Papers of Herbert Marcuse: Vol. 3. Herbert Marcuse: The New Left and the 1960s*. London and New York: Routledge.

Marcuse, Herbert. (1967b). The obselescence of marxism. In Douglas Kellner & C. Pierce (Eds.), *Marxism, Revolution and Utopia: Collected Papers of Herbert Marcuse* (Vol 6, pp. 188–195). London; New York: Routledge.

Marcuse, Herbert. (1969). *An Essay on Liberation*. Boston: Beacon Press.

Marcuse, Herbert. (1972). *Counterrevolution and Revolt*. Boston: Beacon Press.

Marcuse, Herbert. (1978). *The Aesthetic Dimension*. Boston: Beacon Press.

Marcuse, Herbert. (1998). Some social implications of modern technology. In Doulglas Kellner (Ed.), *Technology, War, and Fascism: The Collected Papers of Herbert Marcuse: Vol. One* (pp. 39–66). Routledge.

Marcuse, Herbert. (2001). The problem of social change in the technological society. In Douglas Kellner (Ed.), *Towards a critical theory of Society: Vol. Volume 2* (pp. 37–57). London and New York: Routledge.

Marcuse, Herbert. (2005a). Ecology and revolution. In Douglas Kellner (Ed.), *The New Left and the 1960s: The Collected Papers of Herbert Marcuse*. New York: Routledge.

Marcuse, Herbert. (2005b). New sources on the foundation of historical materialism. In R. Wolin & J. Abromeit (Eds.), *Heideggarian Marxism. Herbert Marcuse*. Lincoln and London: University of Nebraska Press.

Marcuse, Herbert. (2009). Philosophy and critical theory. In J. J. Shapiro (Trans.), *Negations: essays in critical theory* (pp. 99–117). London: MayFlyBooks.

Marcuse, Herbert. (2011a). From ontology to technology: Fundamental tendencies of industrial society. In Douglas Kellner & C. Pierce (Eds.), *Philosophy, Psychoanalysis and Emancipation* (pp. 132–140). Oxon and New Y'ork: Routledge.

Marcuse, Herbert. (2011b). Critique of Dewey's Theory of Valuation. In D. Kellner & C. Pierce (Eds.), *Philosophy, psychoanalysis and emancipation.* (pp. 87–91). London and New York: Routledge.

Martinez-Badía, J., & Martinez-Raga, J. (2015). Who says this is a modern disorder? The early history of attention deficit hyperactivity disorder. *World Journal of Psychiatry*, 5(4), 379–386.

Marx, L., & Smith, M. R. (Eds.). (1994). *Does Technology Drive History? The Dilemma of Technological Determinism*. Cambridge, MA.: MIT Press.

Marx, L. (2010). Technology: The Emergence of a Hazardous Concept. *Technology and Culture*, 51(3), 561–577.

Menand, L. (2001). *The Metaphysical Club*. New York: Farrar, Straus and Giroux.

Miles, M. (2012). *Herbert Marcuse: An Aesthetics of Liberation*. London: Pluto Press.

Minsky, M. (1988). *The Society of Mind*. New York: Simon & Schuster.

Mitcham, C. (1994). *Thinking Through Technology: The Path Between Engineering and Philosophy*. Chicago and London: University of Chicago Press.

Mitcham, C. (2000). On Character and Technology. In E. Higgs, A. Light, & D. Strong (Eds.), *Technology and the Good life?* Chicago and London: University of Chicago Press.

Mitcham, C. (2009). Convivial software: An end-user perspective on free and open source software. *Ethics and Information Technology*, 11(4), 299–310.

Mokyr, J. (1990). *The Lever of Riches: Technological Creativity and Economic Progress*. Oxford: Oxford University Press.
Moor, J. H. (2011). The nature, importance, and difficulty of machine ethics. In M. Anderson & S. L. Anderson (Eds.), *Machine Ethics* (pp. 13–20). Cambridge: Cambridge University Press.
Morozov, E. (2014). *To Save Everything, Click Here: Technology, Solutionism, and the Urge to Fix Problems That Don't Exist*. London: Penguin.
Mumford, L. (1926). *The Golden Day: A study in American Experience and Culture*. New York: Horace Liveright.
Mumford, L. (1934). *Technics and Civilization*. New York: Harcourt, Brace & Company, Inc.
Mumford, L. (1964). Authoritarian and democratic technics. *Technology and Culture*, 5(1), 1–8.
Murphy, D. (2016). *Last Futures: Nature, Technology and the end of Architecture*. London & New York: Verso.
Nietzsche, F. (2009). *On the Genealogy of Morals. A Polemical Tract* (I. Johnston, Trans.). Arlington, Virginia: Richer Resources Publications.
Nissenbaum, H. (2001). How computer systems embody values. *Computer*, 34(3), 117–119.
Noble, D. F. (1998). Digital diploma mills: The automation of higher education. *Science as Culture*, 7(3), 355–368.
Norman, D. (1988). *The Design of Everyday Things*. New York: Basic Books.
Nordmann, A. (2002). Another New Wittgenstein: The Scientific and Engineering Background of the Tractatus. *Perspectives on Science*, 10(3), 356–384.
Nye, D. E. (1996). *American Technological Sublime*. Cambridge, MA.: MIT Press.
Nye, D. E. (2006). *Technology Matters: Questions to Live With*. Cambridge, MA.: MIT Press.
Orr, J. E. (2000). Lessons from Frankenstein on technology and society. In T. Cherkasky, J. Grennbaum, P. Mambrey, & J. K. Pors (Eds.), *PDC 2000 Proceedings of the Participatory Design Conference* (pp. 148–155). Palo Alto, CA: CPSR.
Owen, G. E. L. (1986). Logic and metaphysics in some earlier works of aristotle. In M. Nussbaum (Ed.), *Logic, Science and Dialectic: Collected Papers in Ancient Greek Philosophy* (pp. 180–199). Ithaca, N.Y.: Cornell University Press.
Packard, V. (1957). *The Hidden Persuaders*. Longmans, Green and Co Ltd.
Pariser, E. (2011). *The Filter Bubble: What the Internet Is Hiding from You*. New York: Penguin Press.
Parsons, G. (2016). *The Philosophy of Design*. Cambridge: Polity Press.
Pasquale, F. (2015). *The Black Box Society: The Secret Algorithms That Control Money and Information*. Cambridge, MA: Harvard University Press.
Peterson, M., & Spahn, A. (2011). Can technological artefacts be moral agents? *Science and Engineering Ethics*, 17(3), 411–424.
Pinch, T., & Bijker W. (1987). The social construction of facts and artefacts. In W. Bijker, T. Hughes, & T. Pinch (Eds.), *The social construction of Technological systems* (pp. 17–50). Cambridge, MA: MIT Press.
Poel, I. van de. (2013). Translating values into design requirements. In *Philosophy and Engineering: Reflections on Practice, Principles and Proces* (pp. 253–266). Springer.
Poritz, J. A., & Rees, J. (2017). *Education is not an app: The future of university teaching in the Internet age*. Abingdon, Oxon; New York, NY: Routledge.
Putnam, H. (1981). *Reason, Truth and History*. Cambridge: Cambridge University Press.

Quine, W. v. O. (1953). *From a Logical Point of View.* Cambridge, MA.: Harvard University Press.
Quine, W. v. O. (1960). *Word and Object.* Boston: MIT Press.
Rabinbach, A. (1990). *The Human Motor: Energy, Fatigue and the Origins of Modernity.* University of California Press.
Rabinbach, A. (2018). *The Eclipse of the Utopias of Labour.* New York: Fordham University Press.
Rainie, L., & Wellman, B. (2012). *Networked: The New Social Operating System.* Cambridge, MA.: MIT Press.
Rawls, J. (1971). *A Theory of Justice.* Cambridge, MA.: Belknap Press of Harvard University Press.
Rainie, L., & Wellman, B. (2012). *Networked: The New Social Operating System.* Cambridge, MA.: MIT Press.
Riis, S. (2008). The Symmetry between Bruno Latour and Martin Heidegger: The Technique of Turning a Police Officer into a Speed Bump. *Social Studies of Science, 38*(2), 285–301.
Riis, S. (2016). *(Re)associating Bruno Latour and Martin Heidegger: Interdisciplinary investigations in the fields of philosophy, sociology and history.* Roskilde: Roskilde Universitet
Rockmore, T. (1980). *Fichte, Marx and the German Philosophical Tradition.* Southern Illinois University Press.
Roderick, I. (2016). *Critical Discourse Studies and Technology: A Multimodal Approach to Analysing Technoculture.* London: Bloomsbury Publishing.
Rosenberger, R., & Verbeek, P.-P. (2015). Introduction. In R. Rosenberger & P.-P. Verbeek (Eds.), *Postphenomenological Investigations: Essays on Human-Technology Relations* (pp. 1–6). Lexington Books.
Rorty, R. (1972). The World Well Lost. *The Journal of Philosophy, 69*(19), 649–665.
Russell, A., & Vinsel, L. (2016, April 7). Hail the Maintainers. Retrieved from Aeon website: https://aeon.co/essays/innovation-is-overvalued-maintenance-often-matters-more. Accessed on 18.021.2020
Russell, B. (1903). *Principles of Mathematics* (2nd edition). London: Routledge.
Russell, B. (1912). *The Problems of Philosophy.* London: Oxford University Press.
Russell, B. (1945). *A History of Western Philosophy and Its Connection with Political and Social Circumstances from the Earliest Times to the Present Day.* New York: Simon & Schuster.
Russell, D. C. (2009). *Practical Intelligence and the Virtues.* New York: Oxford University Press.
Sayers, S. (1998). *Marxism and Human Nature.* London; New York: Routledge.
Schatzberg, E. (2018). *Technology: Critical history of a concept.* Chicago and London: The University of Chicago Press.
Schultze, Q. J. (2002). *Habits of the High-Tech Heart: Living Virtuously in the Information Age.* Grand Rapids: Baker.
Schmidgen, H. (2015). *Bruno Latour in Pieces: An Intellectual Biography* (G. Custance, Trans.). New York: Fordham University Press.
Searle, J. R. (1995). *The Construction of Social Reality.* New York: Free Press.
Seigel, J. (2005). *The Idea of the Self.* Cambridge: Cambridge University Press.

Selinger, E. (2009). Towards a reflexive framework for development: Technology transfer after the empirical turn. *Synthese, 168*(3), 377–403.
Selinger, E. (2013). *Facebook Home Propaganda Makes Selfishness Contagious*. Wired, (April 22). Retrieved from https://www.wired.com/2013/04/facebook-home-ads-make-selfishness-contagious/ Accessed on 29.03.2020.
Shakespeare, W. (2009). *The Tragedy of Coriolanus* (J. D. Wilson, Ed.). Cambridge University Press.
Sharr, A. (2007). *Heidegger for Architects*. London: Routledge.
Shaw, W. H. (1979). 'The Handmill Gives You the Feudal Lord': Marx's Technological Determinism. *History and Theory, 18*(2), 155–176.
Siyahhan, S., & Gee, E. (2018). *Families at Play: Connecting and Learning Through Video Games*. Cambridge, MA.: MIT Press.
Slaby, J. (2016). Mind invasion: Situated affectivity and the corporate life hack. *Frontiers in Psychology, 7*, 266.
Slaby, J., & Mühlhoff, R. (2018). Immersion at work: Affect and power in post-fordist work cultures. In B. Röttger-Rössler & J. Slaby (Eds.), *Affect in Relation: Families, Places, Technologies*. Abingdon, Oxon: Routledge.
Slaughter, S., & Leslie, L. L. (1997). *Academic Capitalism: Politics, Policies, and the Entrepreneurial University*. Baltimore, MD: John Hopkins University Press.
Small, G., & Vorgan, G. (2008). *IBrain: Surviving the Technological Alteration of the Modern Mind*. Collins Living.
Smith, A. (1776). *An Inquiry into the Nature and Causes of the Wealth of Nations* (S. M. Soares, Ed.). New York: MetaLibri Digital Library.
Smith, B., & Mark, D. M. (2003). Do mountains exist? Towards an ontology of landforms. *Environment and Planning B (Planning and Design), 30*, 411–427.
Socolow, R. H. (1976). Failures of Discourse: Obstacles to the Integration of Environmental Values into Natural Resource Policy. In L. H. Tribe, C. S. Schelling, & J. Voss (Eds.), *When Values Conflict: Essays on Environmental Analysis, Discourse, and Decision* (pp. 1–34). Ballinger Publishing Company.
Sokal, A. D. (1996). Transgressing the Boundaries: Towards a Transformative Hermeneutics of Quantum Gravity. *Social Text*, (46/47), 217–252.
Stemhagen, K., & Waddington, D. (2011). Beyond the "Pragmatic Acquiescence" Controversy: Reconciling the Educational Thought of Lewis Mumford and John Dewey. *Educational Studies: A Journal of the American Educational Studies Association, 47*(5), 469–489.
Sunstein, C. R. (2007). *Republic.com 2.0*. Princeton: Princeton University Press.
Taylor, C. (1991). *The Ethics of Authenticity*. Cambridge, MA: Harvard University Press.
The Virtues Project. (2019). Retrieved from https://virtuesproject.com/
Thierer, A. D. (2010). The Case for Internet Optimism, Part 1 – Saving the Net from its Detractors. In B. Szoka & A. Marcus (Eds.), *The Next Digital Decade. Essays on the Future of the Internet* (pp. 57–87). Washington, D.C.: TechFreedom.
Thompson, C. (2019). *Coders. Who They Are, What They Think and How They Are Changing Our World*. London: Penguin Press.
Tiles, M., & Oberdiek, H. (1995). *Living in a Technological Culture: Human Tools and Human Values*. London: Routledge.
Toffler, A. (1970). *Future Shock*. London: Pan.

Turkle, S. (2011a). Authenticity in the age of digital companions. In M. Anderson & S. L. Anderson (Eds.), *Machine Ethics* (pp. 62–76). Cambridge: Cambridge University Press.
Turkle, S. (2011b). *Alone together*. New York, NY: Basic Books.
Ure, A. (1835). *The Philosophy of Manufactures*. London: Chas. Knight, 1979.
Urquhart, D. (1855). *Familiar Words. As Affecting the Character of Englishmen and the Fate of England*. London: Trubner & Co.
Vallor, S. (2016). *Technology and the virtues: A philosophical guide to a future worth wanting*. New York: Oxford University Press.
van der Laan, J. M. (2016). *Narratives of Technology*. New York: Palgrave Macmillan.
van Wynsberghe, A. (2016). When should we use care robots? The Nature-of-Activities Approach. *Science and Engineering Ethics*, 2, 1745–1760. https://doi.org/10.1007/s11948-011-9343-6
Veblen, T. (1922). *Engineers and the Price System*. New York: B. W. Huebsch.
Verbeek, P.-P. (2002). Devices of engagement: On Borgmann's philosophy of information and technology. *Techné*, 6(1), 69–92.
Verbeek, P.-P. (2005). *What things do: Philosophical reflections on technology, agency, and design*. University Park, PA: Pennsylvania State University Press.
Vermaas, P. E., Carrara, M., Borgo, S., & Garbacz, P. (2013). The design stance and its artefacts. *Synthese*, 190(6), 1131–1152.
Vogel, S. (1996). *Against Nature: The Concept of Nature in Critical Theory*. Albany: State University of New York Press.
Wallach, W., & Allen, C. (2009). *Moral Machines. Teaching Robots Right from Wrong*. New York: Oxford University Press.
Walzer, M. (1983). *Spheres of Justice : A Defense of Pluralism and Equality*. Basic Books.
Weeks, K. (2011). *The Problem with Work*. Duke University Press.
Weiner, L. Y. (1997). There's a great big beautiful tomorrow: Historic memory and gender in Walt Disney's 'Carousel of Progress'. *Journal of American Culture*, 20, 111–116.
Wendling, A. (2009). *Karl Marx on Technology and Alienation*. London: Palgrave Macmillan.
Westbrook, R. B. (1991). *John Dewey and American Democracy*. Ithaca, N.Y.: Cornell University Press.
Whitchurch, C. (2008). Shifting identities and blurring boundaries: The emergence of third space professionals in UK higher education. *Higher Education Quarterly*, 62(4), 377–396.
White, L. (1962). *Medieval Technology and Social Change*. London: Oxford University Press.
Williams, R. (2003). *Retooling: A Historian Confronts Technological Change*. Cambridge, MA.: MIT Press.
Williams, Raymond. (1977). *Marxism and Literature*. Oxford: Oxford University Press.
Winner, L. (1977). *Autonomous Technology: Technics-out-of-Control as a theme in Political thought*. Cambridge, MA.: MIT Press.
Winner, L. (1983). Technē and politeia: The technical constitution of society. In P. T. Durbin & F. Rapp (Eds.), *Philosophy and Technology* (pp. 97–111). Reidel Publishing Company.
Winner, L. (1986a). Decentralization clarified. In *The Whale and the Reactor. A Search for Limits in an Age of High Technology*. Chicago and London: University of Chicago Press.
Winner, L. (1986b). Do artefact have politics? In *The Whale and the reactor*. Chicago and London: University of Chicago Press.

Winner, L. (1995). Political ergonomics. In R. Buchanan & V. Margolin (Eds.), *Discovering Design: Explorations in Design Studies*. Chicago: University of Chicago Press.

Winner, L. (2017a, July 1). *Frankenstein: Giving voice to the monster*. Retrieved from Langdon Winner. On Politics, technology and the arts website: https://www.langdonwinner.com/technopolis/2017/7/6/frankenstein-giving-voice-to-the-monster. Accessed on 18.01.2020

Winner, L. (2017b, July 12). *The cult of innovation: Its colorful myths and rituals*. Retrieved from Langdon Winner. On Politics, technology and the arts website: https://www.langdonwinner.com//other-writings/2017/6/12/the-cult-of-innovation-its-colorful-myths-and-rituals. Accessed on 18.01.2020

Wittgenstein, L. (1922). *Tractatus Logico-Philosophicus* (Transl. C.). London: Routledge & Kegan Paul.

Wittgenstein, L. (1980). *Remarks on the Philosophy of Pscyhology. Vol 2* (G. H. von Wright & H. Nyman, Eds.). University of Chicago Press.

Wittgenstein, L. (1982). *Last Writings on the Philosophy of Psychology. Vol 2* (G. E. M. Anscombe, G. H. von Wright, & H. Nyman, Eds.). Oxford: Basil Blackwell.

Wolin, R. (2001). *Heidegger's Children: Hannah Arendt, Karl Löwith, Hans Jonas, and Herbert Marcuse*. Princeton, New Jersey: Princeton University Press.

Wood, A. (2004). *Karl Marx* (2nd ed.). London: Routledge.

Wrathall, M. A. (2011). *Heidegger and Unconcealment: Truth, Language and History*. Cambridge: Cambridge University Press.

Wright, C., & Hale, B. (2001). *The Reason's Proper Study: Essays towards a Neo-Fregean Philosophy of Mathematics*. Oxford: Oxford University Press.

Wright, K. (1993). Heidegger's Hölderlin and the mo(u)rning of history. *Philosophy Today, 37*(4), 423–425.

Wyatt, S. (2008). Technological determinism is dead; Long live technological determinism. In E. Hackett, O. Amsterdamska, M. Lynch, & J. Wajcman (Eds.), *Handbook of Science and Technology Studies* (pp. 165–180). Cambridge, MA: MIT Press.

Young, J. (2001). *Heidegger's later philosophy*. Cambridge: Cambridge University Press.

Zimmerman, M. E. (1990). *Heidegger's Confrontation with Modernity. Technology, Politics and Art*. Bloomington & Indianapolis: Indiana University Press.

Zuboff, S. (2015). Big other: Surveillance capitalism and the prospects of an information civilization. *Journal of Information Technology, 30*, 75–89.

Zuckerberg, M. (8/1–2019). *Every year I take on a personal challenge to learn something new. I've built an AI for my home, run 365 miles, visited every US state, read 25 books, and learned Mandarin. Last year, I focused almost all my time* [Facebook status update]. Retrieved from https://www.facebook.com/zuck/posts/10106021347128881. Accessed on 18.01.2020

Index

Achterhuis, H. 9
actant 175f., 178, 180, 183, 185f., 188, 191f., 195
agency 11, 39, 42, 45, 48, 58, 60, 70–72, 74, 76–78, 81, 88, 93, 175f., 178
akrasia 146
akrasia 138, 144, 148
alienation 8, 28–30, 32–34, 36, 38, 40, 43, 46, 48, 50f., 56, 63, 70, 100, 140
animals 19, 24, 37, 57, 64, 66, 94, 116, 139, 161, 164, 175, 181
architecture 11, 117, 123, 132, 145
Arendt, H. 38, 71, 83f., 126
Aristotelian principle 125, 143f., 147
Aristotle 19f., 84, 105f., 167, 192
art 63, 65, 68, 101, 111, 113f., 120, 195
artificial intelligence 16, 18, 93–95
autonomy of technology 41, 70, 73f., 76, 83, 85, 87, 93, 95, 127, 174f.

Babbage, C. 22, 40
Being 99–102, 106–108, 110
Biesta, G. 69
black boxes 85, 176, 180–182, 192
Brey, P. 10

Callon, M. 171, 183
capitalism 17f., 22, 26–28, 31–33, 40–42, 44f., 49f., 52, 55f., 59–61, 63, 71, 92, 135
car 61, 89, 96, 126, 136, 147, 192
cause 8, 53, 85, 107, 109f., 119, 166, 190f.
commodity 31, 51, 60, 127, 129, 136
constructivism 176–179, 187–189, 193
conviviality 11, 96
craft 31, 35, 38, 69f., 85, 110, 166f.
critical theory 13, 42, 47, 62
culture 2–4, 51, 53, 73, 87f., 95, 98, 112, 114, 120, 122–124, 127, 129, 135, 137, 142, 144f.

definition
– and essentially contested concepts 7
– and the laboratory 185
– and vagueness 5–7
– of technology 2f., 88
design 9, 13, 117, 145–149, 155, 168, 174, 193
determinism 39–41, 71–73, 76f., 88, 175
division of labour 22, 25, 27, 39
Dummett, M.A.E. 164, 189–193
dwelling 8, 14, 98, 105, 115–118, 122f., 126, 128, 132, 147f., 174

Ellul, J. 3, 9f., 47, 54, 74, 87f., 140
exchange value 23, 31, 57, 59

Facebook 96, 138, 140
Feenberg, A. 9, 14, 33, 42–44, 47, 69f., 135
Felsenstein, L. 11
Floridi, L. 7, 93
focal things 122f., 130–133, 135, 143, 145
forgetfulness 98, 100, 108f., 113, 188
fourfold 115f., 122, 174
Frankenstein 25, 74, 77, 93–95, 174f.
Frege, G. 155f., 158, 166, 189, 192
Fukuyama, F. 12

games 68, 130, 144
Gestell 44, 98, 109–115, 119–122, 126, 173
GPS 72, 93, 131, 158

Habermas, J. 49, 55–57, 62f.
habit 35, 97, 133, 137–140, 143f., 158, 161f., 164
Hegel, G.W.F. 16, 19, 28f., 36, 43, 84, 154
Hickman, L. 3, 149, 167
higher education 1, 13, 32f., 66f.
human nature 13, 20, 35, 62, 84

Ihde, D. 6, 77, 80, 111
Illich, I. 11, 96
information technology 1, 33, 73, 97, 128, 131, 139

inquiry 149–151, 157, 159f., 162f., 165, 167–169
instrumentalism 46f., 58f., 85, 151, 163
instruments of labour 17, 19, 23, 32, 44, 81

Kant, I. 16, 40, 49, 63, 69, 112, 149
Kellner, D. 52, 54, 134f.
Kuhn, T. S. 127, 176f., 184

Lave, J. 152, 156
learning 32–34, 64, 66f., 69, 132, 135, 152
logic 5, 53, 73, 76, 89f., 99, 105, 151–153, 155–160, 163, 166, 168
logos 3, 53, 60, 110

machine 4, 18, 26–28, 30–32, 34f., 37–41, 46, 48–50, 52, 56, 58f., 74, 79f., 93f., 129, 133, 145, 160, 180, 182, 184, 190
– ethics 9
MacKenzie, D. 39, 73, 77
Marx, L. 4, 49
means 2, 12, 29, 44, 89–92, 110, 150, 158, 160, 163, 167, 174–176, 192
metaphysics 8, 13, 56, 69, 98–100, 102–104, 106, 108f., 112f., 116, 120, 154, 166f., 175, 180, 185–188, 192
Mitcham, C. 86, 127, 149
monster 25, 74, 92, 94f., 173, 175
mood 10, 99, 111, 118, 120, 165, 167
Moses, R. 74, 77, 79
Mumford, L. 47, 52, 54, 58, 81, 84, 150

nature 21, 36, 53, 56, 60, 62, 113, 162, 168
neologism 194f.
network 11, 73, 76, 90, 97, 174, 178f., 181, 183f., 186–189, 192, 194
Nietzsche, F. 2, 84, 101, 172, 186, 194
Nissenbau, H. 68
Nissenbaum, H. 12, 65
Nye, D. 1, 4, 76, 83

objectification 8, 18, 20f., 27, 29, 34–36, 44, 85, 167
optimism 10, 16f., 41, 46f., 58f., 61, 67, 95, 123, 135

Pasteur, L. 183, 186f., 189, 193f.
pessimism 4, 10, 14, 17, 46–48, 54, 63, 127, 146, 150
phenomenology 7, 13, 43, 103
Plato 15, 70, 73, 82, 85, 93, 141, 166f., 190
post-phenomenology 6, 11, 72
principle of symmetry 175
privacy 50f., 60, 66, 72, 82, 96
progress 16f., 43, 46, 61f., 71, 100, 151, 166

Quine, W.V.O. 53, 103–105, 156, 185

Rawls, J. 125, 143f.
realism 149, 151–153, 155, 164f., 169, 172, 177–179, 187–189
reform 1, 119, 123, 128, 146f.
revolution 14, 40, 42–46, 57, 60–63, 71, 81, 177
robot 64f., 85, 93–95, 131
Russell, B. 140, 151, 153, 155–157, 160
Ryle, G. 50, 78, 101

Schatzberg, E. 3f., 49, 54, 58
science 150f., 156, 167–169, 171, 173, 176f., 179f., 182f., 185, 187–191, 193, 195
Smith, A. 16f., 20, 22, 25, 28
stages of history 16–18, 23, 25, 39f., 43f., 56, 60, 63, 95, 165f., 168
subjectivity 11, 14, 22f., 34–36, 48–50, 57, 65, 150, 178
surplus value 17, 23f., 27, 30, 40

technical delegates 176, 192
technocracy 91f.
truth 45, 101–104, 106, 111, 155f., 160, 164–166, 169, 173, 176, 188, 191
Turkle, S. 64f., 139

use-value 21–23, 28, 31

Vallor, S. 124, 140–142
value sensitive design 12, 47, 65–69, 79, 136
van der Laan, J. M. 2, 47
Veblen, T. 49, 58, 91

Verbeek, P.-P. 6, 8, 78, 132, 140, 163
virtue 12f., 17, 82, 124f., 127, 136–142

Wittgenstein, L. 5, 50, 98f., 106, 108, 151f., 155–157, 166, 181, 186, 190

www.ingramcontent.com/pod-product-compliance
Lightning Source LLC
Chambersburg PA
CBHW021141230426
43667CB00005B/208